Other Books from the Author

Archaeology of Orissa, with Special Reference to Nuāpāḍā and Kālāhāṇḍī

Character Assassination in the Modern History of Orissa

Cultural Profile of South Kosala

Eventful Life of an Orissa Province Maker (Diaries of Raja R.N. Bhanja Deo of Kanika, Orissa, 1908–1922)

Origins of Jagannāth Deity

Role of Raja Rajendra Narayan Bhanja Deo of Kanika (Orissa) (in the Indian Legislative Council 1916–1920)

Socio-Cultural History of Orissa: A Case Study of Khariar Estate

Some Tāntric Esotericism of Orissa

Tāntric Art of Orissa

Tāntric Hedonism of Mahānadī Valley (Uḍḍiyāna-Pīṭha)

A Tāntric Scholar and the British Wrath on Bastar State

Sankhya Darshan and Tantra Originated from Mahanadi River Valley of India

Āgneya-Koṇa
of
Bhāratavarṣa

Jitamitra Prasad Singh Deo

DK PRINTWORLD
Publishers of Indian Traditions

Cataloging in Publication Data — DK
[Courtesy: D.K. Agencies (P) Ltd. <docinfo@dkagencies.com>]

Siṁhadeba, Jitāmitra Prasāda, 1946-
Āgneya-koṇa of Bhāratavarṣa / Jitamitra Prasad Singh Deo.
p. cm.
Includes bibliographical references (p.).
ISBN 9788124606636

1. Orissa (India) — Civilization. 2. Orissa (India) — Religious life and customs. I. Title.

DDC 954.133 23

ISBN 978-81-246-0663-6
First published in India in 2013

Printed and published by:
D.K. Printworld (P) Ltd.
Regd. Office: 'Vedasri', F-395, Sudarshan Park
(Metro Station: Ramesh Nagar)
New Delhi-110 015
Phones: (011) 2545 3975; 2546 6019; *Fax*: (011) 2546 5926
E-mail: indology@dkprintworld.com
Website: www.dkprintworld.com

Dedicated to
my wife

Rani Rajshree Devi

Princess of Gajapati Dynasty, Puri

Preface

THE Indians[1] were the educators of the world, when the Indian empire in the remote past covered a large part of Asia,[2] Europe and other continents. This could spread Indian astrology across Asia and Europe. However astrology — the science of sciences — has lost its sheen in our country. Its present status is that of sufferance and neglect. Our approach to astrology should be more constructive, serious and intense. To make this happen, it should be taught across the premier academic institutions in the country. The Government and public should extend financial support to get astrology a new lease of life.

This book deals with *Āgneya-Koṇa of Bhāratavarṣa*, i.e. south-east of India, i.e. Bhāratavarṣa. Agni, i.e. fire,[3] on earth is the mundane, earthly form of the Divine, celestial Sun in the high heavens. The sun fire — principle or the life — animates the body in the form of oxygen (प्राणो वै नृषदग्निः [*prāṇo vai nṛ̀ṣadagniḥ*] says *Śatapatha Brāhmaṇa* VI.7.11 of *Ṛgveda*). The control-centre of the life-fire in the human being is the head which, therefore, is placed at the very top. Being identical in essence with cosmic energy, a properly "turned in" and concentrating human brain can, at anytime, switch itself on to the cosmic currents pulsating the universe.

Seeing meaning in our Vedic teachings, the West is turning to the East. Therefore, Ram Swarup[4] says:

> A fateful thing has been happening. Buddhism, Taoism and Confucianism are becoming available to the world. Already, it is having a transforming effect on the minds of the people, particularly in countries where there is freedom to seek and express. Dogmas are under a cloud; claims on behalf of last prophethood and only sonship, hitherto enforced through great intellectual conditioning, brow-beating and the big stick are becoming unacceptable. Religions of proxy are in retreat. More and more men now seek authentic experience. Borrowed creed will not do. Men and women are ceasing to be obedient believers and are becoming seekers. They no longer want to be anybody's sheep, now that they know that they can be their own shepherds. An external authority, even when it is called God in

certain scriptures, threatening and promising alternately, is increasingly making less and less impression; people now realize that Godhead is their own true, secret status and they seek it in the depth of their own being. All this is in keeping with the wisdom of the east.

At this juncture, one of the great Vedāntists of the West, David Frawley, whose Hindu name is Vamadeva Shastri, has written a book,[5] *Yoga and the Sacred Fire* (*Self-Realization and Planetary Transformation*).

I felt the necessity to write this book, *Āgneya-Koṇa of Bhāratavarṣa*, so that the cultural developments of the region and their contributions to humanity can be known.

The author is grateful to his wife, Rani Rajshree Devi of Khariar, for providing solitariness by taking up all worldly responsibilities. Without her assistance and support, the author could not have devoted to research and written various books listed on the facing title page.

Thanks are also due to D.K. Printworld for accepting publication of this book.

29 August 2012 **Raja Jitamitra Prasad Singh Deo**
Palace of Khariar, Khariar

Notes

1 P.N. Oak, *The Rationale of Astrology*, pp. 6-7, published by author, New Delhi, 1967.

2 P.N. Oak, *Some Blunders of Indian Historical Research*, Delhi: Surya Prakashan, 1969, *passim*.

3 P.N. Oak, *The Rationale of Astrology*, 1967, p. 274.

4 Ram Swarup, "Introduction to the Reprint", in D.S. Margoliouth, *Mohammed and the Rise of Islam*, New Delhi: Voice of India, 1985, p. xx.

5 David Frawley, *Yoga and the Sacred Fire* (*Self-Realization and Planetary Transformation*), Delhi: Motilal Banarsidass, 2006, *passim*.

Contents

Abbreviations

ASCITATTOYAK	*A Systematic Course in the Ancient Tāntric Techniques of Yoga and Kriya* (Paramahansa Swami Satyananda Saraswati)
ATSATBWOBS	*A Tāntric Scholar and the British Wrath on Bastar State* (J.P. Singh Deo (ed.))
AMCPCBD	*A Man Called Prafulla Chandra Bhanja Deo* (Juga Bhanu Singh Deo)
CPOSK	*Cultural Profile of South Kosala* (J.P. Singh Deo)
BSOIHAC	*Bhishma's Study of Indian History and Culture* (S.D. Kulkarni (ed.))
EI	*Epigraphia Indica*
OHRJ	*The Orissa Historical Research Journal.*
OOJD	*Origin of Jagannāth Deity* (J.P. Singh Deo)
SITCOJ	*Studies in the Cult of Jagannātha* (K.C. Mishra (ed.))
THACOTIP	*The History and Culture of the Indian People* (R.C. Majumdar (ed.))
THOMV	*Tāntric Hedonism of Mahānadī Valley* (*Uḍḍīyāna-Pīṭha*) (J.P. Singh Deo)
TTHATROI	*The True History and the Religion of India* (His Divinity Dharm Chakravarti Swami Prakashanand Saraswati)
TCOJATRTOO	*The Cult of Jagannātha and the Regional Tradition of Orissa* (A. Echmann, H. Kulke & G.C. Tripathi)

List of Illustrations

Cover Page

Agni, *c.* fourteenth century CE, Orissa State Museum, Bhubaneswar.

Maps

Figures

Plates

1. *Sòṣṭi-Yantra* (*Yantra* of Creation). Findspot: Patdaraha region of Sunabeda plateau, Dist. Nuāpāḍā, Orissa. Preserved at Khariar Palace Museum of the author, Khariar.
2. "Stone Sockets," Showing the union of male and female principals of nature. Findspot : Kharligaṛh site of Bolaṅgīr district, Orissa. Exibited at Manikyapur Museum, Bhawānīpatna, Dist. Kālāhāṇḍī, Orissa.
3. The Shape of Lord Puruṣottama Jagannātha, traced on the ruin of Sumerian Temple on a raised platform. Courtesy: Vishnu Kant Varma, *Missing Link of World Civilization: Indo-Aryan Colonization*, Delhi: Pratibha Prakashan, 2006, Plate 3 and back cover page.
4. "*Śiva-liṅga* without Śākti," worshipped at the Natural Cave entrance of Guru Ḍoṅger, Dist. Nuāpāḍā, Orissa. Courtesy: Samuel Dani.
5. "Umā-Maheśvara," Flat type of sculptural art, prevalent in South Kosala region. Findspot: Amgura village, Dist. Nuāpāḍā, Orissa. It is kept as household deity and worshipped by Sanlal Herna of Amgura village. Early medieval period.
6. "Narasiṁga," Flat type of Sculptural Art, prevalent in South Kosala region. Findspot: Tank of Nilji village, Dist. Nuāpāḍā, Orissa. Early medieval period. Preserved at Khariar Branch Museum, now functioning at district headquarter, Nuāpāḍā.

7-70. "Sixty-four sexual poses," found in palm-leaf etching of Orissa. Findspot: Gañjam district, Orissa.

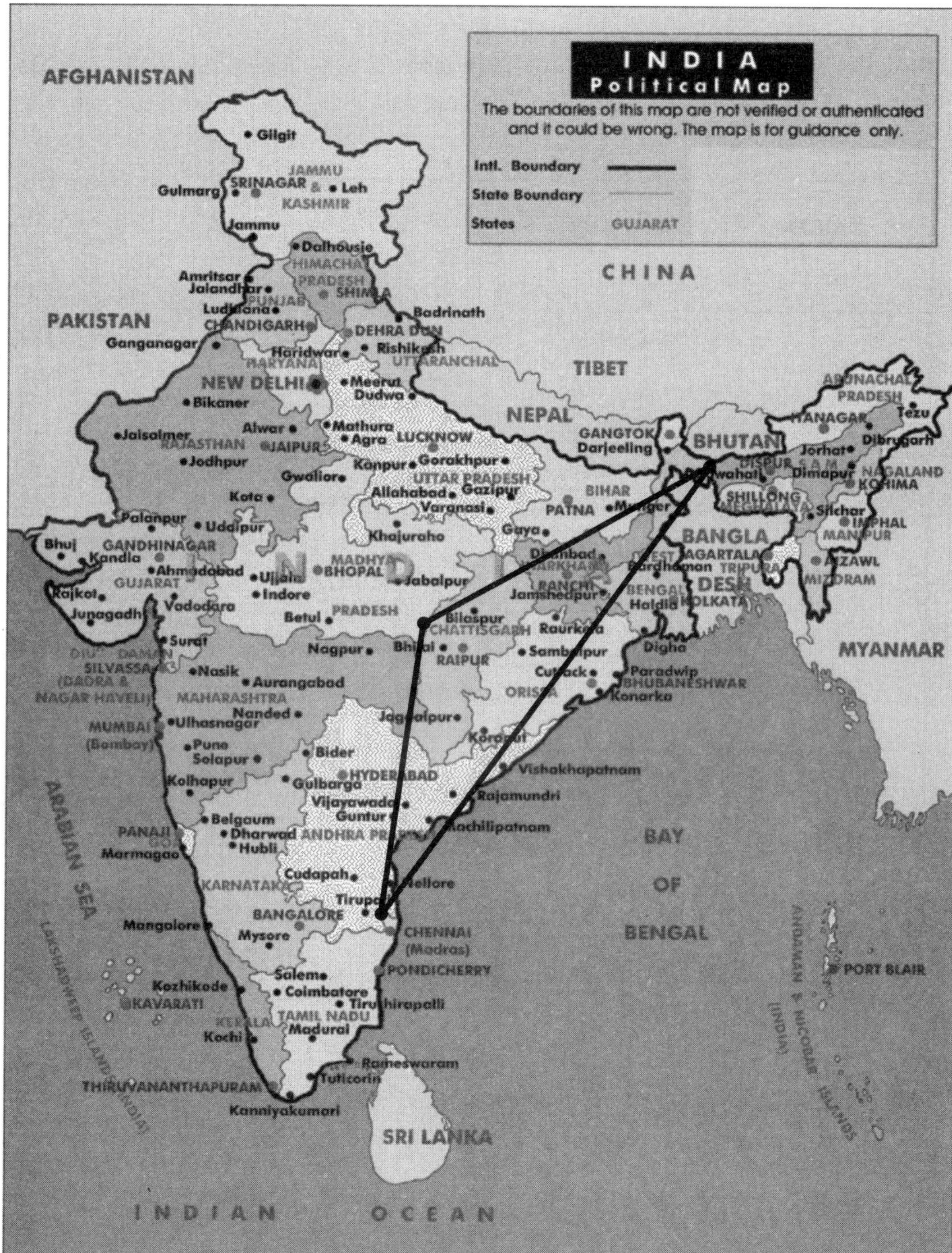

Map 1: Map of India, showing Āgneya-Koṇa, i.e. south-east of India, i.e. Bhāratavarṣa, according to Varāhamihira.

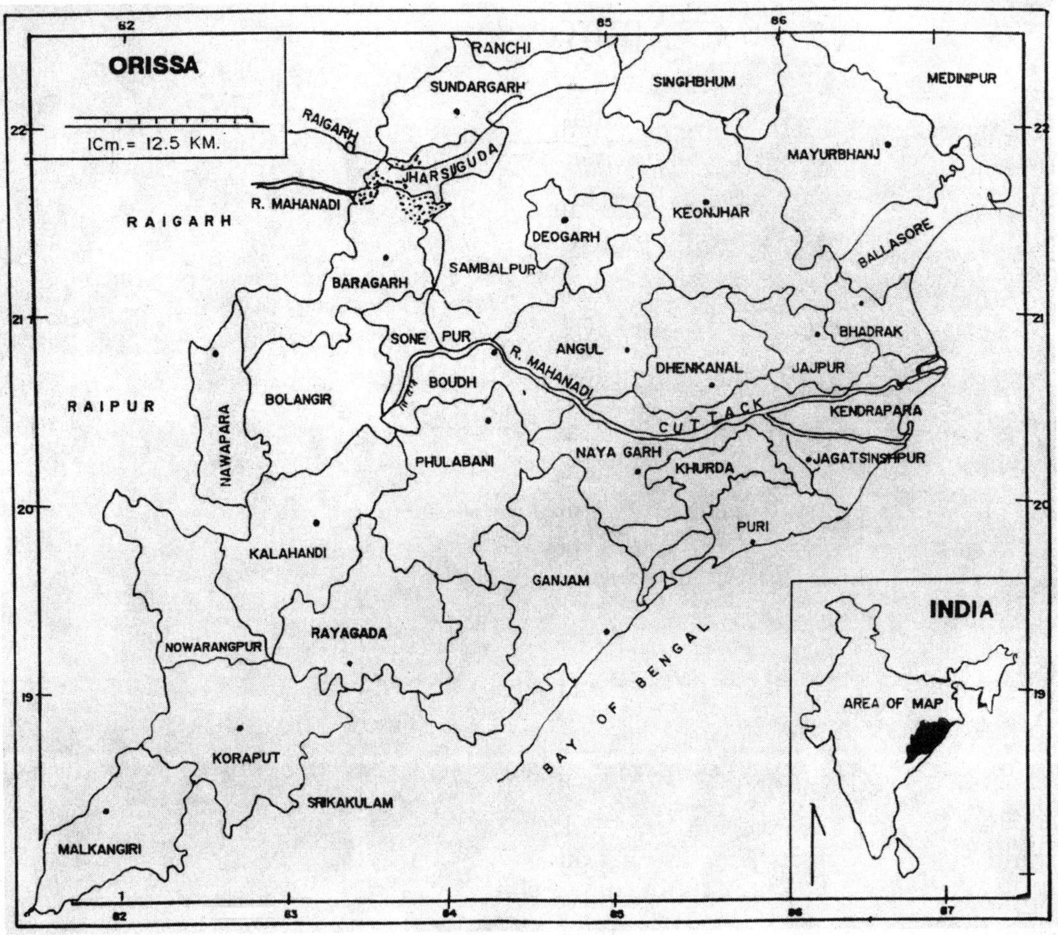

Map 2: Map of Orissa state.

Introduction

THE history of the evolution of Sanātana Dharma, the Hindu philosophy, starts with four Vedas — *Ṛgveda, Yajurveda, Sāmaveda* and *Atharvaveda* and six Darśana Śāstras — Pūrva-Mīmāṁsā of sage Jaiminī, Nyāya by sage Gautama, Vaiśeṣika by sage Kaṇāda, Sāṁkhya by sage Kapila, Yoga by sage Patañjali and Uttara-Mīmāṁsā (*Brahma-Sūtra*) by sage Veda Vyāsa.

In the words of Swami Chinmayananda:[1]

> We have thus in Indian philosophy today altogether six recognized main schools of thoughts, all of them arguing differently to arrive at seemingly independent conclusions, which, when digested by a sincere student (*sādhaka*), would indicate the same truth. To help us gain a comparative estimate of the relative merits of these different systems of thoughts, scholars have provided us with a beautiful classification of all these schools of thoughts.

The chart shown on the next page classifies the different philosophies, according to the Hindu tradition.

Swami Chinmayananda[2] further informs that the Sāṁkhya philosophy is the most scientific in treatment and so, perhaps, the most appealing to the modern mind of our scientific age. The Sāṁkhyans are extremely rational; their scientific approach has the flavour of modernity. The Sāṁkhyans again fall under two groups, marshalled behind two great expounders of this school of thought, Kapila and Patañjali. Kapila's philosophy does not take into consideration the God principle; while Patañjali adds to the fundamental factors of his doctrine, the concept of Īśvara also. On this basis, these philosophies are termed "Nir-Īśvara Sāṁkhya", and "Sa-Īśvara Sāṁkhya".

---

[1] Swami Chinmayananada, *Vedānta: The Science of Life*, vol. I, Bombay: Central Chinmaya Mission Trust, rpt., 1983, p. 5.

[2] Ibid., p. 8.

Chart-1: Classification of Different Philosophies according to the Hindu Tradition

- KNOWLEDGE POSSIBILITIES
  - SECULAR
  - SPIRITUAL
    - ATHEISTIC
      - ATHEISTIC ATHEISM
        - MATERIALISM (Cārvāka)
        - BUDDHISM (Buddha)
      - ATHEISTIC THEISM
        - JAINISM (Mahāvīra)
    - THEISTIC
      - THEISTIC ATHEISM
        - TARKA ŚĀSTRA
          - VAIŚEṢIKA (Kaṇāda)
          - NYĀYA (Gautama)
        - SĀṀKHYA PHILOSOPHY
          - NIR-ĪŚVARA SĀṀKHYA (Kapila)
          - SA-ĪŚVARA SĀṀKHYA (Patañjali)
        - PŪRVA-MĪMĀṀSĀ (Jaiminī)
      - THEISTIC THEISM
        - UTTARA-MĪMĀṀSĀ (VEDĀNTA) (Bādarāyaṇa)

Chart-2: Sāṁkhya Philosophy

PRAKṚTI
(Undifferentiated primal matter)

↓

BUDDHI/MAHAT (The suprapersonal potentiality of experiences)

↓

AHAṀKĀRA (Egoity: A function approaching the date of consciousness and wrongly assigning them to Puruṣa)

↓

The Five Karmendriya (The faculties of action)	Manas (The faculty of thought)	The Five Jñānendriya (The faculties of sense)	The Five Tanmātra ("Merely (*mātra*) that (*tan*)", mere trifle)

(The subtle, primary elements: realized as the inner, subtle counterparts of the five sense experience — sound, touch, colour-shape, flavour, smell, *śabda, sparśa, rūpa, rasa, gandha*)

↓

Parama aṇu
(Subtle atoms: realized in the experiences of the subtle body)

↓

Sthūla bhūtāni
(The five gross elements, ether, air, fire, water, earth, constituting the gross body and the visible tangible world: realized in sense experiences.)

According to Kapila Vatsyayan,[3] the system of Sāṁkhya and Yoga can be summarized, as shown in chart 2.

The early archaeological remains, showing the origins of Sāṁkhya Darśana and Yoga Darśana, are traced in the Great Mahānadī River Valley and they are dealt in Chapters 1 and 2.

---

[3] Kapila Vatsyayan, "Indriya", *Kalātattvakośa*, vol. IV, *Manifestation of Nature, Sṛṣṭi Vistāra*, gen. ed. Kapila Vatsyayan, New Delhi: Motilal Banarsidass, 1999, p. 31.

Great politics has been done to ancient Indian history by English historians.[4] In the words of His Divinity, Dharma Chakravarti Swami Prakashanand Saraswati:[5]

> This is the age of materialism called *Kaliyuga* that started 5,101 years ago (3102 BCE). The effects of *Kaliyuga* are to despise the Divine Truth and to elevate the anti-God elements in the name of God. Its effects have been clearly visible for the last 2,500 years when Jagadguru Śaṅkarācārya descended in India. But in the last 200 years such despisations were much greater when the English regime tried to destroy the culture and the religion of India by all means, and, during that time, they deliberately produced such derogatory literatures in huge quantities that confused and misguided the whole world.
>
> Trying to impose the worldliness of their own culture upon the Hindu faith, they introduced such fictitious theories and disparaging dogmas that produced a derogatory and demeaning view of Hinduism. These publications affected the minds of Hindu writers to such an extent that they also began to think and write on the same lines. As a result of that, the reputed organizations like Ramakrishna Mission and Bharatiya Vidya Bhavan and world-known learned scholars like Sarvepalli Radhakrishnan, produced such books that were the replicas of the same trend that was promoted by Sir William Jones, the associates of the Asiatic Society of Bengal, Max Müller (who was a highly paid employee of East India Company), and many more.

The Indian *r̥ṣis*, *yogīs* and saints through intuitive wisdom and knowledge have dealt in every aspect of human life and wisdom, which are supposed to live with the nature and thereby maintain equilibrium. In the words of Swami Prakashanand Saraswati:[6]

> Seeing such an amazing spiritual greatness of India, which was a ruled colony of the British, their vanity was hurt and their hearts revolted. They couldn't believe that India had such a deep and descriptive divine philosophy since time immemorial whose single ray incorporates the

[4] Navaratna S. Rajaram, *The Politics of History*, New Delhi: Voice of India, 1995, *passim*.

[5] Swami Prakashanand Saraswati, *The True History and the Religion of India*, New Delhi: Motilal Banarsidass, 2001, p. 31.

[6] Swami Prakashanand Saraswati, *The True History and the Religion of India*, New Delhi: Motilal Banarsidass, 2001, p. 279.

> teachings of all the pious religions of the rest of the world. At the same time, recognizing the blemishes of their own culture and of their own religion of the wrathful God of the Bible whose beliefs induced the killing and burning of millions of innocent people, they, as a psychological reaction of their prejudiced minds, decided to crush the Hindu culture to the extremes and bring it as low as possible.

Because of this background, false history of ancient India has been written and taught in the Indian educational institutions. Hence, to showcase the true history, I have taken up the regional study of the Āgneya-Koṇa, i.e. south-east India.

Vedic *ṛṣis* and their disciples had civilized the entire world in ancient period. "The missing link of world civilization: Indo-Aryan colonization" has been worked out in recent years by Vishnu Kant Varma.[7] The author[8] had earlier stated that Varāhamihira, in his *Bṛhat-Saṁhitā*,[9] put Kosala, Kaliṅga, Vaṅga, Upa-Vaṅga, Jaṭhar, Aṅga, Sailik, Vidarbha, Vatsa, Āndhra, Cedi, Udharva, Kant, Brusa, Naliker and Charmadip in the Āgneya-Koṇa (i.e. south-east) of India. The grouping of states indicates that Kosala here refers to Dakṣiṇa Kosala or South Kosala.

From the grouping of states in Āgneya-Koṇa, i.e. south-east India, it seems that the centre of Āgneya-Koṇa is the Great Mahānadī River Valley. With this background, the author[10] had written a book *Tāntric Hedonism of Mahānadī Valley* (*Uḍḍīyana-Pīṭha*). In that book, all aspects of Āgneya-Koṇa could not be dealt. Therefore, comes the endeavour to write the present book.

Each and every corner of India had contributed to the Great Tradition of Bhāratavarṣa.[11] From the archaeological antiquities traced and discovered in this region, it is observed that Tantra and the two main trends which originated in this area are the Sāṁkhya Darśana and Yoga Darśana. This background developed Sapta-Mātṛkā worship, Sixty-four Yoginī cult, sculptures and temple architectures with eroticism and the great Jagannātha cult, which is the syncretic culture, meant for the present world.

---

[7] V.K. Varma, *Missing Link of World Civilization: Indo-Aryan Colonization*, New Delhi: Pratibha Prakashan, 2005, *passim*.

[8] *CPOSK*, 1987, p. 36.

[9] *Bṛhat-Saṁhitā*, Kūrma Vibhāg, 8.

[10] *THOMV*, 2004, *passim*.

[11] Swami Agehananda Bharati, *Great Tradition and Little Traditions*, Varanasi: Chowkhamba Sanskrit Series Office, 1978, *passim*.

K.C. Mishra[12] dealt the theology of the system of Yoga in the Jagannātha cult and states:

> The most important aspect of the Cult of Jagannātha is its elaborate system of Yoga which is mainly based upon the *haṭha-yoga*. The aims of Yoga system are to control diseases, decay and death through physical culture and to realize the Alekha Nirañjana (the formless and the spotless) by transmuting the subtler body into a gross physical superconscious one. The theory of the six plexuses (*ṣaṭ cakra*), the thousand-petalled lotus (*sahasrāra*) and that of the three mystic nerves, i.e. *iḍā, piṅgalā, suṣumṇā* giving the processes of breath control like *pūraka, kumbhaka* and *recaka* together with various practices of *mudrā*s and *bandha*s are taken in more or less modified form by these Vaiṣṇavas from earlier Tantra-Yoga practices. They also name, after *haṭha-yoga*, their Yoga system as *ghaṭa-yoga*, which means the Yoga of the body (*ghaṭa*).

It is impossible to describe here in detail the elaborate yogic processes of the Jagannātha cult, so we simply present below the salient features of it with a view to pointing out its distinctive nature. The yogic philosophers of Orissa seem to have made a thorough survey of the whole nervous system of the human body, and they counted altogether 72,000 nerves from the naval region of the body. Out of these 72,000 only ten nerves are considered to be essential for yogic practices and they are named as *iḍā, piṅgalā, suṣumnā, gandhārī, hastijihvā, pūṣā, yaśasvinī, alambuṣā, kuhū* and *śaṅkhinī*. But only the first three nerves are regarded as the most important ones, and they are located inside the vertebral column — *iḍā* on the left, *piṅgalā* on the right and *suṣumnā* in the middle — running parallel to one another. These three mystic nerves meet together inside the forehead in between the two eyes, where both the nostrils meet; the juncture is known as *trikūṭa*. Above *trikūṭa*, there is a small slit known as the *brahmarandhra*, leading to the region of Alekha, and the valve of the slit is as delicate as the skin of the sesame seed. The *sādhaka* is to raise the vital wind upward through *suṣumnā* and keep it in the *trikūṭa*, and then, opening the gate of *brahmarandhra*, should concentrate upon Alekha, whereby he would easily conquer Yama, the God of Death. The vital energy or the life-force, conceived in the nature of the coiled snake and, hence called *kuṇḍalinī*, is taken to be tending downward in the case of the ordinary human being who fretters it away in various worldly indulgences. In yogic *sādhanā*, this vital force is to be given an upward direction, which is called *ulṭā* or *ujāni* (reverse) *sādhanā*, implying a process of reversal from the world of *pravṛtti* to the state of *nivṛtti*.

[12] K.C. Mishra, *The Cult of Jagannātha*, Kolkata: Firma K.L. Mukhopadhyay, 1971, pp. 165-66.

There are six *cakra*s in the human body, and *kuṇḍalinī* in her reverse (*ulṭā*) ascent towards *nivṛtti* is to gradually pass through them, making the different stages of Yoga. The final stage, however, is reached when the slit at the top of the *trikūṭa* can be opened by constant yogic concentration allowing thus the *kuṇḍalinī* to get through the *vaṅkunāḷa* to the *brahma cakra*, situated inside the cavity of the head below the skull. This *brahma cakra* is also called the *sahasrāra*, the thousand-petalled lotus, which is as luminous as the rays of a thousand suns and is described as the incomprehensible region of Alekha. The upward journey of the *kuṇḍalinī* towards the *sahasrāra* is considered as the march of the finite towards the infinite, and their union is taken to be the alliance of Rādhā and Kṛṣṇa in eternal *rāsa* arena. Moreover, the *brahma cakra* or the thousand-petalled lotus is regarded as the seat of Jagannātha. Acyutānanda in his *Chayālīsa Paṭala* and Balarāmadāsa in *Virāṭa Gītā* identify the human body in all its aspects with temple of Jagannātha, making the *sahasrāra* region the thousand-petalled lotus. The logical corollary is that these Orissan Vaiṣṇavas visualize the union of Rādhā and Kṛṣṇa as the image of Jagannātha. In other words, Jagannātha to them is not only the visible expression of the incomprehensible Alekha Brahma but also the non-dual conception of both Rādhā and Kṛṣṇa.

Because of these reasons while dealing with *indriya* and manifestation in the arts, the opinion of Kapila Vatsyayan[13] is very correct, when she states:

> Ultimately with the creation of Jayadeva's *Gīta-Govinda*, and its interpretation by the Goswamin's Rūpa and Jīva, specially in the *Ujjvalanīlamaṇi*, a new Śāstra of *rāsa* based on sense perceptions and dialogue of *jīva* and *ātmā* is enunciated.
>
> The wheel again comes full circle for the texts of *bhakti* and the theology developed is a consummation of a distinctive comprehension of sense-perceptions and their role in metaphysics, philosophic discourse, medicine, arts and mysticism. This is the holistic system and approach of the Indian tradition, where each concept becomes a hub and felly for radiating into differing interpretations as spokes but all held together and regulated within the circumference.
>
> As has been stated throughout, the special attitude to the body and senses holds a key to the understanding of the Indian arts, not only at the level of

---

[13] Kapila Vatsyayan, "Indriya," *Kalātattvakośa*, vol. IV, *Mainfestation of Nature, Sṛṣṭi Vistāra*, gen. ed. Kapila Vatsyayan, New Delhi: Indira Gandhi National Centre for the Arts, and Motilal Banarsidass, 1999, pp. 66-67.

theory but also at the level of practice, be it literature, architecture, sculpture, painting, music or dance. Sanskrit drama (*kāvya*), employs the language of sense-perceptions to evoke emotive states. The elaborate descriptions on sense-perceptions from *Abhijñānaśākuntalam* to Jayadeva's *Gīta-Govinda* are the artistic counterparts of the philosophic discourse on the subject. The process of externalization and internalization as also the movement from the gross to subtle, from the material to the non-material, from the physical to the psychical are obvious.

A comprehension of the attitude to the senses and its artistic expression will make it clear that while there are differentiated levels, there is no dichotomy between the "profane" and the "sacred". Indian architecture — ancient and medieval — once again manifests this distinctive attitude. The Buddhist *stūpa,* the Jaina temples and the Hindu temples bear testimony to this fact. If the Buddhist *stūpa* from Sāñcī to Borobudur is the concretization of the principles of the *kāya*s and *dhātu*s, the Jaina temples exemplify conception of the *indriya* as expounded in the texts of *Jainendra-Siddhānta Koṣa* of Jinendra Varṇi. Hindu temples — northern, southern, eastern, western — are a celebration of the sense-perceptions in all their effervescence and yet leading the spectator and audience from the gross to the subtle and from the external to the internal. The sheaths (*kośa*) of the outer (*bāhya*) and the inner (*antara*) are concretized as the multiplicity of images on the outer walls where each sense-perception bursts forth in abundance as the motifs of *yakṣī*s, the *surā-sundarī*s, the *kinnara*s, *gandharva*s and *apsaras*. Gradually, the outer walls give place to the inner quietening images melt away and the smell of incense, the sound of bells, the touch of flowers and the light of the lamps take over from the organs to perception and feeling. The countless images of Indian sculpture encapsulate the attitude to the body and the senses, be they Śaiva, Vaiṣṇava, Śākta, Buddhist or Jaina. Outstanding amongst these is naturally the Śiva image Naṭarāja. It symbolizes many conceptions and can be comprehended at the levels of myth, philosophy and dance. The image also encodes the five-sense-perceptions and the five primal elements. The Lord sees and listens, touches and smells as he tramples upon the dwarf of ignorance.

In music and dance, in content form, structure and technique concretise this attitude towards the senses. The overwhelming impression of sensuousness in practically all forms of Indian music and dance is neither accident nor preoccupation with flesh and body. It is another path to *mokṣa* (liberation).

These factors and environment gave rise to *prema-bhakti* (devotion of love). In the words of Chittaranjan Das:[14]

> The special brand of *prema-bhakti* that was once so ostentatiously propounded by Jayadeva and Śrī Ramananda Roy has been described and so lucidly explained to Śrī Caitanya, so as to convince the latter about its superiority to other paths of *bhakti*. It had not been very much accepted in Orissa in spite of all that. But it is interesting to see that for the next almost three centuries it took advantage of the general decadance of the time, and inspired as a theme nearly the entire bulk of Oriya poetry-making. It is a phase in itself and demands a separate treatment. *Prema-bhakti* got itself degenerated into bare erotic and ornamental poetry and before long became court poetry also. From the point of view of literature in relation to a people and the totality that its life stands for, it was a sort of regression. It was as it were half a step from *prema-bhakti* to *kāma-bhakti* which was for all intents and purposes cent per cent *kāma* with a mask of *bhakti*. The gods were dragged down to the pits where frustrated men were intoxicated with *kāma* and wanted to believe that they had not really lost anything at all. The pomposities in literature only suggested nevertheless a poverty that had gone very deep into the heart of a people. Where there is darkness all round, some people try to deny it by appearing pompous and snug.

The impact of the spiritual, yogic, cultural and historical influence of Āgneya-Koṇa can be still found as living traditions of whole South-East Asia. According to Swami Chinmayananda, Sāṁkhya philosophy is the most scientific in treatment, and so, perhaps, the most appealing to the modern mind.

Lord Jagannātha cult has been spread throughout the world mainly by the International Society of Kr̥ṣṇa Consciousness and Yoga, including Āyurveda, has become popular. It seems the vision of Arya r̥ṣis — *kr̥nvanto viśvam āryam*, i.e. "make the entire world Aryan" — is going to be fulfilled. P.N. Oak[15] had correctly said that had the word "Aryan" signified a race, the above dictum would not have come into being because race-conscious people, far from wanting to assimilate the "world" in their fold, believe in maintaining an exclusive identity. Because of this region Chapter 3 of this book deals with the topic, rethinking on Aryan race theory.

---

[14] Chittaranjan Das, *A Glimpse into Oriya Literature*, Bhubaneswar: Orissa Sahitya Akademi, 1982, p. 94.

[15] P.N. Oak, "Arya as Ideal Misconstrued as a Race", *Some Blunders of Indian Historical Research*, New Delhi: Surya Prakashan, rpt., 1969, pp. 223-33.

From the recent archaeological discoveries, it is found that there is no country in the world which had not received India's spiritual and cultural influence or impact.[16] Hence, Chapter 4 deals with the influence of Bhāratavarṣa civilization on the ancient world.

The diplomatic schemes[17] of the British during the eighteenth, nineteenth and twentieth centuries to destroy the culture, religion and ancient history of Bhāratavarṣa had worked. They had their effects on the academic and educational systems of India, including the great writers, historians, educationists, diplomats, politicians, and most of the people of the country. We are still following the same trend.

Because of the British rule, history, religious developments and their true presentations have been affected. Therefore, Chapters 5 to 14 deal with the topics given in the contents and are the results of field discoveries, deep studies and free-lance research of the author. This is a pathway to take up studies on regional basis for the development and representation of the true history, culture and religious studies of Bhāratavarṣa.

This book deals with Sāṁkhya and Yoga Darśana, and their development, their impact on the society, and their contribution to the great tradition of the country the Vedic culture. I hope that the entire mankind will benefit from this earnest endeavour.

---

[16] *BSOIHAC*, vol. XVI, India Abroad, 1995, *passim*.

[17] *TTHATROI*, 2001, pp. 223-34.

1

The Boden Block Area and the Yogic Tradition

STONE Age tools in the form of ring stones and celts are found under the foothills of mountains and streams of Boden Block area in the Nuāpāḍā district of Orissa in plenty. They prove the inhabitation of Stone Age people in this area. Iron slags are also found in this region.

According to *Chamber's Twentieth Century Dictionary*, Yoga means a system of Hindu philosophy showing the means of emancipation of the soul. A Hindu ascetic, who practises the Yoga system, consisting in long continuance in unnatural postures, which is known as *haṭha-yoga,* reaches great spiritual heights and health perfection. Yoga is meant for all and yogic culture of India now finds its popularity throughout the world. It seems, the twenty-first century is going to be the century of Yoga.

The knowledge, which is acquired from teachers and books, is imitative, repetitive, derivative and educative. Another knowledge, which is above these types of knowledge, is intuitive. Only intuitive knowledge reaches the reality *alias* truth.[1] There are nine kinds of Yoga. They are *jñāna-yoga, rāja-yoga, bhakti-yoga, karma-yoga, haṭha-yoga, kuṇḍalinī-yoga, tantra-yoga, japa-yoga* and *laya-yoga*.[2]

The Boden Block area had made great contributions to the yogic world and primal *alias* Ādi Śakti. The origin of Śakti worship is shrouded in mystery. J.N. Banerjea[3] considers that the ring stones, the female figures along with the circular discs and the nude figures of the historical period collectively establish the long continued existence of the worship of the female principle in aniconic and iconic forms. Ring stones are found in plenty in Nuāpādā district, in particular, and Orissa in general.

---

[1] J.P. Singh Deo, *Origin of Jagannāth Deity*, New Delhi: Gyan Publishing House, 2nd edn., 2003, vide: Preface.

[2] J.P. Singh Deo, *Tāntric Art of Orissa*, Delhi: Kalpaz Publication, 2001, p. 29.

[3] J.N. Banerjea, *Purānic and Tāntric Religion*, (?), p. 14.

To know about the earliest primal Śakti conception, attention should be drawn to the period of geological formations. It is true that the course of human history in a region is, in a considerable measure, shaped by its physical and geographical features, which, in turn, in the ultimate, are determined by the geological history the region has passed through in the course of time.[4]

When the geological earth crust was under formation, in many places the Mother Earth had formed the shape of female vulva, the external organ. In the words of O.A. Wall,[5] "The external feminine sexual part, the vulva, is called *yoni* in India; it is still very widely worshipped in Asiatic religions and the worshippers of feminine attributes are called *yonichitas*. In subsequent reference to the vulva, we will speak of it as the *yoni*."

Yoni in Sanskrit means vulva, uterus or origin; it is the female power in Nature. The Supreme Being, wishing to bring creation, divided himself into two parts — Brahmā and Nature. Nature denotes all females, but the females are regarded as the real forces in nature and most deserving of worship.

One such naturally formed female vulva or *yoni* of Mother Earth is found under a bamboo thicket in the Pātālgaṅgā site, near Boden and worshipped as *dvārsani*. It should be regarded as the earliest Śakti Pīṭha (site) of the Orissa province. There are such earthen-formed female vulva or *yoni* sites elsewhere in India, and the entire world. Tantra gives prominence to the female energy of Śakti. Śakti (Kālī) of the Śākta cult is the Mother or the Supreme Being. Śiva of the Śaiva cult is the Father or the Supreme Being. The tantras attempt to blend these two concepts the Motherhood and the Fatherhood of God. Tantra gives importance to the Eternal Mother, for God's love for the creation is like mother's love, deep and pure. So, the earliest tāntric site of Orissa is the Yonigatra (as named in "Yoni Tantra"), worshipped as *dvārsani* deity near Boden (*OHRJ*, vol. XLVII, no. 3, pp. 38-39).

About *Puruṣa* and *Prakṛti* (Spirit and Nature), the *Bhagavad-Gītā*,[6] mentions thus:

> Know that *Puruṣa* and *Prakṛti* are beginningless; and know also that all modifications and qualities (*guṇa*s) are born of *Prakṛti*.

---

4 D.N. Wadia, "The Geological Background of Indian History", *THACOTIP*, vol. I, *The Vedic Age*, 1965, p. 80.

5 O.A. Wall, *Sex and Sex Worship in the World*, Delhi: Inter-India Publication, 1979, p. 464.

6 Sri Sri Paramahamsa Yogananda, *God Talks with Arjuna: The Bhagavad-Gītā*, Kolkata: Yogoda Satsanga Society of India, 1999, p. 889.

Sri Sri Paramahaṁsa Yogananda[7] illustrates it thus:

> *Puruṣa*, the Lord's transcendent presence in creation as the *kūṭastha* intelligence and the individualized soul, and *prakṛti*, nature, indicate two aspects of the same God. He is causeless and eternal, therefore his manifestations as *puruṣa* and *prakṛti* are also beginningless and endless.
>
> The Lord in his transcendental or inactive aspect in creation (*puruṣa*, the *kṣetrajña* or witness) and the Lord in his immanent kinetic aspect as the Creator of the universe and beings (*prakṛti*) are not two but one, the Supreme Spirit, Īśvara, *Parā Puruṣa*.
>
> As the ocean with waves and without waves is the same ocean, so spirit, with or without creation, is ever a unity. *Prakṛti* is the stern of *māyā*, delusion, relativity, that transfers the surface of the calm ocean of God into tumultuous waves of human lives. The vibratory sterns of relativity is God's desireless desire to create. Its force comes from the inherent three *guṇas* of manifestation: *sattva* (good), *rajas* (active) and *tamas* (evil). As they move across the ocean of infinity, individualized waves are whipped into being. The large waves, swept farthest from the quiet oceanic depths, are the waves of evil, those lives most affected by the storms of delusion. The medium waves are the waves, the active lives, surging along in nature's ebb and flow. The small waves of good lives remain closest to the ocean's bosom, buffeted the least by the prevailing winds of change. Yet all waves are of the same essence, and in their own evolutionary time return to their source.
>
> Naught could exist without *prakṛti*'s power of *māyā*. The beam of light from the projector's booth cannot alone create a motion picture, a film of mingled shadows and transparencies is also needed. Similarly, the Lord assumes two aspects *puruṣa* on the undistorted light of *kūṭastha*, intelligence and *prakṛti* with its *māyā* film of shadow relativities, to project the intelligently organized drama of countless worlds and beings. Through the two divine agencies he produces in cosmic cycles through eternity the dream motion picture of creation.
>
> *Prakṛti*, God's *māyā*, is the Lady of Phenomena, the mistress of illusion, the director of the phantasmagoria of the unfolding Universe. What a mysterious magic is her power secret in its working, bold in its displays. *Prakṛti* means "that which can work superbly". Gazing around at the panorama of her

[7] Sri Sri Paramahamsa Yogananda, *God Talks with Arjuna: The Bhagavad-Gītā*, Kolkata: Yogoda Satsanga Society of India, 1999, pp. 889-90.

> inexhaustible hand work, who could dispute the aptness of her Sanskrit name?

Besides *yoni* worship as *dvārsani,* few other *yoni*s as Śaktis are found within the Boden Block area. They are:

1. One naturally formed stone *yoni* was found in Dhaṅgritāl village area, which is now preserved in the author's private museum in the Palace of Khariar.
2. Three *yoni*s have been found on the rock belt, on the left bank of the Indra River, at a distance of 2 km from Chhuipain village, on the foothill of the eastern slope of Sunabeda plateau.
3. Two *yoni*s are worshipped in Kerapadar village area, near Nighagarh area and its vicinity.
4. One stone *yoni* has been found at Soseng village area, on top of the Sunabeda plateau. Its middle portion is damaged because of human vandalism. It is now preserved in the author's private museum at the Palace of Khariar.

These findings prove that Boden Block area had contributed much to the worship of Śakti and Śakti Tantra.

A rare stone has been found from Patdaraha area of Boden Block with *sṛṣṭi* (creation) *yantra*, chiselled on it (Plate 1). The *Indian Express*[8] reported that Rajshree Devi and Deb Prashad Singh Deo of Khariar came across a rare stone in Patdaraha region recently, believed to have enough tāntric significance. During their recent trekking to the Patdaraha region in southern slope of the Sunabeda plateau, the two came across a *Śivaliṅgam* on the mountaintop located at a height of about 2,000 ft. A few furlongs away, they found a chiselled stone with a triangular design, which was later examined by J.P. Singh Deo. In his interpretation, Singh Deo says that the stone signifies Śiva Kāmeśvara, Śakti Kāmeśvarī, and Somarasya, a tāntric formula *alias yantra* of creation *alias sṛṣṭi.* This ideology had influenced the development of three tāntric temples of Bauḍ, which are also situated in a right angle triangular shape of situation.

Trikoṇa consists of *icchā, jhāna* and *kriyā śakti*s. In the *Śāradā Tilaka* (I.78), it is recorded that from Saguṇa Śiva rise *Śakti, Nāda* and *Bindu*. This *Bindu* is threefold: (a) *Bindu* (Śiva), (b) *Bīja* (Śakti), and (c) *Nāda* (Śiva-Śakti).

While dealing on *Phonic Emanation*, Dirk Jan Hoens[9] states:

---

[8] English daily newspaper, *The Indian Express*, Bhubaneshwar, 26 February 2004, p. 4.

[9] Dirk Jan Hoens, "Tantra and Other Constituents of Tāntric Practice", *Handbuchder Orientalistik, II, ABT. IV, Band 2, Abschn, Hindu Tantrism*, Leiden/Koln: E.J. Brill, 1979, p. 95.

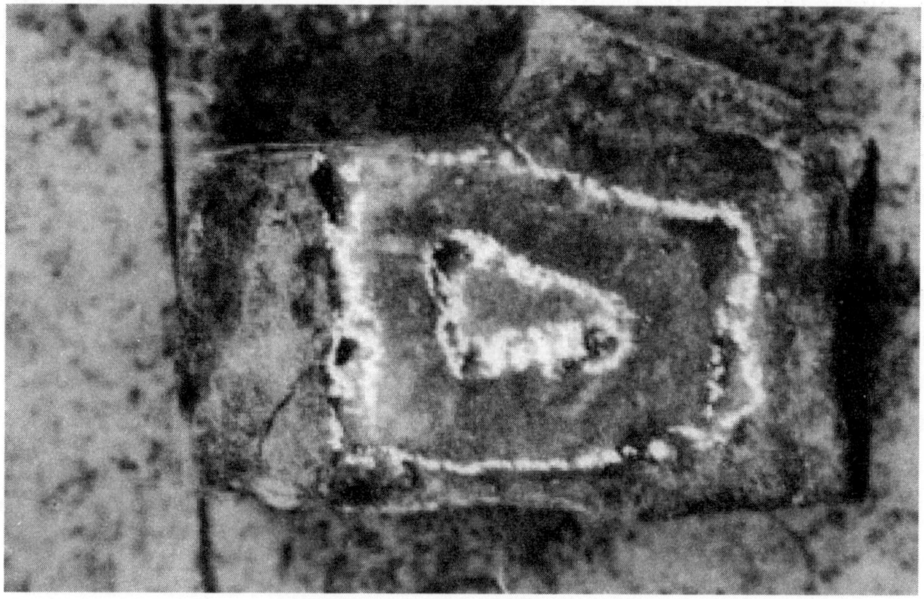

Plate 1: *Sṛṣṭi-Yantra* (*Yantra* of Creation). Findspot: Patdaraha region of Sunabeda plateau, Dist. Nuāpāḍā, Orissa. Preserved at Khariar Palace Museum of the author, Khariar.

Śakti-Siva, is characterized by both Amṛtānanda and Rāghavabhaṭṭa in the mentioned passage of the *Yoginī-Hṛdaya-Tantra* and the *Śāradā Tilaka*, by white and red colours suggestive of semen and menstrual flux, the two factors of reproduction in Hindu (including tāntric) embryology. The Śiva-Śakti-Nāda obtained the name "Kāmakalā", the divine particle (manifesting itself as desire, personified as Tripurasundarī) (*Jhānārṇava Tantra*, 10.8). In this context, Śiva and Śakti are called Kāmeśvara and Kāmeśvarī. The Kāmakalā

Śiva Kāmeśvara (white, Agni) — Śakti Kāmeśvarī (red, Soma)

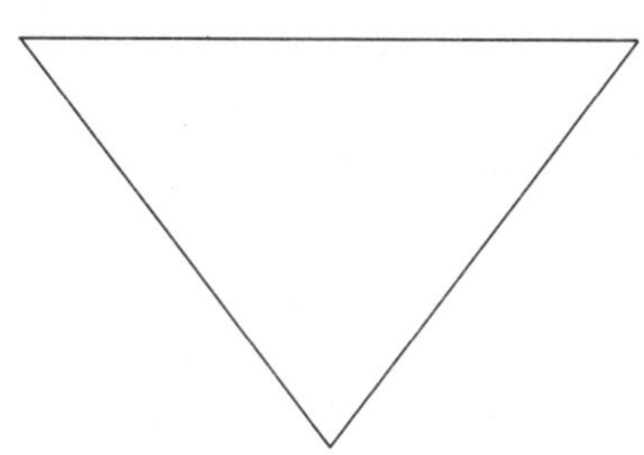

Somarasy
(Ravi, kāma)

> symbolizes the creative union of the primeval parental pair, a pulsating cosmic atom with two nuclei graphically represented by a white and red dot which automatically produce a third point of gravity. This situation is often represented graphically as a triangle. This can be done in two ways, with the point upward or downward. The second variety which expresses the initial cosmic dynamism would look like this:

This supposition of an ordinary triangle of Dirk Jan Hoens is a mistake, because a triangle pointed down is *yoni-yantra* and a triangle pointed up, is *liṅga-yantra*. The above discussed discovery of a rare stone with right-angled *yantra* from Patdaraha area proves that the simple triangular *yantra* as shown by Dirk Jan Hoens is wrong and the Patdaraha finding of *yantra* is correct and should be like this:

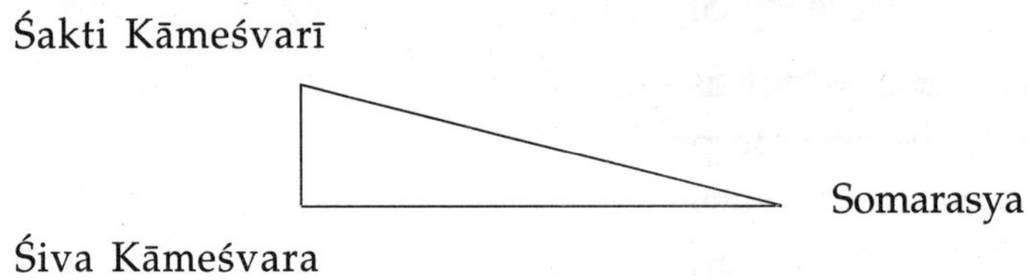

The composition of the great tāntric text *Śāradā Tilaka* is assigned to Lakṣmaṇa Deśikendra. While editing this text, in its introduction, Arthur Avalon (pen-name of Sir John Woodroffe)[10] states that nothing much about Lakṣmaṇa Deśikendra, the author of the *Śāradā Tilaka*, is known. At the end of his book he says that his father was Śrī-Kṛṣṇa, his grandfather was Ācārya Paṇḍita and his great-grandfather was Mahābala. All of them, he says, were men of great piety and erudition and enjoyed great reputation for the same. We are not aware if he wrote any other book. Rāghava places him on a very high pedestal and gives us further information that Lakṣmaṇa was a disciple of Utpalācārya, Somānaṅśa, Vasumanta and Śrīkaṇṭha. He further says that Lakṣmaṇa was impelled to write the book because of his compassion for men who wanted to know something about all the different forms of worship but, he could not do so owing to the voluminousness of the different Tantras, each of which dealt with a single form of worship, and also because of the abstruse character of the same. The majority of men of his time were unable to master these Tantras as they were of limited intelligence and short-lived.

---

[10] Arthur Avalon, *Śāradā Tilaka Tantram*, Delhi: Motilal Banarsidass, rpt., 2001, Introduction, p. vi.

The statement of Arthur Avalon, proves that Lakṣmaṇa Deśikendra was not the original discoverer of the tāntric creation *yantra* and thought, but was a compiler as it was vast and getting lost.

This discussion and finding of *sṛṣṭi yantra* at Patdaraha prove that the original first tāntric *yogī* who discovered the *yantra* of *sṛṣṭi*, which is a rectangular triangle, was residing at the hilltop of Sunabeda plateau. Probably, to commemorate the memory of this great *siddha yogī*, a mountain under which Boden village exists was named as "Guru Ḍoṅger". The author, therefore, boldly declares that the *yantra* of *sṛṣṭi* (creation) war originated in Boden Block area.

The splendid heritage of India are its four Vedas and six Darśana Śāstras.[11]

According to Sāṁkhya Darśana, *puruṣa* is for the entire divine phenomena and *prakṛti* (nature) is for the prime cosmic power *māyā* that evolves itself into the form of this universe with the help of *puruṣa* (God).[12]

The finding of rare stone, which is of ferruginous colour and fossilized stone, proves that it belongs to the remote past of geological years. This is the result of Sāṁkhya Darśana, discovered by sage Kapila in the remote past,[13] because sage Veda Vyāsa says that Svayambhuva Manu and Śatarūpā appeared from Brahmā's body. They started the first human generation on the earth planet, in Bhāratavarṣa. (Taking into account some time for the creation of the atmosphere, the ozone layer and the development of animal life, it could be around 155.5 trillion years ago.) They had two sons, Priyavrata and Uttānapāda, and three daughters, Akūtī; Devahūti and Prasūtī. Akūtī was married to Prajāpat Ruci and Devahūtī was married to sage Kardam. (Their divine son was sage Kapila who revealed the Sāṁkhya Darśana.) The youngest daughter Prasūti was married to Dakṣa Prajāpati: slowly the whole world was filled with their descendants (Appendix I, for the true chronology of the history of Bhāratavarṣa).

It seems, sage Kapila while meditating at the top of Guru Ḍoṅger revealed the *sṛṣṭi alia*s creation *yantra* and chiselled it on this rare discovered stone. On the top of Guru Ḍoṅger there is a natural rock cave, which leads to a natural tunnel. Sage Kapila, who lived here for some time, seems to have been a Śaiva, as the *Śivaliṅga*

---

[11] His Divinity, Dharm Chakravarti Swami Prakashanand Saraswati, *The True History and the Religion of India*, Delhi: Motilal Banarsidass, 2001, pp. 538 and 555.

[12] Ibid., p. 560.

[13] Ibid., p. 457.

worshipped by him still exists near the entrance of the rock cave. There is a Megalithic rock pile, like a wall, nearby. It seems this rocky mountain is named as Guru Ḍoṅger after sage Kapila, the great *yogī*. This spiritual *guru* (master) is nowadays worshipped as "Guru Deva" by the local people. It can be claimed that from this region Sāṁkhya Darśana originated, which deals with *puruṣa, prakṛti* and *sṛṣṭi*.

This could be possible because, according to Varāhamihira, this area is located in Āgneya-Koṇa (south-east), where fire devise spiritually plays the main role (vide Varāhamihira's *Bṛhat-Saṁhitā*, Kūrma Vibhāga, 8.)[14]

Another important finding is the discovery of half portion of stone sockets, near the water pool of Pātālgaṅgā. Such stone sockets of circular shape and with a socket on the lower part owe their origin to the rock art of Yogīmaṭh Ḍoṅger, belonging to the Neolithic period.[15] Such stone sockets have been found from Mohangiri site of Kālāhāṇḍī district and Kharligaṛh site of Bolaṅgīr district (Plate 2). Two sets of such sockets are found in the ruin of eight-handed Mahiṣāsuramardinī stone temple, situated on the left bank of Udanti River, within Baṛgāon village of Sinapali Block area.

The shape of these stone sockets is an artistic expression of yogic vision — the union of male and female principles of nature. These stone sockets finally led to evolution of the form or shape of Lord Puruṣottama Jagannātha. Three such stone images of Balabhadra, Subhadrā and Jagannātha, without hands, have been excavated from the ruined huge temple mound, near Tentelkhuṇṭi village in Bolaṅgīr district.[16] These findings of the author are seconded by a rare finding in Sonepur district. It was reported in *Sambād*, an Oriya daily newspaper, dated 12 October 2005, p. 2, that "on 2 October 2005, Ghasiram Sahu, a resident of Piplikani village within Ulunda block of Sonepur district, while digging the banana plants, by the side of his house, accidentally came across or dug out a stone Jagannātha image, with square hands, measuring 3" each in length. The height of the image is 1' and its width is 5". On the forehead a small half moon shape is chiselled". The studies of these archaeological findings prove that Boden Block area had contributed to the

[14] Siba Prasad Das, *History of Sambalpur* (Oriya), Sambalpur: Viswabharati Press, Madipara, 2nd edn., 1969, p. 20.

[15] J.P. Singh Deo, "Pre-Historic Cave Painting of Jogimath Donger", *OHRJ*, vol. XXII, no. 2, pp. 21-22.

[16] *THOMV*, 2004, *passim.* and Sasanka Sekhar Panda, "Antiquities of Shri Jagannātha: Amazing Finding", *Reference Orissa* (Century edn.), A.N. Tiwari (ed.), Bhubaneswar: Enterprising Publishers, 2005, pp. 72-77.

Plate 2: "Stone Sockets," showing the union of male and female principals of nature.
Findspot: Kharligaṛh site of Bolaṅgīr district, Orissa.
Exibited at Manikyapur Museum, Bhawānīpatna, Dist. Kālāhāṇḍī, Orissa.

formation of the shape of Lord Jagannātha deity, which signifies the union of *puruṣa* and *prakṛti*.

In Amguḍā village, human antiquities are found. Sanlal Herna of this village had found one Umā-Maheśvara image of flat design, which is the peculiarity of Kosala style of sculptural art and is worshipped by him. According to *haṭha-yoga*, Umā-Maheśvara images signify haṭha-yogic *lāṭa-mudrā*. With the help of late Jagabandhu Das, a set of three copperplate with seal of Jayarāja of Śarabhapura, regnal year 3, was discovered.[17] It belongs to sixth century CE. The seal has Gaja-Lakṣmī and it is well known from other copperplate findings that Śarabhapurīyās were Vaiṣṇavas in faith. The archaeological findings at Amguḍā prove that there was synchronization of Śaiva and Vaiṣṇava faiths or Hari-Hara cult.

Near to Amguḍā, from Dumerbahal village, on the bank of Udanti River within Sinapali Block, the author had discovered one Hari-Hara image and towards its east is situated Nilji village. While fishing in a tank of Nilji village, a sculptural flat

---

[17] D.C. Sircar and J.P. Singh Deo, "Amgura Plates of Jayaraja of Sarabhapura, Regnal Year 3", *Indian Museum Bulletin*, vol. XI, no. 1, January, 1976, pp. 57-59

type of stone art of Lord Narasiṁha was found, which is typical to the sculptural arts of South Kośala region. Such sculptural flat-type art excavated from Sirpur site, is exhibited at Mahanta Ghasidas Museum, Raipur. These two flat-type of sculptural arts are now preserved at the private museum of the author in the Khariar Palace.

On 27 October 2003, Ram Ratan Majhi of Kiraijhola village of Boden Block informed the author about a Devī image, found on the embankment of the village tank, Dehelia Bandha. Subsequently, it was collected and is preserved at my private museum. The image is made of stucco art and is about 1.5' in height and 1' in width. It is four-armed standing image of a goddess wearing skull necklace. On the raised upper right hand she holds a bell. On the raised upper left hand, she holds a *khapara* (broken earthen pot piece) and on the lower left hand, a human head. This interesting image of the goddess is not properly identified.

2

Traces of Spiritual Kuṇḍalinī in the Kālāhāṇḍī Region

THE earliest trace of Yoga is found at the pre-historic rock-shelter painting at Guḍahāṇḍī. This painting of human-like figure, standing on an animal, seems to represent Paśupati. Further, this painting has a head which symbolizes a lotus. In *kuṇḍalinī-yoga*, the highest *cakra* of human being is described as a thousand-petalled lotus, i.e. *sahasrāra*. So, it can be claimed that *sahasrāra cakra* is a gift of Kālāhāṇḍī region to the mankind. In reality, going by Swami Satyananda Saraswati, *cakra*s are within the realm of the psyche. Consciousness, manifests at different levels, in accordance with the *cakra* that is predominantly active. *Sahasrāra* acts through nothing and yet again, it acts through everything. *Sahasrāra* is "beyond the beyond" (*parātparam*) and it is right here. *Sahasrāra* is the culmination of the progressive ascension through different *cakra*s. It is the crown of expanded awareness. The power of the *cakra*s does not reside within themselves, but in *sahasrāra*. The *cakra*s are only switches and all the potential lies in *sahasrāra*.[1]

There are four stages of happiness: pleasure, joy, bliss and beatitude. Beatitude is the happiness of the highest kind, it is the heavenly happiness. Beatitude can be compared to *samādhi* in yogic conception. *Samādhi* is a particular type of consciousness whose practicality lies in the rise of *kuṇḍalinī*.

Kuṇḍalinī is a gift of Tantra to mankind. In the words of Paramahamsa Swami Satyananda Saraswati:

> Since the dawn of creation, the tāntrics and *yogī*s have realized that in this physical body there is potential force. It is not psychological, philosophical or transcendental; it is a dynamic potential force in the material body and it is called *kuṇḍalinī*. This *kuṇḍalinī* is the greatest discovery of Tantra and Yoga.[2]

---

1 Paramahaṁsa Swami Satyananda Saraswati, *Kuṇḍalinī Tantra*, Munger: Bihar School of Yoga, 1992, p. 201.

2 Ibid., vide Introduction.

This statement of a realized *yogī*, who has reached the *paramahaṁsa* stage of Yoga and spirituality, is of great importance for the antiquity study of the Kālāhāṇḍī district. It seems the Guḍahāṇḍī rock art (*fig*. 2.1) is of early period and therefore the Gazetteer[3] assigns it to about fifteenth millennium BCE. Sadasiba Pradhan[4] is unable to identify this human figure in red and informs that in the absence of any thematic depictions, the paintings remain, by and large, enigmatic to any viewer.

fig. 2.1: Rock art of Guḍahāṇḍī, Kālāhāṇḍī district, Orissa.

[3] D.C. Kuanr (state ed.), *Orissa District Gazetteers: Kalahandi*, Nilamani Senapati (chief ed.), Cuttack, 1980, p. 36.

[4] Sadasiba Pradhan, *Rock Art in Orissa*, New Delhi: Aryan Books International, 2001, p. 31.

Pradhan's view is completely wrong and he seems to be working within the limits of his educative mind only. Knowledge is of repetitive, derivative, educative and intuitive types. Intuitive knowledge is achieved through any type of yogic process, with which one gets absorbed in different types of consciousness or *samādhis*, with the rise of *kuṇḍalinī*.

When *kuṇḍalinī* rises to *mūlādhāra cakra, savitarka samādhi* takes place; in *svādhiṣṭhāna cakra, savicāra samādhi* takes place; in *maṇipūra cakra, sānanda samādhi* takes place; in *anāhata cakra, sasmita samādhi* takes place; in *viśuddhi cakra, bhāva pratyaya videha samādhi* takes place; and in *ājñā cakra, pūrṇa pratyaya samādhi* takes place.[5]

About *sahasrāra cakra,* Swami Satyananda Saraswati[6] mentions:

> The literal meaning of the word *sahasrāra* is one thousand. For this reason, it is said to be a lotus with one thousand petals. However, the word *sahasrāra,* while literally meaning one thousand, implies that its magnitude and significance is vast. In fact, unlimited. Therefore, the *sahasrāra* should more aptly be described as a lotus with an infinite number of petals.
>
> It is both formless (*nirākāra*) and form (*ākāra*), yet it is also beyond and therefore untouched by form (*nirvikāra*). It transcends logic, for logic compares one thing with another. The *sahasrāra* is the totality, so what is there to compare it with?
>
> It is the supreme experience, but even this statement is completely misleading. Experience implies an individual, separated from the experience, who is experiencing the experience. The *sahasrāra* is beyond experience. It implies that the experience, the experienced and the experiencer are one and the same. The seer, seeing and seen are merged as a unified whole. Even this is a misconception, for they have always been merged. In this situation, who is there to experience? These are only words, but words intended to indicate that *sahasrāra* is beyond all definition . . . beyond description.
>
> Mount Kailāsa is a famous mountain in the Himalayas. It is said to be the abode of Śiva and Śakti, who live in eternal nuptial Bliss. Symbolically, the mountain represents *sahasrāra,* where consciousness and *prāṇa* (Śiva and

[5] S.R. Sengupta, *Mother Cult*, Kolkata: Firma K.L.M., 1977, p. 106.

[6] Paramahaṁsa Swami Satyananda Saraswati, *ASCITATTOYAK*, Munger: Bihar School of Yoga, 2nd edn., 1989, p. 623.

> Śakti) are united. Every mystical and religious system throughout the world has its own unique way of symbolizing *sahasrāra*. Experience of *sahasrāra* is called by different names. Buddhists call it *nirvāṇa*, Hindus call it *kaivalya, turīya, nirvikalpa samādhi* and so forth, Sūfīs call it *baqua*, Christians call it heaven, Kabbalists call it *Ain soph*. It is possible to list hundreds of names, all meaning the same thing — *sahasrāra*.
>
> *Sahasrāra* is not a *cakra* as is often thought. *Cakra*s are within the realms of the psyche. Consciousness manifests at different levels, according to the *cakra* that is predominantly functioning. *Sahasrāra* acts through nothing, and yet again, it acts through everything. It is beyond the beyond (*parātparam*) . . . and yet, it is right here. *Sahasrāra* is the culmination of the progressive ascension through the different *cakra*s. It is the crown of expanded awareness.
>
> Many ancient people worshipped the seven (then known) planets. These represent the six principal *cakra*s and *sahasrāra*. The planets were regarded as living in the sun, for the sun is analogous to white light, which contains the essence of all other colours; it is also the source of the other planets. This symbolises that the power of the *cakra*s does not reside in the *cakra*s themselves, but in *sahasrāra*. The *cakra*s themselves are only switches. All the potential lies in the *sahasrāra*.
>
> Books could be written on *sahasrāra*, but it would be merely words. We therefore feel that we have said enough and if you want more descriptions of *sahasrāra*, we suggest that you read any of the thousands of mystical and religious scriptures. But we warn you: do not become attached to intellectual analysis. It will lead you nowhere except into a bog of misconceptions. It is far better to practise Yoga, or any other spiritual system, and raise your own level of awareness.

It can be definitely mentioned that in early period of human development, great realized *yogī*s or supermen were living in the Kāḷāhāṇḍī region. They have left the trace or antiquity of their realization of *kuṇḍalinī* in its *sahasrāra* stage, in the depiction of Guḍahāṇḍī rock art which was discovered by Kedarnath Mahapatra and Satyanarayan Rajguru jointly, who were working jointly as staff of the Archaeology Department of erstwhile Kālāhāṇḍī state. This rock art of Guḍahāṇḍī was first reported in *The Journal of Kalinga Historical Research Society*, vol. II, p. 243, by Satyanarayan Rajaguru, and it is the earliest of *kuṇḍalinī* antiquity showing or depicting *sahasrāra cakra* of Paśupati.

3

Rethinking on the Aryan Race Theory

THE English regime tried to destroy the culture and the religion of India by all means. They deliberately produced such derogatory literatures in huge quantities that confused and misguided the whole world. "Aryan Race Theory" was one of such attempts.

According to His Divinity, Dharm Chakravarti Swami Prakashanand Saraswati,[1] one such fiction was the Aryan invasion theory. He states:

> The pre-planned scheme of Jones (i.e. Sir William Jones) to introduce the idea that Sanskrit was an outside language gave birth to the speculation of the imagined existence of some Central Asian (Aryan) race who spoke Sanskrit and who brought Sanskrit language to India when they forcefully entered the country. In this way the fiction of the Aryan invasion was created much later some time in the 1800s by the same group of people and was extensively promoted by Max Müller. Let us now probe into the matter and see how the story formulated.
>
> It is a well-known fact that India is called "Āryāvartta". *Manu-Smṛti* (2/2/22) describes the exact location of Āryāvartta which lies from the south of the Himalayas and all the way up to the Indian ocean. Its inhabitants are called Arya. But it is not a locally spoken name. Commonly, we write Bhāratavarṣa for India in general and scriptural writings. The territory of India (or Bhāratavarṣa or Āryāvartta) during the Mahābhārata War (3139 BCE) was up to Iran. So the ancient Iranian people also used to call themselves the Aryans.
>
> People of the British regime using this information, fabricated a story that some unknown race of Central Asia who came and settled in Iran were called the Aryans and they were Sanskrit-speaking people. They invaded India, established themselves permanently, and wrote the Vedas. Those who introduced this ideology never cared to produce any evidence

[1] His Divinity Dharm Chakravarti Swami Prakashanand Saraswati, *The True History and the Religion of India*, Delhi: Motilal Banarsidass, 2001, p. 266.

in support of their statement because it never existed, and furthermore fiction stories don't need evidences as they are self-created dogmas.

If someone carefully looks into the ancient history of India, he will find that there was no such thing as an Aryan invasion. Since the very beginning of human civilization, Hindus (Aryans) are the inhabitants of Bhāratavarṣa (India) which is also called Āryāvartta. In the Bhāratīya history there are descriptions of Śaka and Hūṇa invasions and also of Muslim invasions but never an Aryan invasion. It was simply a figment of the imagination of the British diplomats that fabricated this false story. However, after creating this story, they had to fix the period of the entry of the Aryans into India which needed a careful decision.

The second millennium BCE was the period of migration and the expansion of major civilizations in the Middle East area. The Sumerians were at their peak around 2000 BCE; the Babylonians were expanding their empire around 1700 BCE and the Assyrians established their independent kingdom around 1400 BCE. The Hittite Empire (Turkey) also flourished during the second millennium BCE. The Hittite language used Akkadian cuneiform script of which the earliest known record of cuneiform text goes back to 1700 BCE. The cursive form of the alphabetical writing of early Hebrew and Aramaic languages started taking first primitive shape around 1000 BCE and the Greek around 900 BCE.

Considering these factors of social and literal developments in the Middle East, they randomly fixed the fifteenth century BCE for their speculated Aryan invaders, telling that they came from the Iranian side, forcefully entered the Indus Valley, settled there and spread towards the south.

This is the whole story about the Aryan invasion fiction which was so extensively popularized that it appeared in the writings of every historian.

The earliest recorded literature are the *Ṛgveda* and subsequent Vedas. So, Vedic Sanskrit is the earliest language of mankind. Therefore, P.N. Oak[2] had said that "Arya" is an ideal and is misconstrued as a race. What better proof of this truth can be found than the well-known maxim which enjoins on all Indians the ideal, *kṛṇvanto viśvam āryam,* i.e. "Make the entire world Aryan". Had the word "Arya" signified a race, the above dictum would not have come into being because race-

[2] P.N. Oak, *Some Blunders of Indian Historical Research,* Delhi: Surya Prakashan, 1st rpt., September 1969, pp. 223-33.

conscious people, far from wanting to assimilate the "world" in their fold, believe in maintaining an exclusive identity. The word "Aryan" signified an ideal man and no race.

The influence of British yoke was still there, when B.K. Ghosh[3] wrote on the Aryan problem, which is followed by an Appendix — India, the Original Home of the Aryans by S. Srikanta Sastri.

B.K. Ghosh[4] was of the opinion that it was Florentine merchant Fillippo Sassetti who, after five years stay at Goa (1583–88), declared for the first time that there existed a definite relation between Sanskrit and some of the principal languages of Europe. But that this relation is due to origin from a common source was suggested only in 1786 by Sir William Jones in his famous address to the Asiatic Society of Bengal. He, thus, established the common origin of a number of languages such as Greek, Latin, Gothic, Celtic, Sanskrit and Persian to which the scholars have given the name Indo-European or Indo-German and therewith laid the foundation of the science of comparative philology. The third and the final step in formulating the Aryan problem was taken by Max Müller, who declared in emphatic terms that "Aryan, in scientific language, is utterly inapplicable to race. It means language and nothing but language; and if we speak of Aryan race at all, we should know that it means no more than X+ Aryan speech". Thus, purely linguistic formulation of the problem was, however, never fully accepted by the learned or the laity.

B.K. Ghosh had clearly stated that:

> Max Müller declared in emphatic terms, "Aryan", in scientific language, is utterly inapplicable to race. On the contrary, a romantic reaction, which identified language with race, set in soon and was given powerful expression by Penka, who declared language to be the organic product of an organism subject to organic laws. . . . Today Müller's school is dominant no doubt, but Penka's is yet far from discredited, for it is now realized that, though by no means determined by race, yet as a social phenomenon, a language can assume its particular aspect only within a particular society and that in those very early times, when the original Indo-European language was gradually taking shape, such a particular society could have been based only on racial affinity, purely cultural bonds being out of the question. . . . Penka's attitude is, however, irrational. The Aryan problem, as formulated

[3] B.K. Ghosh, "The Aryan Problem", *THACOTIP*, vol. I, *The Vedic Age*, 1965, pp. 205-21.

[4] B.K. Ghosh, "The Aryan Problem", *THACOTIP*, vol. I, *The Vedic Age*, 1965, pp. 205-13.

> by Max Müller, is a purely linguistic one and it can be connected with ethnology only in the restricted sense. Penka succeeded in proving, at least to his own satisfaction, that Scandinavia was the cradle land of the Indo-Europeans. Modern supporters of Penka's theory have altogether dropped the linguistic arguments and tend to concentrate on pre-historic archaeology.

Great explorations and studies have been going on. P.N. Oak[5] had written a paper, "Role of Sanskrit as Ancient World Language Forgotten".

Swami Prakashanand Saraswati[6] has dealt with the topic and has shown the history of the origin and developments of the languages of the world; and the origin and development of Greek, Roman and Western religions and civilizations, from fourth millennium BCE to twentieth century CE.

This proves that the Vedic people and their disciples had spread the Vedic knowledge and Sanskrit language throughout the world and Sanskrit as the mother language of all the languages of the world has been forgotton.

About the home of Vedic people, S.D. Kulkarni[7] had observed that the Vedic influence was all-pervasive and it spread right from modern Turkey and Egypt, covered the region between the Caucasus mountain and the Caspian Sea down to Syria and Palestine and the Persian Gulf kingdoms of ancient Babylon, Asur, Russian Azerbaizan and the southern regions of the Russian republics — Tajikistan, Uzbek, Turkmen and Kirghis. It extended further east to Hindukush mountains and covered the region around Varasakh River and included the Sindhu region of modern Sindh, Punjab and Kashmir. This was the position in about 5000 BCE. About 2000 years or so earlier, the Daśarājña battle was fought and the Vedics, living together in this vast region, began to spread eastwards and southwards to the present-day India, and towards west to Greece, Italy and northwards.

Discovery of the evolutionary history of the lost river of north-western India, Vedic Sarasvatī River, has been done in recent years.[8] Vedic culture flourished in India and the Vedic culture was spread throughout the world. Latest study of Shripal Dhattatraya Kulkarni and his following scholars[9] show that there is no

[5] P.N. Oak, op. cit., 1969, pp. 301-09.

[6] Swami Prakashanand Saraswati, op. cit., 2001, pp. 95-222.

[7] S.D. Kulkarni (gen. ed.), *BSOIHAC*, vol. I, *Beginning of Life, Culture and History*, 1988, p. 147.

[8] B.P. Radhakrishna and S.S. Merh (eds.), *Memoir 42, Vedic Saraswati*, Bangalore: Geological Society of India, 1999, *passim*.

[9] S.D. Kulkarni (gen. ed.), op. cit., vol. XVI, *India Abroad*, Bombay, 1995, *passim*.

country in the world where Vedic culture, both spiritually and materialistically, has not reached. Therefore, Will Durant, the famous American scholar, was of the opinion:

> India was the Motherland of our race and Sanskrit the mother of Europe's languages. She was the mother of our philosophy, mother through the Arabs of much of our mathematics, mother through the village communities of self-government and democracy. Mother India in many ways is the mother of us all.

With the spread of science, great researches are continuing and international scholars like Georg Feuerstein, Subhash Kak and David Frawley[10] are in search of the cradle of civilization, which they have found out to be Sarasvatī River, its Vedic culture and Sanskrit language. Because of such advanced studies and observations, they have set forth seventeen arguments to prove that the Aryan invasion never happened.

So, the story of Aryan race and Aryan invasion or Aryan penetration to India is now invalidated by latest researches. Now, let us peep into the Arya conception. David Frawley of Mexico is a direct disciple of Raman Maharṣi and his Hindu name is Vamadeva Shastri. He is very much accepted as a Vedic scholar of the western world by the Indians. In his latest book, *Wisdom of the Ancient Seers : Mantras of the Ṛgveda*, David Frawley[11] writes about the Aryan seers thus:

> Spiritual culture of India's mythical Golden Age called itself "Aryan", and it is from here that this term originally derives. Aryan originally means noble, people of noble character, inner values, integrity and honesty, the nobility of self-knowledge. It was in this sense that even the Buddha (who criticized much of the Vedic religion which by his time had degenerated from its spiritual base) called his religion Aryan (Aryan Dharma), his wisdom Aryan (Arya Prajñā) and his path Aryan. This original sense of Aryan has little to do with Germanic sense of the term invented by nineteenth-century European thinkers and further warped by the Nazis. Aryan is a term for a higher spiritual humanity based on the principles of truth, giving self-sacrifice and the consciousness of unity and universality. It is unfortunate that it has been debased and that these negative and inappropriate associations, which

[10] G. Feuerstein, S. Kak and D. Frawley, *In Search of the Cradle of Civilization*, Delhi: Motilal Banarsidass, 1999, pp. 153-61.

[11] David Frawley, *Wisdom of the Ancient Seers* (*Mantras of the Ṛgveda*), Delhi: Motilal Banarsidass, 1995, pp. 33-35.

are really ignoble, unspiritual and un-Aryan, should be projected upon it. Yet this is often the way of the world, as the Vedas say, wherein the dark forces take upon themselves and use falsely the powers and appellations of the light.

The highest human type in Aryan society, the culture bearer and guide, is the seer and sage. Aryan society was ruled by men of spiritual knowledge, the enlightened and illumined who lived in cosmic awareness. The values of Aryan society were arranged hierarchically to lead all human beings to become seers. Material and commercial values were regarded as inferior and kept in check. The prime value of Aryan society was the worship of the divine, outwardly and ritualistically for the ignorant, inwardly in meditation for the wise.

The Aryan seer is a higher order of human being, a man of spiritual knowledge like Buddha or Christ. At that time such seers were not rare individuals outside of society, but the highest level of the society whose place was recognized and revered by the culture as a whole. These seers manifested the love of truth, a free and open creativity, and a great ardour of life and awareness. In stature they were like great mountains and in movement like mighty rivers. Their powers of perception extended through all the realms of Cosmic existence. Their creative force manifested in many worlds. Yet they were as yielding and serviceable as a cow, as impartially beneficent as the sun. Reaching in mind the highest heavens, they remained as humble as the earth. Knowing the supreme beyond, they could still reveal in the simple beauties of life in the here and now. They were men of the greatest simplicity, yet of vast comprehension, which is why their hymns frequently became too multiple and magical in meaning for us to grasp. They were our spiritual fathers, the makers of civilization, and as long as civilization upheld their inner and spiritual values, there was true harmony on earth.

The Vedic hymns are, in a way, merely a means of introducing us to our ancestors, that we might comprehend the heritage of spiritual humanity we also possess. Our true human legacy is not just of violence and sorrow. All the origins of our civilization are the seers and their great meditations. Recognizing them again, we can once more call up their power within us and again become true human beings, men of cosmic awareness, instead of animals or machines out of control. A true understanding of ancient culture discovers the work of these seers and a true vision of the future shows their influence returning again.

> Our present idea of man as a purely physical entity with purely material drives and our idea of history as the development of material tools and capacities is false and degrading. Our true and original human heritage from which we have fallen is as seers, cosmic beings of spiritual awareness. A proper understanding of the *Ṛgveda* restores this original and higher heritage of ours and returns to us that capacity of seeing in which alone we can realize our potential, a condition happier and wiser than anything modern culture has yet to imagine. It is to bring the Aryan seer out in us that this book is written, to stimulate our true nobility of character and capacity to perceive the truth. It is not for some cultural or intellectual interest, but to link us upwardly to the ancient spiritual forces that once had great power on earth and are needed again today for us to survive this difficult transitional period of the race.

It is seen that people of all walks of life in the West are fascinated on India and are conducting research in every field of life or in all fields of Indology.[12] Many scholars are working on the Aryan problem. Some scholars — of both East and West — have worked on Aryan topic. They are: K.D. Sethna,[13] S.K. Patel,[14] P. Bandyopadhyay,[15] S.G. Talageri,[16] David Frawley,[17] V.K. Verma,[18] N.S. Rajaram,[19]

---

12 F. Wilhelm and H.G. Rawlinson , "India and the Modern West", *A Cultural History of India*, ed. A.L. Basham, Delhi: Oxford University Press, 2nd impression, 1984, p. 486.

13 K.D. Sethna, *The Problems of Aryan Origins*, New Delhi: Voice of India, 1989, *passim.*

14 Satyavrata R. Patel, *East and West: A Cultural Dialogue*, Bombay: Bharatiya Vidya Bhavan, 1992, *passim.*

15 Pranab Bandyopadhyay, *The Aryans and the Holy Vedas, United Writers, Selling Agent*, Kolkata: Firma K.L.M., 1993, *passim.*

16 Shrikant G. Talageri, *The Aryan Invasion Theory: A Reappraisal*, New Delhi: Voice of India, 1994, *passim; Aryan Invasion Theory and Indian Nationalism*, New Delhi: Voice of India, 2003, *passim.*

17 David Frawley, *The Myth of the Aryan Invasion of India*, New Delhi: Voice of India, 1994, *passim; Gods, Sages and the Kings* (*Vedic Secrets of Ancient Civilization*), Delhi: Motilal Banarsidass, 2nd rpt., 1995, *passim.*

18 Vishnukant Verma, *Indo-Aryan Colonization of Greece and Middle East*, 2 vols., Delhi: Pratibha Prakashan, 2000, *passim; Missing Links of World Civilization, Indo-Aryan Colonization*, Delhi: Pratibha Prakashan, 2004, *passim.*

19 Navaratna S. Rajaram, *The Politics of History*, New Delhi: Voice of India, 1995, *passim*; N.S. Rajaram and David Frawley, *Vedic Aryans and the Origin of Civilization*, New Delhi: Voice of India, 2nd edn., 1997, *passim.*

L.N. Renu,[20] Michel Danino,[21] and K. Elst.[22] Their books may be referred for more details.

This discussion proves that there was never an Aryan race in the world. The Vedic *ṛṣis* called themselves Aryans and had wished or desired to Aryanize the human beings of the earth, as the term, *kṛnvanto viśvam āryam*, as mentioned in *Ṛgveda.*

Purushottam Lal Bhargava,[23] who is a Sanskritist, historian and Indologist since early 1950s, had worked on the topic "India in the Vedic Age" and had shown the homeland of the Aryan Vedic *ṛṣis*. B.B. Lal[24] gives ample evidence and proves that all the trees mentioned in the *Ṛgveda*, such as the *aśvattha*, *khadira* and *nyagrodha* do not belong to a cold climate but to a tropical one. Likewise the Ṛgvedic fauna, comprising such species as the lion, elephant and peacock also belong to a tropical climate.

In recent years, the Sindhu-Sarasvatī Valley Civilization has been studied as the later Vedic civilization by Bhagwan Singh.[25] The Aryan invasion theory is the greatest folly of Indological study, which was forced by the imperialistic historians.

---

20 L.N. Renu, *Indian Ancestors of Vedic Aryans*, Bombay: Bharatiya Vidya Bhawan, 2nd impression, 1996, *passim.*

21 Michel Danino, *The Invasion that Never Was*, Mysore: The Mother's Institute of Research, Mira Aditi, 1996, *passim.*

22 Koenraad Elst, *Update on the Aryan Debate*, New Delhi: Voice of India, (?), *passim.*

23 P.L. Bhargava, *India in the Vedic Age*, 1st edn., 1956, 2nd edn., 1971 and 3rd rev. and enlarged edn., New Delhi: D.K. Printworld, 2001, *passim.*

24 B.B. Lal, *The Homeland of the Aryans (Evidence of Ṛgvedic Flora, Fauna and Archaeology)*, New Delhi: Aryan Books International, 2005, *passim.*

25 Bhagwan Singh, *The Vedic Harappans*, New Delhi: Aditya Prakashan, 1995, *passim.*

4

Bhāratavarṣa Civilization and Its Impact on the Ancient World

THE adjective of "orient" means rising as the sun, eastern, bright or pure in colour, the part where the sun-rises, sunrise, purity of lustre and the countries of the East.

The East was influenced by the great tradition of India,[1] i.e. Vedic culture and faith. Sarasvatī River Valley was the centre or the cradle of Vedic civilization. The impact of Vedic culture had extended far and wide. In the words of S.D. Kulkarni,[2] the Vedic influence was spread right from modern Turkey and Egypt, covered the region between the Caucasus mountain and the Caspian Sea down to Syria and Palestine and the Persian Gulf kingdoms of ancient Babylon, Asur, Sumer, Akkad, Ur, Kassite and included the modern Iran-Afghanistan, the Russian Azerbaizan and the southern regions of the Russian republics — Tajikistan, Uzbek, Turkmen and Kirghis. It extended further east to Hindukush mountains and covered the region around Varasakh River and included Sindhu region of modern Sindh, Punjab and Kashmir. This was the position in about 5000 BCE. About 2000 years or so earlier, the Daśarājña battle was fought and Vedics living together in this vast region, began to spread eastwards and south-wards to the present-day India and towards west to Greece, Italy and northwards.

About the geography of the Vedic period, P.L. Bhargava[3] says that the region in which the hymns of the *Ṛgveda* originated was known as Saptasindhu or the land of the seven rivers as one verse of the *Ṛgveda* clearly indicated (*ṚV*, VIII.24.27). The *Ṛgveda* mentions the names of about forty rivers, though the ones most frequently mentioned are the Sindhu, the river *par-excellence* and the Sarasvatī. The largest number of rivers mentioned at one place is to be found in a late hymn occurring in

---

[1] Swami Agehananda Bharti, *Great Tradition and Little Traditions (Indological Investigations in Cultural Anthropology)*, Varanasi: Chowkhamba Sanskrit Series, 1978, *passim*.

[2] S.D. Kulkarni (ed.), *BSOIHAC*, vol. I, *Beginnings of Life, Culture and History*, 1983, p. 147.

[3] P.L. Bhargava, *India in the Vedic Age*, New Delhi: D.K. Printworld, 3rd rev. edn., pp. 70-71.

the tenth Maṇḍala of the *Ṛgveda* (*ṚV*, X.75). This is the only hymn of the *Ṛgveda* which directly mentions the river Gaṅgā.

Vedic Sarasvatī River has dried and in recent years much archaeological and scientific surveys of this great river are going on and Geological Society of India[4] has published its research studies in *Memoir 42*. Being so great the spread of the Vedic India, one has to firmly believe that our civilization has definitely influenced the life of people in many countries across the globe. However, this truth has been concocted by biased and prejudiced historians mostly from the West. But, the recent researches are paving the way for finding the ultimate truth. It is noteworthy to recapitulate the developments so far to underline the impact of our civilization. A research paper of David Frawley,[5] "The Myth of the Aryan Invasion in India" deserves a special mention. The Aryan invasion theory has become outdated and no more accepted by the serious intellectual scholars,[6] but is still taught in schools and many universities. This shows the inefficiency of Indian History Congress and education departments of our country.

David Frawley[7] draws the attention of the egoistic, mundane, ignorant and arrogant humanities in his book *Awaken Bharata — A Call for India's Rebirth*. With this background L.N. Renu[8] has written a book, named *Indian Ancestors of Vedic Aryans*, wherein he proves that originally Aryans were Indians and there was no migration.

Reality of ancient Indian history is long suffering because it was politically

---

[4] B.P. Radhakrishna and S.S. Merh (eds.), *Memoir 42, Vedic Saraswati* (*Evolutionary History of a Lost River of North-Western India*), Bangalore: Geological Society of India, 1999, *passim*.

[5] Ibid., 1999, pp. 57-62.

[6] Michel Danino, *The Invasion that Never Was*, Delhi: The Mother's Institute of Research; Mysore: Mira Aditi, 1996, pp. 9 and 82;

Pranab Bandyopadhyay, *The Aryans and the Holy Vedas*, Kolkata: United Writers, 1993, *passim;*

David Frawley, *The Myth of the Aryan Invasion of India*, New Delhi: Voice of India, 1995, *passim;*

Navaratna S. Rajaram, *The Politics of History* (*Aryan Invasion Theory and Subversion of Scholarship*), New Delhi: Voice of India, 1995, *passim*; and

Navaratna S. Rajaram and David Frawley, *Vedic Aryans and the Origins of Civilizations*, New Delhi: Voice of India, 1995, *passim.*

[7] David Frawley, *Awakened Bharata: A Call for India's Rebirth*, New Delhi: Voice of India, 1998, *passim*.

[8] L.N. Renu, *Indian Ancestors of Vedic Aryans*, Bombay: Bharatiya Vidya Bhavan, 2nd edn., 1996, *passim*.

deframed and degraded by the imperialistic oriental scholars and how it was done has been described shown by His Divinity Dharm Chakravarti Swami Prakashanand Saraswati[9] in Chapter 3, "Demeaning the History and the Religion of India: Misguiding the Whole World and Destroying and Fabricating the Historic Records", in his famous book, *The True History and the Religion of India*. This book has received much accolade from great freelance scholars of the world, who are in search of true history, culture, and human and religious developments of the ancient world.

No doubt, there were eminent savants, antiquarians, archaeologists and historians of Indology of Europe and America belonging to diverse times,[10] but they wrote history with politics in mind. But some of them were true to their observations of India's past. One of them was Lord Curzon. Rev. Jebez T. Suderland[11] of America had mentioned Lord Curzon, who, as the Viceroy of India, said in his address at the Great Delhi Durbar in 1901:

> Powerful empires existed and flourished here (in India) while English men were still wandering painted in the woods, and while the British colonies were still a wilderness and jungle. India has left a deeper mark upon the history, the philosophy and the religion of mankind than any other terrestrial unit in the Universe.

In recent years, Vishnukant Verma[12] has written two volumes — *Indo-Aryan Colonization of Greece and Middle-East* and *Missing Link of World Civilization: Indo-Aryan Colonization*.[13]

Through yogic, spiritual and cultural migrations, the disciples of Vedic *ṛṣis* had civilized the mankind. The archaeological discoveries are fast confirming this fact with the help of modern technologies. Shripad Dattatraya Kulkarni[14] edited eighteen volumes of *BSOIHAC*. His effort is worth visualizing, because these publications

---

9 *TTHATROI*, Delhi, 2001, pp. 281-404.

10 G.G. Sengupta, *Indology and Its Eminent Western Savants* (*Collection of Biographies of Western Indologists*), Kolkata: Punthi Pustak, 1996, *passim*.

11 Rev. Jabez T. Suderland, *India in Bondage: Her Right to Freedom*, Calcutta: R. Chatterjee, 1928, p. 6.

12 Vishnukant Verma, *Indo-Aryan Colonization of Greece and Middle East*, vols. I and II, Delhi: Pratibha Prakashan, 2000, *passim*.

13 Vishnukant Verma, *Missing Links of World Civilization, Indo-Aryan Colonization*, Delhi: Pratibha Prakashan, 2004, *passim*.

14 *BSOIHAC*, vol. XVI, *India Abroad*, Bombay, 1995, *passim*.

deal with India's influence on the world. People who revealed the Vedas through their intuitive wisdom and knowledge are known as *ṛṣis*. Intuition is achieved through yogic path and body alchemy takes place with the rise of *kuṇḍalinī*. In *THOMV*, thus author has observed:[15]

> The spiritual culture of India, i.e. Bhāratavarṣa, reached its zenith through Vedic wisdom, which is meant for the entire human community. Tantra is a parallel cultivation of this Vedic wisdom which brought much refinement to the art of Vedic civilization. As the overall development of Indian spirituality is based on truth, it brought about a synthesis in all aspects of life. It is for this reason that Indian civilization is eternal and a vibrant composite culture. As the Vedic civilization mostly developed in the Sarasvatī Valley, Indians claim that though this river of north-west Indians has dried up, Sarasvatī still flows on, i.e. Indian culture or civilization is perennial. This is Vedic culture.

According to Will Durant,[16] an American scholar:

> India was the motherland of our race and Sanskrit the mother of Europe's languages. She was the mother of our philosophy, mother through the Arabs of much of our mathematics, mother through the village communities of self-government, and democracy. Mother India in many ways is the mother of us all.

French and Russian scholars had also done much studies on India, but many of their works are not yet translated into English. American scholars are very advanced in the latest studies. Therefore, G. Feuerstan, S. Kak and D. Frawley[17] have jointly written a book *In Search of Cradle of Civilization*. More archaeological discoveries using scientific methods and sincere human efforts have made a paradigm shift in representing India in European discourses.[18] With the help of American Institute of Indian Studies, New Delhi,[19] a book has been published to felicitate the people

---

[15] *THOMV*, Delhi, 2004, preface.

[16] *BSOIHAC*, vol. XVI, *India Abroad*, Bombay, 1995, inner cover page.

[17] G. Feuerstein, S. Kak and D. Frawley, *In Search of the Cradle of Civilization*, Delhi: Motilal Banarsidass, 1999, *passim*.

[18] Vibya Maurya (ed.), *Encountering the Indian: Contemporary European Images of India*, New Delhi: Aryan Books International, 1999, *passim*.

[19] Joseph W. Elder, Edward C. Dimok Jr. and T. Ainslie Embree (eds.), *India's Worlds and U.S. Scholars 1947–1997*, New Delhi: Manohar, 1998, *passim*.

and Goverment of India on the fiftieth anniversary of India's Independence, to acknowledge the ways in which the study of India has stimulated the U.S. scholars during the period and to express gratitude on behalf of American Institute of Indian Studies to people and the Government of India for their help in the scholars' endeavours. Geoffrey Bobby[20] considers "Indus Valley Civilization the Cinderella of the ancient world."

Friedrich Wolhelm and H.G. Rawlinson[21] are of the opinion that the influence of India, where the accent has always been on spirituality, is having a second renaissance.

The present focus on Vedic research, without biasness, is definitely going to fill up the missing links of Vedic influence on the entire mankind.

Injustice was done to the ancient history of India by imperialistic historians of British India. Navaratna S. Rajaram[22] has clearly exposed it in his work, *The Politics of History* (*Aryan Invasion Theory and the Subversion of Scholarship*).

C.K. Kareem,[23] the then state editor of *Kerala Gazetteers*, in 1971 had written a book, *What Happened in Indian History*. He had felt distressed by the distortions that have crept into the Indian history and, hence wrote the book.

After 60 years of India's independence, our historical world is not yet free from the British influence and we are still following the path of ancient Indian history, paved by imperialistic historians.

"Time and tide wait for no man", says an old adage. The time has created spiritual and yogic historians who work with one's Intuitive knowledge and wisdom. One of them is His Divinity Dharm Chakravarti Swami Prakashanand Saraswati,[24] who has drawn the attention of oriental scholars and exposes the organized plannings and workings of the British administration to destroy Hindu culture and religion, mutilate the history, fabricate the historic dates, and to totally demean and misrepresent the theme of Bhāratīya scriptures with the help of Max Müller, the people of the Asiatic Researchers' and many others.

His Divinity Dharm Chakravarti Swami Prakshanand Saraswati,[25] who dates

[20] Geoffrey Bobby, *Looking for Dilmun*, New York: New American Library, 1974, p. 161.

[21] Friedrich Wilhelm and H.G. Rawlinson, "India and the Modern World", *A Cultural History of India*, A.L. Basham (ed.), Bombay: Oxford University Press, 1975, p. 486.

[22] Navaratna S. Rajaram, *The Politics of History*, New Delhi: Voice of India, 1995, *passim*.

[23] C.K. Kareem, *What Happened in Indian History*, Cochin: Paico Publishing House, 1971, *passim*.

[24] *TTHATROI*, 2001, *passim*.

[25] Ibid., 2001, pp. 501-02 and 668-69.

the Descension of Lord Kṛṣṇa in 3228 BCE and ascension in 3102 BCE and about the first tribal migration in the world, says:

> After the ascension of Kṛṣṇa *Kaliyuga* started, and fierce sea deluge destroyed Dvārikā. Much before that the kṣhatriyas of Bhāratavarṣa (i.e. India) had been going out to settle in other countries and to have their own domain. However, there is a big question in the minds of certain intellectuals that how did the migration of the tribes start in the world? When they try to probe into the migration problem, the scanty historical information prior to 3500 BCE and then a dead stop caused by the latest ice age obscure the situation. However, the scriptures give a reference to this situation and explain that the existing human civilization was re-established by Vaivasvata Manu 120.533 million years ago on the plains of the Ganges. We had the same Purāṇas, *Gītā* and the *Bhāgvatam* all the time. When the population increased and stretched towards the Indus Valley and the eastern side of India, the prideful youths, desirous of conquering new lands and territories, spread out all over Asia, Middle East and also Europe. This could have happened before the last ice age and would have kept on happening even prior to the Mahābhārata War.
>
> The *Manu-Smṛti* gives a brief account of such a tribal movement when these prideful people went out of India and settled in the other parts of the continent long ago. It says:
>
> शनकैस्तु क्रियालोपादिमाः क्षत्रियजातयः ।
> वृषलत्वं गता कोके ब्रह्मणादर्शनेन च ॥
> पौण्ड्रकाश्चौड्रद्रविडाः काम्बोजा यवनाः शकाः ।
> पारदापह्मवाश्चीनाः किराता दरदाः खशाः ॥
>
> Because of the non-association of the Vedic teachings of India, the people of Draviḍa, Kāmboja, Śaka (Central Asia), became worldly and lost their original Indian culture. — *Manu-Smṛti*, 10.43.44
>
> When they left India, they had our locally spoken Sanskrit language with them and the stories of the Purāṇas and our religious customs were also in their minds. But the prolonged lapse of time and no social and spiritual relations with India made them forget India and they all started their new culture and religion and also a new style of language. In this way, a number of cultures started in the world whose remote prime origin was India (Bhāratavarṣa).

Ancient India had produced great scientists. Atharvan was the first discoverer of fire and propounder of the finding that fire leads to mechanical devices. Dīrghatamas, the discoverer of the Vedic era; Garga, the first enumerator of constellations; Bharadvāja, the one who presided over the first medicinal plants symposium, are noteworthy. Ātreya was the Punarvasu and his academy was of medicines. Suśruta was the father of surgery. Kaṇāda was the first expounder of realism, law of causation and atomic theory. Medhātithi was first to extend numerals to billions. Āryabhaṭṭa laid the foundations of algebra. Lagadha was the first to rationalize astronomy. Laṭadeva and Śrīsena introduced Greek astronomy to India and Baudhāyana was the first great geometer (Satya Prakash, *Founders of Science in Ancient India*, New Delhi, 1965, *passim*).

As stated, Ṛṣi Kaṇāda discovered atomic theory. Very interestingly, a Soviet scholar A.A. Gorbovsky's[26] finding has been reported thus:

> This academic foraging in far thresholds discovered a human skeleton 40 centuries old, restless in its fossilhood, with a disconcertingly high level of radiation.

Gorbovsky, at the end of numerous hypotheses, was forced to conclude that this was the skeleton of a man who died in a nuclear war, which ravaged the Indo-Gengetic basin somewhere in unrecorded history. Gorbovsky quotes the *Mahābhārata*'s description of *brahmāstra*:

> A blazing shaft which possessed all the effulgence of smokeless fire was let off . . . all directions were enveloped by darkness . . . the very elements seemed to be perturbed . . . the Sun seemed to turn . . . the universe, scorched with the heat, seemed to be in fever . . . the weapon mowed down entire population, reducing them to ashes . . . the survivors lost their hair and nails, and their food became unfit for eating . . . for years the sun and sky remained shrouded with clouds.

Gorbovsky goes on to state that this race knew the use of flying machines, but kept all that knowledge hidden from posterity, fearing its misuse. The Soviet scholar's information was O.V. Vijayan's article "Troublesome Fossil", published in *The Illustrated Weekly of India*, 3-9 January 1988, p. 30. This definitely proves that *brahmāstra* mentioned in Sanskrit literature was an atomic nuclear weapon. Because of its evil effects, the ancient Indians had destroyed the formula of making *brahmāstra*.

---

[26] A.A. Gorbovsky, "Ancient India May Have Had N-Arms", *Statesman*, Moscow, 8 September 1986, *passim* (vide *The Illustrated Weekly of India*, 3-9 January 1988, p. 30).

The glory of ancient India has been duped by the imperialistic English historians. Therefore, Amarnath,[27] the then member of Institute for Rewriting Indian History, wrote a book, *Some Missing Chapters of World History*, and was of the opinion that the Hindus, i.e. the Aryans, had a world empire and that the world then spoke Sanskrit. That is why most people in the world call themselves Aryans and speak Sanskritized language like Latin and Persian.

> To call European languages and others like Persian and Paśtu Indo-Aryan is a terminological monstrosity. Because, if according to blundering Western concepts Aryans spread all over the world, including India, from outside India, European languages and Persian and Paśtu should have been called Aryan languages and not Indo-Aryan. Since those languages are all of Sanskritic origin, they must be termed not Indo-Aryan but simply as Indian or Aryan or Sanskritic. All those three terms mean the same thing.

P.N. Oak[28] had very bluntly written a research paper, "Role of Sanskrit as Ancient World Language Forgotten". Recently, Swami Prakashanand Saraswati[29] has written about the lucid style, history of the origin and the development of the languages of the world, and the origin and development of Greek, Roman and Western religions and civilizations from fourth millennium BCE to twentieth century CE.

Kumar Prafulla Chandra Bhanja Deo,[30] not a very popular tāntric scholar of Mayūrbhañj in Orissa province, had also mentioned that, so far, because of the shackles of imperialism, it has been the fashion of our conquerors (except in a notably few instances) to treat our religion, our culture and the thought of life of our ancestors as dead museum pieces, which all self-styled dabblers in this field could claim the absolute right with impunity to ridicule, malign and distort according to their own preconceived notions and inclinations. The wonderful continuity of Indian civilization and its study as living dynamic culture as a whole, which was played, is played and is irrevocably destined to play a dominant role in the thought, words and deeds of our planet have been sacrificed to a senseless

---

27 Amarnath, *Some Missing Chapters of World History*, New Delhi: Itihas Shodh Sansthan, 1973, p. 4.

28 P.N. Oak, "Role of Sanskrit as Ancient World Language Forgotten", *Some Blunders of Indian Historical Research*, Delhi: Surya Prakashan, 1969, pp. 301-09.

29 *TTHATROI*, 2001, pp. 95-222.

30 Kumar Prafulla Chandra Bhanja Deo, "Om Mani Padme Hum", *OHRJ*, vol. I, no. 1, April 1952, pp. 20-25.

vivisection of our ideals and our way of life in order to emphasize their so-called crudities as contrasted with the superficial varnish of Europe which has a long score to settle as far as the East and especially India is concerned. The spirit in which our erstwhile masters approached subjects connected with our art and culture is patent front and aims with which the Boden Chair of Sanskrit in Oxford University was founded in that university and I have myself seen a distinguished scholar in this field, of international fame who condescended to fill a recent vacancy in this direction, rejected, because (1) he was an Indian and (2) he was not a protestant Christian of the Church of England.

> These are the defects in studies in this field that we should now try to remedy, now that independence and the self-respect arising from that blessed state are ours. The study of a few items connected with our cultural heritage in these pages is meant to give more indication in this direction.

With the scientific developments, when human beings have conquered space and time, global thinking is taking place and scholars have come to know that Bhāratavarṣa had civilized the mankind. It is worth quoting Marcus Schmieke, a German scholar, who is working on Vāstuvidyā. About the origin of Vāstu, Schmieke[31] remarks:

> The great science of Vāstu, the art of building your home in harmony with nature's laws, originated in India. Vāstu is a part of the Sthāpatyaveda that comes from the *Atharvaveda*, which is one of the four Vedas. The Vedas are the oldest writings on India's ancient history, science, philosophy and culture. Five thousand years ago, the great sage Śrīla Vyāsadeva compiled the four Vedas which contain millions of verses.
>
> The word v*eda* means complete knowledge and the original Veda is said to have been spoken by God of the time of the material creation trillions of years ago. According to Vedic world history, prior to 5000 years ago, books were not required: the memories of the people were so powerful that they could remember all they had heard throughout most of their lives. The brilliant sages throughout the ages would teach the unwritten Veda to their disciples and in this way the Veda descended through numerous generations intact. This system of preserving ancient knowledge is called *paramparā*, or disciple succession. Books became a necessity at the dawning of the Iron Age, 5000 years ago when people's memories began to rapidly deteriorate.

[31] Marcus Schmieke, *Vastu the Origin of Feng Shui*, New Delhi: New Age Books, 2003, pp. 11-13.

The massive Veda was too difficult for people to remember or even comprehend, so the Vedas were compiled for this Age.

The essence of the Vedas is to teach about the human need for spiritual development. Many parts of the Vedas additionally teach us how to improve ourselves materially in order to make spiritual progress easier. A few examples are the Gāndharvaveda, containing the ancient Indian science of music; the Āyurveda, depicting medical knowledge; Dhanurveda, presenting the military science of weapons and warfare; the Jyotiṣaveda, prodding astronomy and astrology; and the Sthāpatyaveda and other such scriptures also referred to as the Vāstu-Śāstras which expound the ancient art of constructing buildings auspiciously in harmony with nature.

The science of Vāstu originated when Lord Brahmā, a demi-god, empowered by God to create, was creating a multitude of auspicious and inauspicious beings at the beginning of the Creation. While so engaged, Lord Brahmā and other demi-gods attempted to create the "Aura" but instead a formless demon named Vāstu-Puruṣa appeared. He was the manifestation of unrestrained chaotic energy. This demon needed to be contained since he was threatening to wreak havoc throughout the universe. Lord Brahmā and the demi-gods devised a plan to stop him. They threw him to earth and sat on him. Being pinned down in this way, with Lord Brahmā in the middle and many exalted demi-gods and sages surrounding him, the Vāstu-Puruṣa was completely purified and thereafter was celebrated as a Mahābhāgavata, a great devotee of God. This is confirmed by the ancient Vedic *mantra*: ***oṁ mahābhagavatāya vāstupuruṣāya svāhā.***

The purified Vāstu-Puruṣa thereafter surrendered himself to Lord Brahmā, and said, "My Lord, how can I serve you?" Lord Brahmā replied: "I want you to stay here on earth and be the Lord in all houses and buildings".

After agreeing to serve Lord Brahmā, the Vāstu-Puruṣa inquired: "In the Satya (Golden), Tretā (Silver), and Dvāpara (Bronze) *yugas* (ages), people will build their houses according to Vāstu and will offer loving services to Lord Viṣṇu, and I will enjoy a share of those offerings. But in the Kaliyuga (the age we are in now), people will build houses in which I will suffer (with bad Vāstu) and they will not offer any services to my Master, Lord Viṣṇu. Nor will they offer me any food which has been offered to Lord Viṣṇu. What shall I do and what will I eat?" Lord Brahmā replied: "If people in the Kaliyuga cramp you into inauspiciously built buildings and neglect to offer God food

> which you will enjoy, then you may eat them." How the Vāstu-Puruṣa does this within dwellings, and how you can appease him, is all explained herein. Later, a disciple of Lord Brahmā named Maya Dānava founded the science of Vāstuvidyā which is still prominent throughout north India today.
>
> The inside and outside area of every building is portrayed in a Vāstu-Puruṣa Maṇḍala grid that contains 81 different energy fields. In the centre is the Brahma-sthāna, the place where Lord Brahmā resides. In the fields surrounding Lord Brahmā reside many other great demi-gods and sages who are all positioned on various parts of the Vāstu-Puruṣa's body. In the north-east of all buildings lies the head of the Vāstu-Puruṣa and it is therefore very inauspicious to have a toilet in the north-east. Later chapters in this book explain the consequences or various serious Vāstu defects, as well as the rewards of having good Vāstu, and most importantly how Vāstu defects can easily be corrected.
>
> Compared to Feng Shui, which is considered to be around 3000 years old, Vāstu's written history is at least 5000 years old. "Living witnesses" of Vāstu's age are the 5500 years old cities of the Indus-Sarasvatī culture in India which were discovered in 1921. The first city was found near the Village Haṛappā and hence their culture became known as the Haṛappā Civilization.
>
> One well-known city from this era is Moheṅjo-Dāṛo. This city was planned in a grid system with streets going perpendicularly from north to south and from west to east, dividing the city into rectangular blocks. The houses of Moheṅjo-Dāṛo were built with their square or rectangular sides facing the main directions and each house possessed a central courtyard. These features are found in every city of the Haṛappā Civilization. All their cities were planned like chessboards and were divided into squares of like dimensions, purposely forming various city areas with different functions. The temple was always placed in the city centre.

It is no coincidence that every detail in all those cities conforms to strict Vāstu principles. The cities did not grow organically but were planned systematically, following clear geometrical Vāstu concepts. All these facts prove irrefutably that the science of Vāstu existed even before the 5000 years old Haṛappā city was developed. Schmieke continues:

> Few are aware of Vāstu's previous application in the western hemisphere, dating back to the famous Roman architect Marcus Vitruvius. The energetic codes known to European geomancy and its modern scientific tradition over the last few hundred years (Victor Schauberger, Wilhelm Reich, Von

> Reiehenbach) also correspond to Vāstu principles. This verifies that Vāstu principles were applied in Western countries in the past and are therefore just as relevant in the present. According to authoritative sources of Vedic history, Greece and Italy were controlled by King Parīkṣit from Hastināpura (now Delhi), 5000 years ago. Verification of this can be found in the precise Vāstu architecture found in the ancient ruins of both these cities.
>
> We are living in an era, where our activities are thoughtlessly dominated by economic and pragmatic decisions. Most of us live without any consideration for nature's inescapable subtle laws that constantly and exactingly reward and punish us at every moment. Even a thousand years ago it was customary to build houses according to natural principles of harmony, the same principles Western countries are now adopting from China and India. Humankind over the last century has tried to violate nature's laws like never before, celebrating ourselves as the centre of the Universe, as if we were more powerful than God. Now nature's laws are beginning to severely reprimand our past mistakes in the form of global warming and many unnatural diseases and disturbances. But there is hope, there is a current growing worldwide trend of concern for environment. The increasing interest in Vāstu and Feng Shui demonstrates that the more sensitive and sensible sectors of human society want to re-establish harmonious connections with nature.
>
> According to Vedic texts, the world 5000 years ago didn't have anywhere near the amount of diseases and problems that we face today. Without machines and endless pollution, they built beautiful houses and cities that were auspicious places to live in, all according to the science of Vāstu, the ancient Vedic art of living in perfect harmony with nature.

These findings prove that Bhāratavarṣa had civilized the entire world, at the dawn of civilization. After careful critical studies and observations, oriental scholars of modern time[32] express their view that rather, we can look upon India's spiritual heritage as a consistent cultural system, which happens to be the oldest surviving civilization in the world. It will be wise to quote two scholars and conclude. Toward the end of his life, Max Müller[33] wrote:

---

[32] G. Feuerstein, S. Kak and D. Frawley, *In Search of the Cradle of Civilization*, Delhi: Motilal Banarsidass, 1999, p. 194.

[33] Ibid., p. 259; M. Mòller, *India: What Can It Teach Us?* London: Longmans, Green and Co., 1883, p. 29ff.

> We all come from the East — all that we value most has come to us from the East, and is going to the East . . . everybody ought to feel that he is going to his "Old Home", full of memories, if only he can read them.

R. Panikkar,[34] a Roman Catholic priest and professor of religious studies, was one of the most appreciative interpreters of the Vedas. In his book *The Vedic Experience*, we find the following passage that fittingly describes our present endeavour as well:

> The Vedic experience introduces nothing alien to modern man, but helps him realize his own life and emphasizes on often neglected aspect of his own being. In this sense the Vedas occupy a privileged position in the crystallized culture of man. They are neither primitive nor modern. Not being primitive, they present a depth, a critical awareness and a sophistication not shown by many other ancient cultures. Not being modern, they exhale a fragrance and present an appeal that the merely modern does not possess.

The American scholars[35] further state:

> The *Ṛgveda* is the oldest book in the Sanskrit language. More than that, if we are correct, it is the oldest book in the world, and for this reason alone deserves our attention.

Further they state:[36]

> This is the first time that these amazing developments in archaeology and history are reviewed in a comprehensive and comprehensible fashion. Why has it taken so long to recognize the significance of ancient India in the saga of human civilization? In his book, *Looking for Dilman*, Geoffrey Bibby[37] rightly remarked that the "Indus Valley Civilization is the Cinderella of the ancient world". Indeed for a variety of reasons, ancient India has been sorely neglected by archaeologists and historians. Prevailing misconceptions and biases have long hampered the study of ancient India's civilization.

---

[34] G. Feuerstein, S. Kak and D. Frawley, op. cit., p. 275; R. Panikkar, *The Vedic Experience: Mantramanjari*, London: Darton: Longman and Todd, 1979, p. 9.

[35] G. Feuerstein, S. Kak and D. Frawley, op. cit., p. 29.

[36] G. Feuerstein, S. Kak and D. Frawley, *In Search of the Cradle of Civilization*, Delhi: Motilal Banarsidass, 1999, p. xviii.

[37] G. Bobby, *Looking for Dilmun*, New York: New American Library, 1974, p. 161.

Fortunately this regrettable situation is beginning to change, and the new attitude in scholarly circles has already proven enormously productive. Quite likely, the recent successes in reinterpreting ancient India's civilization will further speed up this promising process of revisioning ancient history that a handful of daring historians and archaeologists have begun.

5

Spiritual and Yogic Cultures of Orissa

In the first edition of *The History of Orissa*, vol. I, H.K. Mahtab[1] states that the origin of the present state of Orissa can be traced back to the hoary antiquity, when in fact it comprised of three distinct regions, Uḍra or Oḍra or Auḍra, Utkal and Kaliṅga.

Here, he had overlooked or neglected the study of South Kosala in his early interpretation of history of Orissa. During the later part of his life, Mahatab[2] had mentioned:

> Orissa as it is today consists of portions of three ancient regions, Kaliṅga, Utkala or Oḍra and Kosala which in course of centuries under political, social and economic pressure joined together in the twelfth century and developed to form the Oriya Society as a distinct entity in the realm of India. Of all the regions, Kaliṅga was the most prominent and advanced in all aspects. The original inhabitants of these regions belong to the Sabar tribe which had distinct civilization of its own.

In this statement, "of all the regions, Kaliṅga was the most prominent and advanced in all aspects", is completely wrong, as the latest archaeological discoveries prove.

Most of the rock arts of Orissa are in the districts of western Orissa — Jharsuguḍa, Sundergaṛh, Sambalpur, Sonepur, Kālāhāṇḍī and Nuāpāḍā. These rock arts have triangles pointed down with a spot at the centre.[3] Such triangles are found in engraving also. *Bhairavī* is one of them.[4] Bhairavī is a benign manifestation

---

[1] H.K. Mahatab, *History of Orissa*, vol. I, Cuttack: Prajatantra Prachar Samiti, 1959, p. 1.

[2] H.K. Mahatab, "Culture of Orissa", *OHRJ*, vol. XXX, nos. 2-4, 1984, p. 1.

[3] Sadasiba Pradhan, *Rock Art in Orissa*, Delhi: Aryan Books International, 2001, pp. 27-44.

[4] David Frawley, *Tāntric Yoga and the Wisdom Goddesses*, Delhi: Motilal Banarsidass, 1996, p. 103.

of Śakti and is considered as the giver of knowledge, according to *Śākta Pramoda*, a tāntric text.[5]

Latest findings and studies show that the eastern part of ancient South Kosala region now forms the western part of modern Orissa province. The earliest traces of Yoga are found in the pre-historic rock-art painting at Guḍahāṇḍī of Kālāhāṇḍī district and Yogīmaṭh Ḍoṅger of Nuāpāḍā district (*fig*. 5.1). The painting of human-like figure of Guḍahāṇḍī has a head which symbolizes a lotus. In *kuṇḍalinī-yoga*, the highest *cakra* of human being is described as a thousand-petalled lotus, i.e. *sahasrāra*. So, it can be claimed that *sahasrāra cakra* is a gift of the Central Mahānadī River Valley to the mankind. The Yogīmaṭh Ḍoṅger art shows the myth of creation and runs right to left. So, it can be claimed that the Central Mahānadī Valley, which comprises the present western Orissa, which is the eastern part of South Kosala is the epi-centre of the Mahānadī Valley, from where spirituality and yogic cultures were flashed, focused and spread.[6]

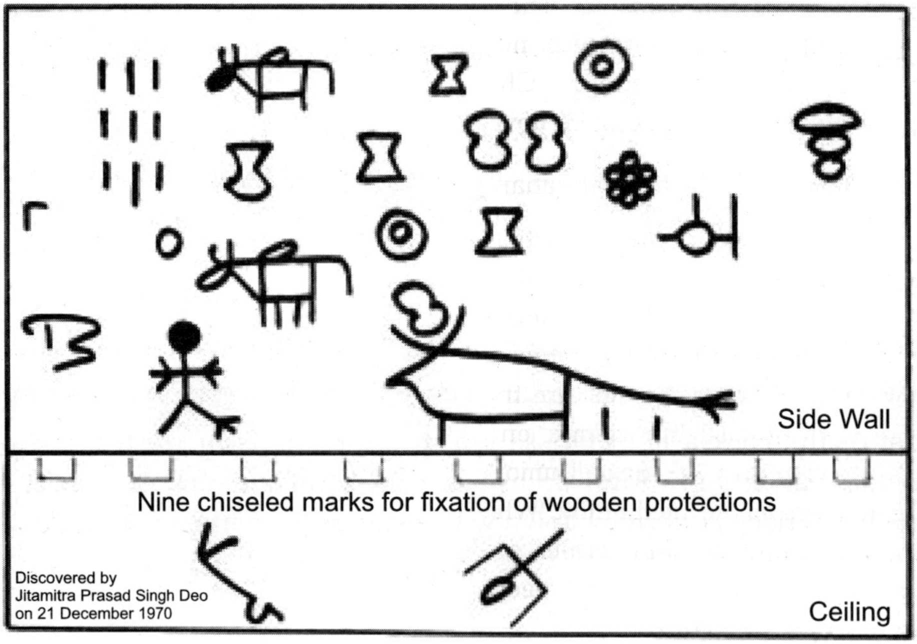

fig. 5.1: Rock art of Yogīmaṭh Ḍoṅger, Nuāpāḍā district, Orissa.

[5] *Śākta Pramoda*, Bombay: Venkatesvara Press, 1951;

Pushpendra Kumar, *Śakti Cult in Ancient India*, Varanasi: Bharatiya Publishing House, 1974, p. 157.

[6] *THOMV*, pp. 22-23 and 71.

Varāhamihira in his *Bṛhat-Saṁhitā*, Kūrma Vibhāga, 8, astronomically puts Kosala, Kaliṅga, Vaṅga, Upa-Vaṅga, Jaṭhar, Aṅga, Sailik, Vidarbha, Vatsa, Āndhra, Cedi, Udharva, Kant, Brusa, Naliker and Charmadip in the Āgneya-Koṇa. The grouping of states indicates that Kosala here refers to Dakṣiṇa (South) Kosala.

So, it is definite that because of the effect of Āgneya-Koṇa, according to Vāstu-Śāstra, i.e. south-east location of the great Mahānadī Valley, the fire device plays a major role in the spirituality and yogic culture of this region. The fire element of fire device leads to sexuality. About this fact, one of the prominent Vedāntists of the Western world, David Frawley,[7] states:

> Sexuality is one of the most sacred aspects of our nature and the very basis of our physical existence — has also been turned into another form of indulgence, escape and domination. Sex has become the basis of social manipulation, advertising and the promotion of every sort of artificial want. We have cultivated and exaggerated sexual desire, which covers over our natural love and poisons it. The fire of such unsacred sex creates an unsanctified progeny, born with no real place in life, merely an unwanted by-product of selfish pleasure. Children born of such a legacy naturally find it hard to either love or be loved.

In tāntric-yogic sense, Swami Satyananda Saraswati[8] says:

> Tantra aims to transform every action in life into ritual, so that the individual performs every action and thought with a feeling of worship and awareness. The action of bathing, dressing, sitting for worship, offering various symbolic sacrifices, sexual relations, stages of development from inception in the womb, birth to marriage, etc. are transformed into worship. . . . The aim of Tantra is to unleash the cosmic energy in man, so that he rises to higher levels of awareness. . . . Sexual union is also a powerful *maṇḍala*. That is why it can be a means to meditation. When a man and a woman make love, then they are creating a magic circle, a *maṇḍala*. . . . A *yantra* is a particularly powerful form of *maṇḍala* and deep concentration on it can lead to higher realization of its nature.

According to Tantra, interaction between man and woman has three purposes — pleasure, pro-creation and *samādhi*.[9]

---

[7] David Frawley, *Yoga and Sacred Fire*, Delhi: Motilal Banarsidass, 2006, pp. 188-89.

[8] *ASCITATTOYAK*, pp. 335-36.

[9] J.P. Singh Deo, *Tāntric Art of Orissa*, Delhi: Kalpaz Publication, 2001, p. 31.

The grace of excellence of aesthetic pleasure is that Sāṁkhya Darśana and Yoga of sexual transformation, which is sexual *samādhi*, first originated or came into existence *alias* discovered, in the Central Mahānadī Valley.

On 18 February 2004, Rani Rajshree Devi of Khariar discovered a rare stone[10] in the Patdaraha region which believed to have enough tāntric significance (see Chapter 1, p. 14 for details).

The concept of *puruṣa* and *prakṛti* is given first in Sāṁkhya Darśana. Sāṁkhya-Sūtras explain the extent of māyic creation and the divinity beyond that. Sāṁkhya Darśana of Kapila calls *puruṣa* for the entire divine phenomena and *prakṛti* for the prime cosmic power *māyā* that evolves itself into the form of this universe with the help of *puruṣa* (God).[11]

It seems, while the great master saint *Yogī* Kapila was meditating on the Guru Ḍoṅger (mountain) of Boden Block area in Nuāpāḍā district, he revealed the Sāṁkhya Darśana. Therefore, the *yantra* of creation or the sign of cosmic origin was chiselled by him on a fossilized quartzite stone of ferruginous colour, as reported and discovered in the vicinity of Guru Ḍoṅger, in the Patdaraha region of the southern hilly area of Sunabeda plateau in the Nuāpāḍā district. This is a great discovery and proves the first effect of the fire device.

The second discovery of the effect of fire device is the stone sockets showing the union of male and female principles of nature. The author[12] had earlier mentioned that the earliest conception of Śakti and Śiva in union has also been discovered in the Mahānadī Valley in the form of stone sockets. These are on circular shape with a socket on the lower part and has components in the upper part which fits into the lower socket. The shape of this socket owes its origin to the rock-shelter painting of Yogīmaṭh Ḍoṅger. Such a stone socket was collected by the author from the Mohangiri site and is preserved at the Manikyapur Museum of Bhawānīpatna. It can be interpreted as the union of Śiva and Śakti, which represents the Yoga of sexual transformation. Later, it developed as *vajrolī, sahajolī, uḍḍiyāna bandha* and *khecarī mudrā*s in the tāntric *haṭha-yoga* practice. Such a socket set was jointly collected by Baba Mishra and Pradeep Mohanty from the Kharligaṛh site of Bolaṅgīr district in Orissa and exhibited at the Manikyapur Museum of Bhawānīpatna.

---

[10] *The Indian Express*, English daily newspaper, Bhubaneswar, 26 February 2004, p. 4.

[11] *TTHATROI*, 2001, p. 560.

[12] *THOMV*, pp. 31-32.

More such sockets were traced it recent years at Baṛgāon village of the Sinapali Block, on the left bank of the Udanti River and at Pātālgaṅgā site of the Nuāpāḍā district. The shape of these sockets used represents Lord Buddha at Sāñcī *stūpa*, Bharhut *stūpa* and Amarāvatī *stūpa*. The critical and comparative studies of the author[13] suggest that Ādi Śaṅkarācārya had visited Purī, defeated the Buddhist scholars and established the sockets shape of Lord Buddha image as Jagannātha deity and made it the male presiding deity of Govardhana Maṭha, established by him at Purī. Ādi Śaṅkarācārya in his commentary of *Prasthānatrayī*[14] established that Īśvara or the Puruṣottama stands for *Akṣara*. *Akṣara* is the *Para-Brahman*, the Supreme Being, "He does not perish when all beings perish." This Jagannātha deity of Govardhana Maṭha of Purī evolved into Puruṣottama Jagannātha deity, during Somavaṁśī King Yayāti Keśarī I's ruling period in the tenth century CE whose full name was Mahāśivagupta Yayāti I.

The author's research gives support to the writing of Satchidananda Misra:[15]

> On a pillar of Jagamohana of the temple of Jagannātha is a depiction of Ādi Śaṅkarācārya in painting. The significance of the painting is explained in a legend which is described in *Śrī Jagannātha Mandira*, written by Pandit Sadasiva Misra in Bengali and published in 1911. Some Oriya books of later date also depict the legend. According to the legend: Before the present temple was built, Govardhana Maṭha of Śaṅkarācārya was located at the place where the present Jagamohana is. The *ācārya*s of the *maṭha* were in-charge of the worship of Jagannātha. In those days the *āśrama* of the *saṁnyāsī*s was in Bali Sahi. To allow enough space for the construction of the massive temple (the earlier temple must have been a small one without Jagamohana), Govardhana Maṭha was shifted to the *āśrama* in Bali Sahi. The legend further states that the painting of Śaṅkarācārya on a pillar of Jagamohana was designed as a momento.
>
> Basing on the legend it may be said that Śaṅkarācārya did initiate the worship of Jagannātha. Otherwise, how was his *maṭha* allowed space within the precincts of an already established temple? Why was the charge of the

---

[13] J.P. Singh Deo, *Origin of Jagannātha Deity*, New Delhi: Gyan Publishing House, 2nd edn., 2003, Appendix II, pp. 193-99.

[14] Phani Mohanty, *The Concept of Purusa and Puruṣottama in Commentary of Śaṅkara on the Prasthānatrayī*, New Delhi: Garg Publication, 1986, p. 49.

[15] Satchidananda Misra, "Installation of Puruṣottama-Jagannātha", *Studies in the Cult of Jagannātha*, K.C. Mishra (ed.), Bhubaneswar: Institute of Orissan Culture, 1991, p. 137.

> temple given to heads of the Govardhana Maṭha? As no king of Orissa is known to be a votary of the Smārtta faith, it is not probable that the *maṭha* was thrust into a functioning temple with royal patronage. The head of the *maṭha* could be in-charge of the temple only because the installation of the deity and the founding of the *maṭha* were done by the same person.

Śaṅkarācārya of Purī *maṭha* is the president of Mukti Maṇḍapa of Purī Puruṣottama Jagannātha temple, which looks after the form of worship prevalent, rituals and spirituality in the temple and is the authority in spiritual values. This practice is still continuing.

K.C. Mishra,[16] as the editor, gives the following note on the research paper of Satchidananda Misra:

> The writer in this short paper has touched on a new point and has arrayed facts to substantiate his position. The paper, as such, is characterized by novelty.

So, the new archaeological discoveries of western Orissa are answers to the challenging problem of the history and culture of the Mahānadī Valley in general and the Orissa province in particular.

Recent archaeological discoveries by Trilochan Bhai[17] at Tentelkhunti village of handless stone images of Balabhadra, Subhadrā and Jagannātha prove that the Trinity conception of this cult also originated in Kosala part of the modern Orissa province. The author is interested to point out that the Trinity conception also owes its origin to the rock art of Yogīmaṭh Ḍoṅger, because three lines have been painted thrice in parallel lines. Among the antiquities dug out from this huge temple mound, many broken temple stone pieces, including anthropoid form of Goddess Dakṣiṇa Kālikā, Anantaśayana Viṣṇu panel, doorjamb with lotus and vase motifs, Gaja-Lakṣmī and fragmentary pieces were found.

A stone image of Lord Jagannātha — 1' in height, 5" in width — which was dug out from Pipilikani village has two square hands and a half moon at the head. This proves that this stone image belongs to the formative period of the shape of Lord Jagannātha's image and finally this shape was originated in the Central Mahānadī Valley, comprising South Kosala.

---

16 Satchidananda Misra, "Installation of Puruṣottama-Jagannātha", *Studies in the Cult of Jagannātha*, K.C. Mishra (ed.), Bhubaneswar: Institute of Orissan Culture, 1991, p. 140.

17 Sasanka Sekhar Panda, "Antiquities of Śrī Jagannātha: Amazing Findings", *Reference Orissa* (Century edn.), A.N. Tiwari (ed.), Bhubaneswar: Enterprising Publishers, 3rd edn., 2005, pp. 72-77.

There are archaeological ruins connected with Lord Jagannātha in many caves in the Court Samlai hill, Sonepur district. They require proper surveys and studies to connect the findings of the area with this study.

The third impact of the fire device can be traced in the temple architecture. Simple square temples were first built throughout the Mahānadī Valley. The Māṭharas ruled coastal southern Orissa during the fourth and fifth centuries CE and the Nalas ruled the Upper Mahānadī Valley during the third to fifth centuries CE known as South Kosala. It can be claimed that these two dynasties were responsible for building square temples with *triratha* plan, throughout the Mahānadī Valley.[18] None of these temple architectures is surviving in its standing position.

The temples of the Mahānadī Valley were built generally in Nāgara style. Some temples of Orissa constructed during Śailodbhavas and Bhauma-Kara ruling period are still existing. Most of them are fallen and few survive in dilapidated shape. Temple of Gokarṇeśvara Śiva, on the summit of Mahendragiri, built during the Śailodbhava period is usually regarded as the earliest surviving temple of Orissa. According to Sarat Chandra Behera,[19] "On the summit of the mountain Mahendragiri there is the temple of Gokarṇeśvara, which in our opinion marked the beginning of temple architecture in Orissa". The author considers this opinion as wrong, because it is known that the Māṭharas and Nala dynasties had started temple constructions[20] earlier, though none of them survives now.

Going by Mahesh Prashad Dash,[21] the earliest existing temple, dedicated to the worship of Durgā, is found on the top of a small hill near Paṭiā-Kilā, which can definitely be assigned to the Gupta period. Here, the deity is carved on a single stone, which forms the back wall of the temple.

In the Upper Mahānadī Valley, lots of experimentation of stellate-planned temple constructions were continued. Such stellate on star-like plans are found in Rāma temple of Sirpur, the Indal Deul at Kharoḍ, the Siddheśvara temple at Palari, the Śabarī temple at Kharoḍ, a temple of Nakṣapali village near Sambalpur, Dadpur in Kālāhāṇḍī district and fallen brick temple inside the fort area of Patnagaṛh.

18 *THOMV*, 2004, p. 226.

19 S.C. Behera, *Rise and Fall of the Śailodbhavas*, Kolkata: Punthi Pustak, 1982, p. 199.

20 K.C. Panigrahi, *History of Orissa* (*Hindu Period*), Cuttak: Kitab Mahal, 1981, pp. 46-48; C.B. Patel, *Dynastic History of Nalas*, Kolkata: Punthi Pustak, 1990, pp. 229-57.

21 M.P. Dash, *A Descriptive Catalogue of Sanskrit Manuscripts of Orissa*, vol. V (*Tantra Manuscripts*), Bhubaneswar: Orissa State Museum, 1965, p. iv.

Another group of temples having the plans of two squares placed diagonally and intersecting each other at 45° angle, which gives the shape of an eight-point star are: the Pātāleśvara brick temple at Būḍhī-Komnā in Nuāpāḍā district, the Chitawari Devī temple at Dhobnī near Damakeda village of Raipur district, two ruined brick temples at Kansil village area in the Rānīpur-Jharial complex of Bolaṅgīr district and ruined temple at Adhabhara village, situated about 8 km south of Kharsia in Bilaspur district. A single temple with different types of stellate plans is found and five temples with the plans of two squares placed diagonally and intersecting each other at angles of 45° are traced in the South Kosala region. It will be proper for the temples, which are more in number with the same plan, to be identified with the Rekha type of Kosali style of temple architecture.[22]

The plan of Rekha variety of Kosali style is based on the *yantra* of Kāmakalā, whose *mantra*s are found in *Ānandalaharī*, v. 20 and *Saundaryalaharī*, vs. 20 and 42 of Ādi Śaṅkarācārya.[23] With these findings, the author[24] was of the opinion that:

> From the above study, it is understood that the Kosali style of temple architecture developed in South Kosala during early Somavaṁśī *alias* Pāṇḍuvaṁśī rule or period and influenced the neighbouring territories. Thus, they influenced the Mukteśvara temple of Bhubaneswar, the temple within the Nurpur Fort and Thousand-Pillar temple of Warangal. It seems, the Kosali style of temple architecture had influenced the Lakṣmaṇa temple at Sirpur and Indralāṭh temple at Rānīpur-Jharial, to some extent, as these temples also consist of the sanctum proper and a *maṇḍapa* in front, with an antechamber (*antarāla*) connecting the two. The *kumbha*-shaped moulding of Kosali style of temples, connecting the *maṇḍapa* and the *antarāla* of these two temples are practically same. The pillared *maṇḍapa* of Indralāṭh temple at Rānīpur-Jharial complex has fallen since long. The scattered stone pillars are now utilized as seats by the Orissa State Archaeology Department. Some influence is also noticeable between the Kosali temples and temples of *pañcaratha* plan, when the sharp edges of early Kosali style rounded up in later years. Nīlakaṇṭheśvara temple of Dadpur, in the district of Kālāhāṇḍī is a stone structure and seems to be a late medieval structure, with influence of Kosali style of Rekha temple architecture, in its plan. Hence, it will be

[22] J.P. Singh Deo, *Cultural Profile of South Kosala*, New Delhi: Gyan Publishing House, 1987, pp. 329-32; *THOMV*, pp. 185-210.

[23] J.P. Singh Deo, *Some Tāntric Esotericism of Orissa*, Kolkata: R.N. Bhattacharya, 2003, pp. 301-08.

[24] J.P. Singh Deo, "Kosali Style of Temple Architecture", *OHRJ*, vol. XXIV, XXV & XXVI, pp. 175-76.

interesting to know the view of K.S. Behera, on the Brāhmanical temples of Orissa, under Somavaṁśīs. While giving the account, K.S. Behera[25] mentions that the Somavaṁśīs, who succeeded the Bhauma-Karas, came from South Kosala but they did not introduce any unfamiliar line of development in art and architecture. The pillared *maṇḍapa* of Kosaleśvara temple at Baidyanath with lateral transepts and large sculptures in the interior, seems to suggest that when the Somavaṁśīs were ruling in the Upper Mahānadī Valley, there was some central Indian influence of the temple architecture but as they proceeded towards the coastal region, they strengthened the traditional temple style. Here, it is to be noted that there was influence of the plan of Kosali style of Rekha temple architecture.

As mentioned above, the number of intersecting squares developed, particularly in the Cāḷukyan monuments of the eleventh-twelfth centuries CE in Gujarat. Even in the Hoysala temples of Mysore, the star-shaped plan became the usual fashion. The maturity of structures influenced each other and developed to such an extent that Cāḷukya-Hoysala school of architecture gradually developed in eleventh, twelfth and thirteenth centuries CE. This shows the plan of intersecting two squares of Kosali style of Rekha temples in early phase to have prevalence over these styles of architectures later.

Bhuvanapradīpa,[26] the earliest text of temple architecture of Orissa, mentions two varieties of Kosali style of temple architecture as "Kosali Rekha Temple" and "Kosali Khakhāra Temple". The observation proves that Kosali style of both varieties had influenced the development of temples in all directions of Bhāratavarṣa.

Being located in Āgneya-Koṇa, fire device plays the main role in this region and South Kosala belt had given another fourth gift to Orissa and to the Indian culture, that is the Yoginī cult.

The Sixty-four Yoginī temple at Rānīpur-Jharial is the first or premier of such temples in India, because, according to *Yoginī Tantra*,[27] the Ādi-pīṭha of Yoginī is

[25] J.P. Singh Deo, "Kosali Style of Temple Architecture", *OHRJ*, vol. XXIV, XXV & XXVI, pp. 175-76; *Orissa Review* (Monument Special), January 1976, p. 60.

[26] Nirmal Kumar Bose, *Canons of Orissan Architecture*, New Delhi: Cosmo Publications, 2nd rpt., 1982, pp. 124 and 172-73.

[27] K.L. Mishra (ed.), *Yoginī Tantra*, Lakshmi Venkatesvar Press, Saṁvat 2013 and Śakābda 1878, Uttara Khaṇḍa, Prathama Paṭala, pp. 241-42, verses 15-19; R.P. Mishra, "Primal Yoginī Pīṭha Rānīpur-Jharial and Its Influence on the Culture of Western Orissa", *Souvenir*, Bolaṅgīr Loka Utsav, Bolaṅgīr, 2001, pp. 106-17.

situated where Someśvara-liṅga is worshipped. Someśvara temple is situated at Rānīpur-Jharial. So, one can believe that the premier Yoginī temple is located at Rānīpur-Jharial site.

It is interesting to know the circumstances in which the Yoginī cult developed in South Kosala. Because of being located in Āgneya-Koṇa, there was development of *yoga* of sexual transformation in this locality. According to *Haṭha-Yoga-Pradīpikā*,[28] a Yoginī is a woman who practises *vajrolī*. This *haṭha-yoga* practice is done because of the *yoga* practice of sexual transformation. So, it can be said that Yoginī is a lady who practises the *yoga* of sexual transformation. This proves that *yoga* of sexual transformation first began in South Kosala region. In modern period Acharya Rajneesh[29] took full advantage of this *yoga* in his speeches and became world famous.

Verse 55 of chapter 22 of *Haṭha-Yoga-Pradīpikā*[30] goes thus:

योगिनी चक्रसंमान्यः सृष्टिसंहारकारकः ।
न क्षुधा न तृषा निद्रा नैवालस्यं प्रजायते ॥ ५५ ॥

yogini cakrasaṁmānyaḥ sr̥ṣṭisaṁharakarkaḥ ।
na kṣudhā na tr̥sā nidrā naivālasyaṁ prajāyate ॥ 55 ॥

He is adored by the circle of Yoginīs and becomes the controller of creation and dissolution, being without hunger, thirst, sleep and laziness.

According to this *śloka*, the perfectionist of *śītkāri* is adored or worshipped by the *cakra* or circle of Yoginīs, but what exactly is the *cakra* of Yoginī? *Cakra* is usually referred to a particular circle which is a source of energy. *Yoginī* is a female *yogī*, the embodiment of Śakti, the cosmic creative force. In Tantra, there is an order of Sixty-four Yoginīs who represent sixty-four Tantras and sixty-four perfections of *yoga*.

The aspects and evolution of cosmic Śakti from its source are represented by the *śrī-yantra* or *cakra*. *Śrī-yantra* is the formula of creation, manifestation and dissolution of the macro and micro cosmos. It is constituted by a number of interlacing triangles which are known as Yoginīs. They represent the cosmic Śakti and manifestation of human existence. *Śrī-yantra* also represents each individual.

[28] Swami Muktibodhananda Saraswati (Commentary), *Haṭha-Yoga-Pradīpīka*, Manager: Bihar School of Yoga, 2nd edn., 1993, p. 362.

[29] Bhagwan Shree Rajneesh, *From Sex to Super-Consciousness*, New Delhi: Orient (paper back), 2nd edn., 1976, *passim*.

[30] *Haṭha-Yoga-Pradīpīka*, pp. 221-22.

> The *cakra* of Yoginīs symbolizes every function of the gross and subtler bodies, the functions of mind and integration with the soul. Our entire existence is controlled or operated by various forms of Śakti or specific Yoginī or Devī. Each individual person is a manifestation of the *cakra* of Yoginīs.
>
> Thus it is said that through the practice of *śītkāri* the whole body comes under the control of the practitioner. In fact, perfection of any of the *prāṇāyāmas* leads to the control of the body mechanisms, stabilization of the mental tendencies and deeper awareness of the mind-body complex.
>
> *Śītkāri* particularly works on the heat/cold aspect of the body. Control of any two opposite forces in the body/mind leads to the control of the other aspects of the physical, mental, emotional and psychic make up. Svātmarāma (the author of *Haṭha-Yoga-Pradīpikā*, who completed the work started by the great *yogī* Gorakhnāth), specifically mentions that *śītkāri* eliminates indolence and the need and desire to eat, drink and sleep.

According to Pranab Bandyopadhyay,[31] *śrī-yantra* (*fig*. 5.2) is a diagrammatic embodiment of the creative sexual activity of the universe. Because of this background Yoginīs are first worshipped in *yantra* worship, as they are the guardian deities of the spiritual *alias* yogic world *alias* creation of nature.

fig. 5.2: *Śrī-yantra*.

[31] Pranab Bandyopadhyay, *The Goddess of Tantra*, Kolkata: Punthi Pustak, 1987, p. 48.

Very interestingly, Mahesh Prasad Dash[32] states that epigraphic evidences of the cult of Yoginīs are not found in Orissa; but such evidences are found in other parts of India. For instance, an inscription from Ankalgi in the Jath taluk of the south Satara district of Maharashtra dated CE 1174 refers to the village Ankulage as the abode of Mahāyogeśvarī Ugra Cāmuṇḍā, the presiding deity of the Sixty-four Yoga Pīṭhas.[33] Mahāsāmanta Cauṇḍarasa, a subordinate of the western Cāḷukya King Vikramāditya VI, is described as "one who had obtained the gracious boon of the Sixty-four Yoginīs". In an epigraph from Halagoṇḍi[34] in the Hadajalli taluk of the Bellary district, now in the Karnataka state, which is assignable to CE 1093. The expression "Sixty-four Yoga Pīṭhas" is of frequent occurrence in the *praśasti* of the great mercantile corporation Ayyavale, five hundred figuring in the inscriptions of Karnataka.[35]

> *Yoginīs* are especially the Mother Goddesses, who are worshipped at the beginning of every *saṁskāra*.[36] The principal Yoginīs are seven or eight but their number is at times raised to sixty-four.[37]

As the Primal Yoginī Pīṭha (site) is located at Rānīpur-Jharial, a study on its presiding two deities will be of interest. It is a known fact that the eight-handed Naṭarāja on a pavilion at the centre of Sixty-four Yoginī temple is the presiding deity. But, in fact there were two presiding deities — eighted-handed Naṭarāja and Cāmuṇḍā. Image of Cāmuṇḍā, larger than the Yoginī images, was installed at the southern wall of the circular temple. There are traces of the ruin of projection of a *maṇḍapa* or pavilion at the south, on the back of which the broken image of Cāmuṇḍā is found. Mahāyogeśvarī Ugra Cāmuṇḍā is the presiding deity of the Sixty-four Yoga Pīṭhas. The Sixty-four Yoginīs represent the sixty-four qualities of nature and Sixty-four Yoga Pīṭhas. Therefore, two presiding deities representing Śiva and Śakti (i.e. *puruṣa* and *prakṛti*) were installed in the Cauṅsaṭh Yoginī temple of Rānīpur-Jharial. In *Devī Mahātmya*,[38] the centripetal Goddess Cāmuṇḍā is called Mahākālī,

[32] M.P. Dash, *A Descriptive Catalogue of Sanskrit Manuscripts of Orissa*, vol. V (*Tantra Manuscripts*), p. ix.

[33] Ibid.; *Bombay-Karnatak Collection*, no. 93, of 1940 , p. 41.

[34] Ibid.; *South Indian Inscriptions*, vol. IX, part I, no. 163.

[35] Ibid., *South Indian Inscriptions*, vol. IX, part I, no. 139.

[36] Ibid.; *Sodasa Ratnamālā*, p. 18.

[37] Ibid.; *Indian Historical Quarterly*, vol. XXXI, p. 367.

[38] Pundit R.N. Dattasastri (ed.), *Śrī Durgā Saptaśatī* (*Devī Mahātmya*) verses, 1-31, XXth edn., Gorakhpur: Gita Press, pp. 192-97.

Mahālakṣmī and Mahāsarasvatī. Mahālakṣmī is described as the primal source of all phenomenal existence.

According to Ram Prashad Mishra,[39] in Rānīpur-Jharial, on the obverse of a tall and huge rock, the image of Goddess Cāmuṇḍā is found well carved. . . . Around the tāntric cult of Siddheśvara Śiva or Siddheśvarī Cāmuṇḍā, cult of *siddhi* conferring Yoginīs continued to evolve in this place, although its primary concept crept into this area as early as sixth century CE.

Śilpa Prakāśa, written by Ramchandra Mahapatra Kaula Bhaṭṭāraka, is an important text on temple architecture. This text[40] mentions about *Yoginī-yantra* thus:

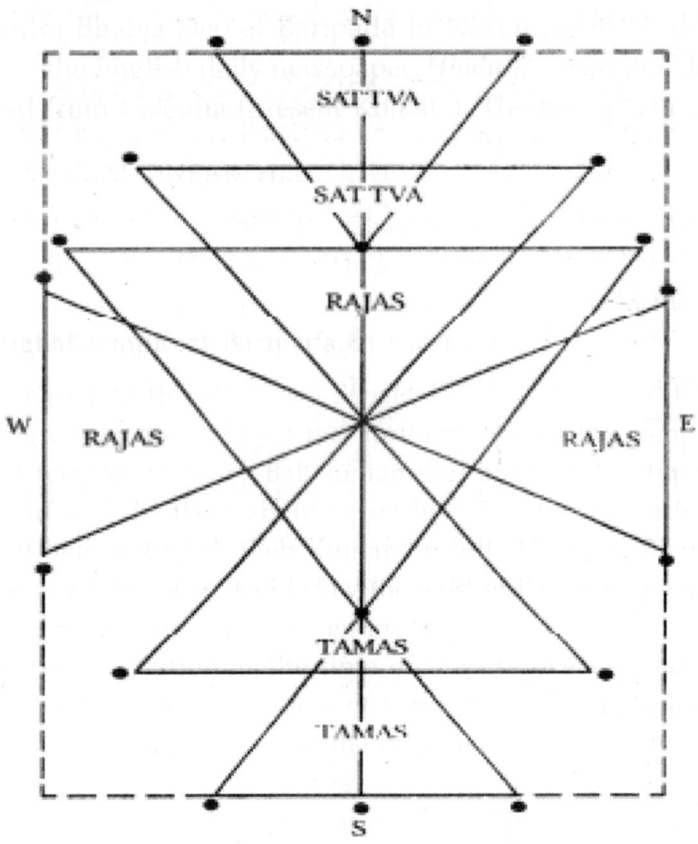

fig. 5.3: *Yoginī-Yantra* (vide *Śilpa Prakāśa*)

[39] Ram Prashad Mishra, *Fragments of Indian Culture* (*Rānīpur-Jharial*), Kolkata: Punthi Pustak, 1995, pp. 66 and 68.

[40] *Śilpa Prakāśa*, Bettina Bäumer, R.P. Das and S. Das (eds.), 2nd rev. edn., Delhi: Motilal Banarsidass, 2005, p. 73.

The shape of *Yoginī-yantra* (*fig.* 5.3) is rectangular with sub-sections, showing the three natural qualities of nature, *sattva, rajas* and *tamas*. So, it can be claimed that Khakhāra temples are based on the *Yoginī-yantra* plan and the two Khakhāra temples of Rānīpur-Jharial site are the earliest Khakhāra temples of India. This proves that originally Khakhāra temples were meant for the Cāmuṇḍā deity. With the flux of time, Khakhāra temples[41] were built in many places throughout India and have different Śakti deities as their object of worship.

Origin and Development of the Yoginī Cult

Without keeping in view or observing the gradual development of Śakti cult in Āgneya-Koṇa, i.e. the great Mahānadī River Valley, earlier scholars like Kedarnath Mahapatra,[42] Satya Narayan Rajguru[43] and Harish Chandra Das[44] were of the opinion that Bhauma-Kara Queen Hīrā-Mahādevī is known to have established a village named Hirapur near Jajpur after her name and constructed the Sixty-four Yoginī temple there, which can be dated back to eighth century CE. This view is blindly followed by later scholars like Rajnath Singh,[45] Ekadashi Padhi[46] and many others. This shows the lack of original investigation, exploration and critical research of scholars nowadays.

As already observed, South Kosala region is in the west, Bengal in the north and Andhra Pradesh in the south, the three extreme corners, which forms the Great Triangle comprising Āgneya-Koṇa as pointed out by Varāhamihira. In this belt, fire device plays the main role as the sublime undercurrent of the cultural heritage. As dealt in chapter 1, Sāṁkhya Darśana originated from Guru Ḍoṅger of the Boden Block area of Nuāpāḍā district of western Orissa. Fire worship is very popular among the tribals of western Orissa. Their usual saying is that Fire is *sat*

---

41 Debala Mitra, "Four Little Known Khākarā Temples of Orissa", *Journal of the Asiatic Society*, vol. II, no. 1, 1960, *passim.*

J.P. Singh Deo, *Tāntric Art of Orissa*, Delhi: Kalpaz Publications, 2001, pp. 180-83.

42 *OHRJ*, vol. II, no. 2, p. 40.

43 S.N. Rajguru, *Odisa-ra-Itihasa* (Oriya), Cuttack, p. 453.

44 H.C. Das, *Śākta Piṭhas*, A Bharti Prakashan, Bhubaneswar, 1999, pp. 197-98.

45 Rajnath Singh, *Religious Tāntricism*, vol. II, New Delhi: Dominant Publishers and Distributors, 2001, pp. 111-13.

46 Ekadashi Padhi, "State and Society During Bhaumakara Rule", *Exploring Orissan History*, Niharranjan Patnaik (ed.), Cuttack: Kitab Mahal, 2005, p. 107.

bahinī jal kāminī. In crude form of *yantra,* the tribals make seven squares or rectangles and worship the seven sisters as fire.

Let us peep into the tribal fire worship and its connection with Vedic fire worship. David Frawley narrates his experience thus:[47]

> I had not always connected native and tribal forms of spirituality with the yogic traditions that appear more philosophically and psychologically complex. However, my recent travels to India helped me bring the two together. I visited the north-east of the country (greater Assam) for the first time in early 2002. I had a rare opportunity to visit the tribal people of Arunachal Pradesh, the eastern-most Himalayas in India, and the Khāsī and Jaintiā hills of Meghalaya to the south, above Bangladesh. Later the same year, I participated in a conference in Assam that featured leaders from all the main tribal groups of the region.
>
> Various tribal cultures remain in these areas, continuing their ancient ways with not only similar customs and dress but with similar facial features as native Americans. Clearly they were kindred souls on the other side of the planet. I became involved with efforts to help preserve such native cultures, which even in that remote part of the world are under siege by the forces of modern civilization (many it seems emanating from the United States).
>
> Such contacts with native traditions helped me understand the Vedic tradition as perhaps the world's best preserved ancient native tradition and Yoga as a manifestation of our global native or earth heritage. The Vedas provide a link between tribal practices like fire worship and the great meditational systems of *yoga* and eastern philosophy that rest upon an inner fire. The sacred is usually more obvious to those who live close to the earth. It arises from life and from the land, not from ideas, beliefs or dogmas.

Muṇḍaka Upaniṣad[48] belongs to the *Atharvaveda* and is called a Mantra Upaniṣad because it is written in verse. The word *Muṇḍaka* is derived from a root that signifies shaving. The instruction given in this Upaniṣad has the sharpness of a razor; it cuts off a man's error and ignorance, like a razor. The name also suggests that this Upaniṣad is meant only for the shaven-headed *saṁnyāsīs*, who renounce all the

---

[47] David Frawley, *Yoga and the Sacred Fire (Self-Realization and the Planetary Transformation)*, Delhi: Motilal Banarsidass, 2006, pp. 16-17.

[48] Swami Nikhilananda, *The Upanishads* (Abridged edn.), New York and Evanston: Harper & Row Publishers, 1964, pp. 7, 110 and 113.

actions prescribed for householders and devote themselves to the cultivation of *brahma-vidyā*, or the knowledge of Brahmā.

This Upaniṣad talks about the seven tongues of the fire and names the seven flames as Kālī, Karālī, Manojavā, Sulohitā, Sudhūmravarṇā, Sphuliṅginī and the luminous Viśvaruci. This is a beautiful example of the great tradition and little tradition.

In the words of David Frawley:[49]

> Kālī is the consort of Lord Śiva, who is also Kāla or the Lord of time and eternity. Kālī is the active power coming from Lord Śiva, who as transcendent reality is beyond action or motivation. Kālī represents the flow of grace from the heart of Śiva. Surrendering to her thus brings us the eternal peace and immortal life of Śiva himself. Śiva is the corpse on whom Kālī dances, who is herself the life and energy of Śiva.
>
> Hence we see that Kālī is known to all of us in some form or another. She is not the deity of some strange religion but an objective portrayal of essential reality in symbolic form. . . . In her higher and benefic form as Bhadra (auspicious) Kālī, she is located in the spiritual heart centre, on the right side of the chest. Here she is the giver of the highest transformation, which is Self-realization.

As mentioned earlier, stone sockets, depicting the union of male and female, are mostly found in Nuāpāḍā, Kālāhāṇḍī and Bolaṅgīr districts of western Orissa. Such a pair of stone sockets is also found from layer III (early historic phase) from Veerapuram of Andhra Pradesh, where it is interpreted as a votive *liṅga*.[50] This cannot be accepted because, as already observed, the socket shape finally evolved to the shape of Lord Puruṣottama Jagannātha. This proves that the Andhra region of Āgneya-Koṇa had a role to play in the development of the shape of Lord Jagannātha and its cult.

The seven tongues of fire gradually developed to Sapta-Mātṛkās[51] worship, which are found in many places of the Orissa province and Bhāratavarṣa. The

[49] David Frawley, *Tāntric Yoga and the Wisdom Goddesses* (*Spiritual Secrets of Ayurveda*), Delhi: Motilal Banarsidass, 1996, pp. 70-71.

[50] T.V.G. Sastri, M.K. Bai and J.V.P. Rao, *Veerapuram*, Hyderabad: Bhavani Printers, 1984, *passim.*

[51] M.P. Dash (ed.), *A Descriptive Catalogue of Sanskrit Manuscripts of Orissa*, vol. V (*Tantra Manuscripts*), Bhubaneswar: Orissa State Museum, 1965, pp. XXVII-XXXVII; J.P. Singh Deo, *Tāntric Art of Orissa*, Delhi: Kalpaz Publications, 2001, pp. 51-57.

notable feature of the Mātṛkās images of Orissa is that the Mātṛkās are never depicted in the shape of killing the demon for whom they were created but are found sitting at ease in their motherly affection on their mounts with babies in laps.

In interaction between man and woman (i.e. male and female principles), Tantra has three purposes — pleasure, procreation and *samādhi*.[52] The *yoga* of sexual transformation, which originated in the Central Mahānadī Valley, paved the way for the beginning of Yoginīs and Yoginī cult, which became popular. A Yoginī is one who practises *vajrolī*. *Vajrolī-mudrā* is a *haṭha-yoga* practice, which means "thunderbolt attitude", in which the muscles of male sexual organ and lower urinary tract are contracted, redirecting sexual energy upwards. A practice of *haṭha-yoga* and Tantra called *Sahajoli mudrā* is practice of *vajrolī* by a woman, involving contraction of the lower urinary muscles.

In *Haṭha-Yoga-Pradīpikā*,[53] it is mentioned:

> पुंसो बिंदु समाकुध्य सम्यगभ्यासपाटवात् ।
> यदि नारी रजो रक्षेद्वज्रोल्या सापि योगिनी ॥९९॥
>
> *puṅso bindu samākudhya samyagabhyāsapāṭavāt* ।
> *yadi nārī rajo rakṣedvajrolyā sāpi yoginī* ॥ 99 ॥
>
> — Chapter 3, Verse 99

With this background, the Yoginī cult originated, developed and spread throughout India — Hirapur in Orissa province; Lokhari, Varanasi, Rikhian and Dudhai in Uttar Pradesh; Bherāghāṭ, Khajurāho, Mitavali, Naresar, Badoh, Hiṅglājgaṛh and Shahdol in Madhya Pradesh; Andhra Pradesh, Karnataka, Tamil Nadu, Maharashtra, Gujarat and Rajasthan.[54]

Shantilal Nagar[55] talks about the Yoginīs and states:

> But this number of Sixty-four Yoginīs was not always followed. In some texts, the number of Yoginīs has been spelt out variously as well. As for example, the sixteenth-century Oriya text entitled *Batavakāśa* gives the number of Yoginīs much more than sixty-four, the details of which are given here. According to that text, Lord Jagannātha at Purī is surrounded,

[52] J.P. Singh Deo, *Tāntric Art of Orissa*, New Delhi: Gyan Books, 2001, p. 31.

[53] Swami Muktibodhananda Saraswati (ed.), *Haṭha-Yoga-Pradīpīka*, Munger: Bihar School of Yoga, 2nd edn., 1993, p. 362.

[54] Shantilal Nagar, *Indian Gods and Goddesses*, vol. 4, *Yoginī Shrines and Śakti Pīṭhas*, part I, Delhi: B.R. Publishing Corporation, 2006, pp. 54-92.

[55] Ibid., 2006, pp. 46-47.

in addition to the Sixty-four Yoginīs, by seven Mātṛkās besides Virajā, Vimalā and seventy-two local goddesses as noted below:

> Śākambarī, Kauṭanī, Durgeśvarī, Kālī, Raṇacaṇḍī, Koṭeśvarī, Bhagavatī, Vaisālī, Hadimakṣī, Kotama-Caṇḍī, Brahmāṇī, Indrākṣī, Sāvitrī, Sarala-Caṇḍī, Jeyunehi, Aparājitā, Rupai, Campai, Piṅgalā, Sarakamā, Marakamā, Bhagavati, Hiṅgulā, Kalapati, Kālikākṣī, Kālarātri Kālikā, Pātālī, Mādhavīśvarī, Kālasun, Kaṣikā, Chāyā, Māyā, Vijayā, Caṇṭaghaṇṭā, Karaṇi, Kulaghaṇṭā, Kālamukhī, Khakayī, Ekyamahi, Ṣoṣiṇī, Piścayi, Trutikhayi, Śānti-Sarpamukhī, Jagulayi, Hadobayi, Samalai, Somasānī, Sthiti, Abalā, Mohasarvāṇī, Tarasuni, Bimcabacin, Maṅgalā, Sāraṅgayi, Naragoyi, Samcoyi. Bimcoyi, Olamayi, Polamayi, Karuṇāyī, Varuṇāyī, Rataskānti, Ratnamālā, Caturbhujī, Jitāyī, Virojayī, Ketukayī, Ravanayi, Mahimāyī, Virasohantā, Kalataṇḍī, Dokani, Ailasuni, Tāriṇī, Jariṇī, Māriṇī, Sapanaciti, Nārāyaṇī, Kāmkeśvarī.

Shantilal Nagar[56] further states:

> It may be stated here that A.K. Banerjee (*Discourses on Hindu Spiritual Culture*, vol. II, pp. 57-58) highlighting on the philosophy of Guru Gorakṣanātha, or Gorakhanātha, as he is commonly known, has expressed his views on the union of Śiva and Śakti according to which, "Śiva and Śakti in external union represent the nature of absolute reality. This is ultimate nature of *Brahman* or *Paramātman* or *Bhagavān*. The *yogīs* realize the truth which is identified with it at the stage of the highest perfection of *yogasādhanā*. He then becomes Avadhūta of Śrī Nātha. This view is distinguished from Absolute non-Śāktism (Viśuddha Advaitavāda) inasmuch as Śakti is not here regarded as false or illusory and as not ultimately pertaining to the true nature of *Brahman* or Śiva and Śiva or Brahmā, i.e. the absolute reality is not regarded as an altogether differenceless, attributeless, manifestationless and enjoymentless *existence*. It is also distinguished from Dualism (Dvaitavāda), inasmuch as it does not regard Śakti as a distinct form, though related to and under the control of Śiva. It is distinguished from qualified non-dualism (Viśiṣṭādvaitavāda) as well because it does not hold that Śakti is in reality different from Śiva, though internally and inseparably pertaining to Śiva, as his Absolute or embodiment. The *yogīs* therefore proclaim that the absolute truth, as realized at the highest stage

[56] Shantilal Nagar, *Indian Gods and Goddesses*, vol. 4, *Yoginī Shrines and Śakti Pīṭhas*, part I, 2006, pp. 105-06.

> of spiritual experience, is above Dualism and non-dualism and all other isms, that is incapable of being adequately expressed or understood in terms of any of these metaphysical theories and convincingly established by the methods of formal logic. All these theories assume in the very beginning the distinction and the antagonism as well as the relations between the substance and attribute, cause and effect, unity and diversity, rest and action, changelessness and change, i.e. between Śiva and Śakti on the basis of normal, mental and sensuous experience. Then they move upward to bring about a logical reconciliation of these distinct and related concepts in the plan of absolute truth.

The author[57] had earlier mentioned that the literatures of the Vedic and post-Vedic period often mention the names of Yoginīs as manifestations of female principles. But Yoginīs in the shape of a Śākta-Tāntric cult came into existence in the sixth-seventh centuries CE when the efflorescences of Śāktism, Tāntricism and Śaivism either in individual form or in combination swayed the religious realm of India. Whatever might be the time of origin of this cult, it continued to flourish as an important manifestation of Śākta-Tāntricism and the propitiators acquired magical and super-natural faculties through the helps of Yoginīs with a view to becoming destroyers of enemies. Through the process of transformation over the ages, the Yoginīs finally multiplying into sixty-four gained supremacy, particularly in the eastern zone of India. Matsyendranāth, in view of popularity of this cult gained over the period, systematized and expounded it in his famous work *Kaulayānanirṇaya*, which has become the authoritative text of the cult.[58]

> Matsyendranāth was born in Candradvīpa, identified with Chandavali-Dhamra region of Bhadrak district in Orissa.[59] R.P. Mishra[60] identifies the site of Rānīpur-Jharial as the Ādi Pīṭha (site), as mentioned in Yoginī Tantra. . . . One ferry *ghāṭ alias* bathing *ghāṭ* of Mahānadī River side within Sonepur is named as Matsyendranāth Ghāṭ. One Matsyendranāth temple exists at Amarkaṇṭaka[61] and this proves the popularity of Sixty-four Yoginī cult in this region.

---

[57] J.P. Singh Deo, *Some Tāntric Esotericism of Orissa*, Kolkata: R.N. Bhattacharya, 2003, pp. 289-90.

[58] Ibid., H.C. Das, *Tāntricism: A Study of Yoginī Cult*, New Delhi: Sterling Publishers, 1981, p. 3.

[59] Ibid.; R.P. Mishra, *Sahajayana: A Study of Tāntric Buddhism*, Kolkata: Punthi Pustak, 1991, pp. 122 and 165.

[60] Ibid.; R.P. Mishra, *Fragments of Indian Culture*, Kolkata: Punthi Pustak, 1995, p. 207.

[61] Minoti Chakravarty, *Religious Life in the Kalachuri Empire*, Kolkata: Punthi Pustak, 1999, pl. 42.

In the words of Shantilal Nagar,[62] "The Yoginī-Kaula of Matsyendranāth had a syncretic character. The doctrine of this school, as could be ascertained from the *Kula-jñāna-nirṇaya*," has something in common with the Buddhist Tantra of Sahaja class. Matsyendra was also honoured by the Buddhist mystics as the first of the *siddhas* under the name of Lui-pada. The fundamental doctrine of the Buddhist Sahaja school is the doctrine of Sahaja. The ideal state of *yogin*, a state in which the mind enters the vacuity, becomes free from duality and rejects the illusory character of the world the Yoginī-Kaula also advocates the doctrine of Sahaja. The Yoginī-Kaula variously agrees with the Buddhist Sahajīya in several other aspects too.

The Impact of Sṛṣṭi-Yantra in Orissa Province

As dealt in Chapter 1, the *sṛṣṭi* (creation) *yantra* of Sāṁkhya Darśana is a right angle triangle, whose three corners signify "Śiva Kāmeśvara", "Śakti Kāmeśvarī" and "Somarasya".

This tāntric formula seems to have been carried to coastal Orissa, by the Somavaṁśīs, as at Bauḍ, three temples — Bhubaneswar, Kapileśvara and Paścima Somanātha — stand in right angle triangle. On the bodies of Kapileśvara temple and Bhubaneswar temple, images of Buddha are found and on the body of Paścima Somanātha temple images of Digambara Mahāvīra are found. Even these three temples are Śiva temples, placed in *sṛṣṭi-yantra* formation; these images prove the synchronization of Śaivism, Buddhism and Jainism at this site.

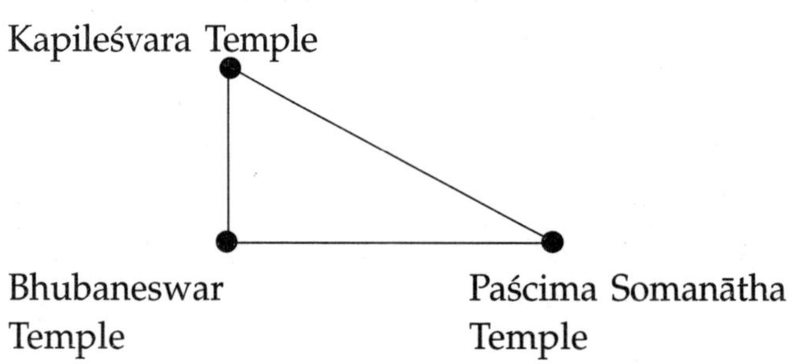

In coastal Orissa, Jajpur (ancient Jaipur) is famous for Goddess Virajā. Besides Virajā temple, one finds temples of Śiva scattered all over the town and its vicinity, of which the most important are those of Akhaṇḍaleśvara, Aṅgeśvara and Trilocaneśvara. The Virajā-Kṣetra is triangular. In each corner, there is one *Śiva-*

[62] Shantilal Nagar, op. cit., p. 108.

liṅga almost at equal distance from one another. These three *Śivaliṅga*s are Bileśvara, Khilateśvara and Baruṇeśvara.[63]

This Śaiva tāntric formula (i.e. *yantra* of creation) of Śiva-Kāmeśvara, Śakti Kāmeśvarī and Somarasya had extended its influence to Gañjam district also,[64] as at the centre of Asika is seen a Śiva temple, Tribidheśvara. Three *liṅga*s are found on the single Śakti deity of this temple. The local people have a belief that it was the abode of the holy trinity — Brahmā, Viṣṇu and Maheśvara.[65] In spiritual sense, the deity of this temple of Asika signifies the tāntric formulae of Śiva-Kāmeśvara, Śakti Kāmeśvarī and Somarasya. The three *liṅga*s in a single Śakti are drawn inside like a tortoise head, which symbolizes the *vajrolī haṭha-yogic-mudrā*, which is meant for *yoga* of sexual transformation.

---

[63] N.C. Behuria (chief ed.), *Gazetteer of India, Orissa State*, vol. II, Cuttack, 1991, p. 315.

[64] *THOMV*, 2004, p. 223.

[65] A.K. Rath, *Studies on Some Aspects of the History and Culture of Orissa*, Kolkata: Punthi Pustak, 1987, p. 209.

6

Form of Lord Puruṣottama Jagannātha at a Sumerian Temple Ruin Site

WITH the established norms of European historians of the eighteenth, nineteenth and twentieth centuries CE, which are taught in Indian schools, colleges and universities, the early civilizations are traced in Egypt, Sumeria, Babylonia, Assyria, China, Persia and Indus Valley of India.[1] Much water has flown and much progress has been made in all walks of life nowadays. Great archaeological and historical discoveries have been made. The lost Sarasvatī River of the Vedic period is now traced scientifically.[2] By observing latest discoveries and by making path-breaking findings, a group of scholars — Georg Feuerstein, Subhash Kak and David Frawley[3] — while writing the Preface of the book, *In Search of the Cradle of Civilization*, mention:

> In this book we are trying to answer some of the questions in regard to a civilization that has a very special place in the story of human cultural evolution and that nonetheless is barely known. Ever since Napoleon's days, we in the West have been dazzled by the splendour of pharaonic Egypt — with its impressive pyramids, the mysterious sphinx, and the magnificent treasures of Tutankhamen. We have also been impressed with the intellectual achievements of the learned elite of Sumer, which, according to our school books, was responsible for the invention of writing, the potter's wheel, wheeled carts, cylinder seals, cosmology, formal law, and bicameral political congress.
>
> Most of the "first time ever" claims made for the Sumerians have in recent years been exposed as exaggerated or absurd. There is mounting evidence

---

[1] H.A. Davies, *An Outline History of the World*, London: Oxford University Press, 1959, pp. 1-83.

[2] B.P. Radhakrishna and S.S. Merh, *Memoir 42 — Vedic Sarasvati* (*Evolutionary History of a Lost River of North-Western India*), Bangalore: Geological Society of India, 1999, *passim*.

[3] G. Feuerstein, S. Kak and D. Frawley, *In Search of the Cradle of Civilization*, Delhi: Motilal Banarsidass, 1999, pp. xvii-xix.

that neither Sumer nor Egypt quite deserves the pride of place among the ancient civilizations. Rather, the cradle of civilization appears to lie beyond the fertile valleys of the Nile, Tigris and Euphrates rivers. We invite the reader to join us in a journey of discovery, which in its implications seems far more thrilling to us than the discoveries of Troy, the Elamite civilization in Iran, the "lost" civilization of Dilmun on the island of Bahrain in the Arabian/Persian Gulf, or most recently the discovery of what may have been the kingdom of Sheba in the extreme south of the Arabian peninsula.

As we will show, India is the giant that looms behind these early urban cultures. This astonishing finding completely revolutionizes our understanding of ancient history. It challenges us anew to look for the cradle of human civilization. We do not claim to have solved the riddle of the big bang of our civilized universe, merely that we are possibly closer to it than ever before. In this book we introduce exciting new evidence that sheds light on a hitherto obscure phase of ancient history. We believe the recent findings are significantly narrowing the gap between the early Neolithic civilizations and the end of the Ice Age and its Palaeolithic cultures.

This is the first time that these amazing developments in archaeology and history are reviewed in a comprehensive and comprehensible fashion. Why has it taken so long to recognize the significance of ancient India in the saga of human civilization? In his book *Looking for Dilmun*, Geoffrey Bibby rightly remarked that the "Indus Valley Civilization is the Cinderella of the ancient World".[4] Indeed for a variety of reasons, ancient India has been sorely neglected by archaeologists and historians. Prevailing misconceptions and biases have long hampered the study of ancient India's civilization. Fortunately this regrettable situation is beginning to change and the new attitude in scholarly circles has already proven enormously productive. Quite likely, the recent successes in reinterpreting ancient India's civilization will further speed up this promising process of revisioning ancient history that a handful of daring historians and archaeologists have begun.

While dealing with the extent, connections and survivals of the Indus Valley Civilization, A.D. Pusalkar[5] had remarked:

The Indus Valley Civilization seems to have embraced the whole of Sind

[4] G. Feuerstein, G. Bibby, *Looking for Dilmun*, New York: New American Library, 1974, p. 161.

[5] A.D. Pusalker, "The Indus Valley Civilization", *THACOTIP*, vol. I, 1965, pp. 199-200.

> and the Punjab, the bulk of Kāṭhiāvāṛa, a part of the coastal region, the valleys of North-West Frontier Province, and a part at least of the Gangetic basin.[6]
>
> The extent of the Indus Valley Civilization indicates its connections practically with the whole of northern India, and in the west, with all the contemporary cultures. Immediately after the discoveries in the Indus Valley were published, sumerologists came forward with affinities of the Indus Valley Civilization with Sumer, and at the outset the Indus Valley Civilization was designated Indo-Sumerian. But despite its close contact with ancient Sumer, the Indus Valley Civilization has peculiarities of its own. It has recently been shown that the similarities between the two cultures have been over-emphasized and the differences overlooked. At any rate there is an overwhelming mass of evidence showing that a flourishing trade, probably through the land routes in Baluchistan, existed between the Indus Valley and Sumer in ancient times. Numerous seals of Indian design and workmanship have been found at various Sumerian and Elamite sites. Importations from Sumer recovered in the Indus Valley, however, are comparatively very few. A white marble seal, an engraved steatite vessel, an etched carnelian bead, a model ram, an adze axe, and small pottery rings used as net-weights have been recorded as probable importations from Sumer, indicating trading intercourse. The most important piece of evidence testifying to the influence of the Indus Valley on Sumer is the fashion of hair-dressing adopted by Sumerian women from the Indus Valley.[7]

This was the expression of A.D. Pusalker during the first half of the twentieth century CE. But the recent findings show that the Vedic culture of India had spread throughout the world. Therefore, scholars like Shripal Dattatraya Kulkarni[8] and Viṣṇukant Verma[9] have written on the topic. The oriental scholars were aware of this and therefore Will Durant,[10] a very eminent and balanced historian, had observed,

---

[6] A.D. Pusalker, op. cit.; *Journal of the Indian History*, Madras, vol. XVI, p. 12.

[7] Ibid.; P. Carleton, *Buried Empires*, London, 1939, p. 161.

[8] *BSOIHAC*, vol. XVI, *India Abroad*, 1995, *passim*.

[9] V.K. Verma, *Indo-Aryan Colonization of Greece and Middle East*, 2 vols., Delhi: Pratibha Prakashan, 2000, *passim*;

V.K. Verma, *Missing Link of World Civilization, Indo-Aryan Colonization*, Delhi: Pratibha Prakashan, 2005, *passim*.

[10] Quoted in *Aryan-Tarangini*, A. Kalyanaraman, vol. I, Asia Publishing House, 1969, Preface, p. viii.

"India was the Motherland of our race and Sanskrit the mother, of European languages. She was the mother of our philosophy, mother through the Arabs of much of our mathematics, mother through Buddha of the ideals embodied in Christianity, mother through the village community of self-government and democracy. Mother India, in many ways, is the mother of us all."

About Sumerians, S.D. Kulkarni[11] observes:

SUMERIANS

Sumeria was the land between the twin rivers Tigris and Euphrates like Gaṅgā-Yamunā Doab, the most fertile land, the land of the crescent. It is, by no means improbable, that the Sumerians were an Indian race, which passed by land and sea into the valley of the two rivers. It was in their Indian home, perhaps in the Indus Valley, that their culture developed. There, their writing might have been invented, progressing from a pictorial to a simplified ideographic, which later on, in Babylonia, took on its peculiar cuneiform appearance, owing to its being written with a square-ended stilus on soft clay. There is little doubt that India must have been one of the earliest centres of civilization. This is the opinion of Francois Lenormant (quoted in *Āryataraṅgiṇī*). It echoes our theory that the Indo-Aryans were autochthonous of the vast region — the home of the Vedic people.

Sumer is SU = the beautiful, MERU = the plateau land, the seat of the Gods. It is said that Onez (Pr̥thu-Venya) came to this land and as he was from the mount Sumeria from which Yamunā takes its source, this land was then known as Sumeria. Chaldeans were one of the families of Sumeria and their king became the king of Sumeria. "The Chaldeans, the Babylonians and the inhabitants of Colchis derived their civilization from India," says Count Bjorstjerna. Chaldea, it is said, is a corruption of Cul — family or tribe and Deva (a God or a Brāhmaṇa). Chaldea was a land of the pious and upright people.

Chaldea's capital town was Ur. In its ruins were found pieces of Indian teak. The Babylonian name for cotton muslin was "Sindhu". This shows that cotton-weaving industry flourished in India since hoary antiquity. Bible records some rare articles being imported from India — ivory, apes, pearls, peacocks, incense and hard wood in King Soloman's time, i.e. since about 900 BCE. A.C. Das in his *R̥gvedic India* observes that there was a very close

[11] S.D. Kulkarni (ed.), op. cit., *India Abroad*, 1995, p. 139.

connection between the Coḷas and Mesopotamia and that Chaldea is a corrupted form of Indian Caḷa-Deśa.

When the global awareness is developing, a Vedic scholar of the West, David Frawley,[12] states:

> There were two main Vedic cultures in ancient India. The first was a northern kingdom centered on the Sarasvatī-Dṛṣadvatī River region dominated by the Purus and the Ikṣvākus that produced the existent Veda texts that we have. The second was a southern culture along the coast of the Arabian Sea and into the Vindhya mountains, dominated by the Turvaṣas and Yadus and extending into groups yet further south. These northern and southern groups vied for supremacy and influenced each other in various ways as the Vedas and Purāṇas indicate. The northern of Bhārata culture ultimately prevailed, making India the land of Bhārata or Bhāratavarṣa and its main ancient literary record the Vedas, though militarily the Yadus remained strong throughout history. The southern culture was the older of the two, with the Vedic people coming originally from the south, not the north-west. This was the basis of the maritime symbolism at the core of Vedic thought, which reflects an ancient heritage.
>
> In addition, there was a third or north-west Vedic culture in Punjab and Afghanistan, that of the Anus and Druhyus, which was at first part of the northern kingdom but gradually developed its own identity. It was partly assimilated by the Bhāratas that became the dominant northern people. Another portion of it extended to the north and west outside of the Indian subcontinent. Its influence was secondary to that of the northern and southern kingdoms and much of it passed out of the Indic sphere of culture. However, it was the basis of most of the Indo-European and Iranian people and cultures that we find in Europe, Central Asia and the Middle East.
>
> Therefore, we must look at the south and east connections to understand not only Indic civilization and Hinduism, but also the Vedas themselves. The western connections to the Europeans and Iranians were more an outflow, while the southern connections were more original and enduring. Western scholars, dominated by a European mindset, only traced Indo-European culture from Europe and the Middle East to India as its eastern border. They failed to see that the boundary was only in their minds.

[12] David Frawley, *The Ṛgveda and the History of India* (*Ṛgveda Bharata Itihas*), New Delhi: Aditya Prakashan, 2001, Vide Inner Cover flaps.

I have[13] collected one broken stone *liṅga* in the actual human *liṅga* shape, from Baṛīgāon village and preserved it in my private possession. It has similarity with those found at Haṛappā and Moheṅjo-Dāṛo. . . . A seated figurine of steatite has been discovered at Khariar and is preserved in author's private possession. It proves the contact of the Indus Valley Civilization with the area of Upper Mahānadī Valley. New evidences of the Indus Valley Civilization, found in Pakistan, reveal that one seated figurine, with bent legs extending out in the front and having pinched applique facial features and breasts, has been found at Gumla. Seated figurines have also been discovered at Jalilpur in Pakistan.[14]

While searching archival records in the library of the great tāntric scholar Prafulla Chandra Bhanja Deo at Baripāḍā in November 1992, this author came across a copy of the English daily newspaper, *Hindustan Standard,* dated 13 October 1953, published from Calcutta (present Kolkata). The newspaper wrote:

> BABYLONIAN SEAL UNEARTHED
>
> Baripada Oct. 11 — Sri Prafulla Chandra Bhanja Deo, M.P. yesterday communicated to the *Hindustan Standard* correspondent here over phone that "an Ivory Babylonian Seal" has just been unearthed in the precincts of the Barunighat temple at Baripada.
>
> Sri Bhanja Deo told the *Hindustan Standard* that while excavation of a tank was in progress on the land on the northern side of the compound of the Barunighat temple, an Ivory Babylonian seal of the roller type was found underground at a depth of about seven feet. The temple and the grounds adjoining it belong to Lalsaheb Kumar Prafulla Chandra Bhanja Deo and are situated at a level of six feet below the level of Baripada town. Fortunately the proprietor who himself is an eminent archaeologist was present near the site of the excavation at the time of the discovery as labourers were about to throw this away as a piece of bone from the mass mud in which it was embedded. The labourers told the proprietor that on previous occasions several similar objects including strange skulls and skeletons had been unearthed on the same spot and that all such objects had been thrown into

13 *THOMV*, 2004, pp. 26-28; J.P. Singh Deo, "Orissa's Contact with First Civilization of the World", *Some Tāntric Esotericism of Orissa*, Kolkata: R.N. Bhattacharya, 2003, pp. 39-42.

14 Ibid.; J.G. Shaffer, "The Indus Civilization: New Evidences from Pakistan", *Essays in Indian Proto-History*, D.P. Agrawal and D.K. Cakrabarti (eds.), Delhi: B.R. Publishing Corporation, 1979, pp. 18-22.

> the river as being inauspicious and undesirable objects after consultation with the temple authorities. Henceforth the proprietor gave strict orders that all finds, however seemingly insignificant or inauspicious, should be kept apart for his personal scrutiny before their disposal in this manner by ignorant individuals. The seal is now in the possession of Sri Bhanja Deo who has preserved it for his new museum which contains many rare objects and discoveries.
>
> This much information confirms that there was cultural, spiritual, and trade and commerce link between the Mahanadī Valley, Sindhu/Indus Valley Civilization and Babylonia.[15]

With this information, the author[16] had also disclosed that the earliest conception of Śakti and Śiva in union has also been discovered in the Mahānadī Valley in the form of stone sockets. These are in circular shape with a socket on the lower part and has components in the upper parts which fit into the lower socket. The shape of this socket owes its origin to the rock-shelter painting of Yogīmaṭh Ḍoṅger (hill). Such a stone socket set was collected by the author from the Mohangiri site of Kālāhāṇḍī district and is preserved at the Manikyapur Museum of Bhawānīpatna. It can be interpreted as the union of Śiva and Śakti which represents the *yoga* of sexual transformation. Later it developed as *vajrolī* and *sahajolī* in the tāntric *haṭha-yoga* practice. Such a socket set was jointly collected by Baba Mishra and Pradeep Mohanty from the Kharligaṛh site of Bolaṅgīr district in the Orissa province and exhibited at the Manikyapur Museum of Bhawānīpatna. Such an object had also been found from layer III (early historic phase), from Veerapuram in Andhra Pradesh, where it is interpreted as a votive *liṅga*.[17] The shape of such stone sockets had been utilized for the shape of Lord Buddha in the Amarāvatī crossbar railing, which shows the presentation of Rāhula.[18] Later this shape was evolved to be the image of Lord Jagannātha at Purī and the composite tāntric figure of Mahākāla and Mahākālī

---

[15] J.P. Singh Deo, "Orissa's Contact with First Civilization of the World", *Reference Orissa*, A.N. Tiwari (ed.), Bhubaneswar: Enterprising Publishers, 2nd edn., 2000, pp. 673-74.

[16] *THOMV*, 2004, pp. 31-32.

[17] Ibid.; T.V.G. Shastri, K.N. Bai and J.V.P. Rao, *Veerapuram*, Hyderabad: Bhavani Printers, 1984, *passim*.

[18] Ibid.; E.R. Shastri, *The Buddhist Art of Nagarjunakonda*, Delhi: Motilal Banarsidass, 1994, Illustration No. 32.

at Tala site in Bilaspur district of Chhattisgarh province, depicting all haṭha-yogic features throughout the body,[19] relating to the *yoga* of sexual transformation.

This area had contact with the Sumerian Civilization also, where trace of the form of Lord Puruṣottama Jagannātha is also found. While dealing with "The Characteristics of the Sumerians", Vishnu Kant Verma[20] states:

> It is established by history that the people, who entered the valley of Tigris and Euphrates and settled there, were the torchbearers of an advanced civilization, foreign to the land of Mesopotamia. Their traits that have come to light were firstly their liking for wooden architecture, secondly their fondness for building temples on natural hills or artificially raised platforms, and thirdly their expertise in sea faring. These apart, the similarity in their seal design and its script with the Sindhu Valley is noteworthy. The Sumerian forefathers brought with them a system of writing and a corpus of law when they entered the valley from a land foreign to Sumer. Endeavour to trace the original home of the Sumerian forefathers is a great step towards writing human history.
>
> The frequent use by the Sumerians of such names as are closely associated with the Paurāṇic narration leaves no doubt as to the Sumerian civilization being an off-shoot of the Vedic civilization of the Sindhu Valley. . . .
>
> It is surprising that the name Sumeru is connected with the legendary Sumeru mountain of the Paurāṇic narration. The word Sumeru is of Sanskrit origin. SU means good and MERU is the name of north pole (Uttarī Dhruva) which is a term of Hindu astronomy. In Hindu mythology it is supposed to be the abode of the *deva*s (Gods).

The most remarkable finding is the form or shape of Lord Puruṣottama Jagannātha found in the plates of a Sumerian temple on a raised platform (*Plate* 3).[21]

This proves that the Central Mahānadī River Valley had cultural and spiritual

---

[19] *THOMV*, J.P. Singh Deo, *Origin of Jagannāth Deity*, New Delhi: Gyan Publishing House, 1991 and 2nd edn. 2003, *passim;* and

J.P. Singh Deo, "Composite Tāntric Yogic Figure of Māhākāla and Māhākālī", *Riddle of Indian Iconography* (*Zetetic on Rare Icon from Tala*), L.S. Nigam (ed.), Delhi: Sharda Publishing House, 2000, pp. 127-34.

[20] V.K. Verma, *Missing Link of World Civilization, Indo-Aryan Colonization*, Delhi: Pratibha Prakashan, 2005, pp. 134-35.

[21] Ibid., Plate 3 and Plate on the back cover page.

Plate 3: The Shape of Lord Puruṣottama Jagannātha, traced on the ruin of Sumerian Temple on a raised platform. Courtesy: Vishnu Kant Varma, *Missing Link of World Civilization: Indo-Aryan Colonization*, Delhi: Pratibha Prakashan, 2006, Plate 3 and back cover page.

contacts with Sindhu-Sarasvatī Valley Civilization and through migrations, the shape of Puruṣottama Jagannātha deity had reached the Sumerian Civilization. So, it can be claimed that much before the installation of this deity at Puri, its worship, which originated and developed in the Central Mahānadī Valley, had spread and was popular in the Sumerian Civilization of 3000 BCE.[22]

Lord Puruṣottama Jagannātha has two large eyes. V.K. Varma,[23] traced evidences pertaining to a period ranging between 2620 to 1700 BCE of Indo-Aryan settlements

[22] V.K. Verma, *Missing Link of World Civilization*, *Indo-Aryan Colonization*, Delhi: Pratibha Prakashan, 2005, p. 131.

[23] Ibid., pp. 179-82.

in northern Babylonia and in parts well within Syria. He details the "The Sahasra Akṣiṇī — The Thousand Eyed Temple".

In Veda, God is described as omnipresent. Just as a living-being requires (eyes, ears, etc.) five conscious organs to see, hear, touch, smell and taste and five motor organs to produce muscular activity to walk, work with hand, etc. God does not suffer from this limitation. He although possesses no physical form, by his very intrinsic nature he is vested with all powers of all the sense organs, as an attribute, in his formless form. He sees, hears, feels the touch without eyes, ears and skin and moves and works without hands. Thus, he has at each point a eye, a nose, a tongue, a hand, a foot for himself. This is described in the Vedic hymn (*R̥V*, Maṇḍala X, hymn 90; verse 1) in an allegorical manner that he has thousand heads, thousand eyes, thousand feet. In fact, thousand is a symbolic figure to denote innumerable quantity.

This idea connotes that God has no face but he has everywhere eyes to see the deeds of the souls in the forms of human or other living beings.

The same idea that God is present everywhere in the form of a power, which can see everything, finds its expression in a temple, at Tell Brak which lies 300 miles east of the Mediterranean Sea and 130 miles west of Tigris on the border of Syria and Iraq.

The two nearest towns are Nisibin and Hasakaen the former 25 miles to the north, while the latter the same distance to the south.

Here a dominant mound stands, roughly oval in plan, covering 120 acres of land. The highest point stands 40 meters above the level plain. This mighty mound cannot fail to attract the attention of a passer-by for it looms over the plain and dominates it. This huge mound hides in its womb the history of ancient Mesopotamia from the period 1900 to 3200 BCE as one descends downwards from the top encountering different levels.

When excavated by the famous archaeologist Maz Mallowan, the second layer from the top revealed a temple of late Jambat Nasr period (around 3300 BCE) which had hundreds of eyes made on the walls in black and white Alabaster. Below this temple there was another temple in which only traces of white plaster were the only remains but still below found a temple of gray brick wall. The walls of the principal temple were overlaid with copper panels on which designs of eyes were embossed. It was due to this prominent feature of the presence of thousands of eye images, made in mixed white and black marble on the walls, and those embellished on copper panelling in repousse, that tempted the archaeologists to call it an Eye temple.

This idea of the Urak period people of representing God as a witness who is present everywhere to observe the deeds of all creatures is at once a familiar idea of the Vedic sages.

The purpose of fixing thousands of eye images on walls on all sides is to represent the all seeing power of God present at every point of space. In this connection the remark, which the archaeologist himself felt to make, is worth quoting. He says:

In summarizing our conclusions I would repeat that the Eye form was merely intended to emphasize the all seeing nature of God and that there was some taboo against representing the divine face.

Even it is not clear to the modern refined Englishman why it is objectionable to represent divine face and that is why he suspects the persistence of some taboo — some sort of curse of prohibition amongst the Urak people for showing divine face.

As against this one can see how clearly the Vedic sages imbibed the principle that God is formless and without physical body, limbs and sense organs yet possesses all the functions of all sense organs at every point of space.

Vedic sages who visualized the super concept of the formless omnipresent existence of God possessing all the attributes of the senses were the original seers of that magnificent idea. Thus the Sumerians borrowed this thought from the Vedic Aryans and reduced this thought into physical representation by engraving thousands of eyes all over the surface of walls of the temple. That this conjecture is correct is supported by the find of thousands of beads at Tell Brak of Mesopotamia, most of which were glazed and painted. Beads of similar nature but more improved than those of Sumer were found in the Sindhu Valley excavations.

The above description of Vishnu Kant Verma proves the form or shape of Lord Puruṣottama Jagannātha to have Vedic confirmation.

From the Gazetteer source,[24] it is known that in *Jagannātha Caritāmṛta*, a work

[24] Durga Charan Kuanr (state ed.), *Gazetteer of India, Orissa, Puri,* Nilamani, Senapati (chief ed.), Cuttack, 1977.

of post-Pañcasakhā period, Jagannātha has been described as the Supreme Lord or Pūrṇa Brahmā, whereas Kṛṣṇa, the son of Nanda, represents only a part of his glory.[25]

> Thus the synthetic cult of Jagannātha is an epitome of divergent religious creeds and schools of philosophy that prevailed in India at different periods of her long cultural history. In the historic process of adjustments, Jagannātha has assimilated strange contradictions in a manner that is most amazing in the history of religious thought.

"There is no discarding any in this Religion of Man," wrote Pandit Nilakantha Das,[26] "and all the gods and goddesses attracting and appealing have found a place in the compound of the temple. Jagannātha has welcomed and embraced all, but been overwhelmed by none and has lost Himself in none."

This study emphasizes the fact that the Central Mahānadī River Valley had cultural and spiritual contact with the Sindhu-Sarasvatī Valley Civilization and, through migrations, the form *alias* shape of Puruṣottama Jagannātha deity had reached the Sumerian Civilization. So, it can be claimed that much before the installation of this deity at Purī, its worship, which originated and developed in the Central Mahānadī Valley, had spread and was popular in the Sumerian Civilization of a period beyond three thousand years BCE.

[25] Durga Charan Kuanr, *Jagannātha Caritamṛta*, Cuttack: Union Printing Work, 1913, chapter XVIII, lines 29-30, p. 169.

[26] Pandit Nilakantha Das, "Cult of Jagannāth", *Orissa Review*, vol. XXVI, no. 12, p. 18, Public Relations Dept., Government of Orissa, Bhubaneswar.

7

Koṭsamlai Area and the Formative Phase of the Puruṣottama Jagannātha Cult

KOṬSAMLAI[1] is a village in Birmaharaj police station limit, in Sonepur district of Orissa province, notable for the hill caves near it. A big cave about 45' wide is known by the name Rānīkhol and the hill is called Trikūṭa. Going by the tradition, when Raktabāhu, the Yavana general, invaded Purī, the images of Jagannātha, Balabhadra and Subhadrā were removed to this cave. Some time after that Yayāti Kesarī defeated Yavanas and drove them out of Orissa. He brought back the images of the deities and installed them in the temple of Purī. This cave also offered shelter to Rājā Pr̥thvī Singh Deo of Sonepur and his family in CE 1799 when the Marāṭhā General Nanasaheb invaded Sonepur and subsequently Pr̥thvī Singh Deo was made captive. . . .

The name Trikūṭa seems to have some relation with a rare stone found in the Patdaraha area, the southern part of Sunabeda plateau of Nuāpāḍā district as described in Chapter 1. The rare stone with *sr̥ṣṭi* (creation) *yantra* is of ferruginous colour and is preserved in the Palace Museum of the author at Khariar. Because of this finding, the author[2] was of the opinion that this discussion and finding of *sr̥ṣṭi yantra* at Patdaraha area proves that the original first tāntric *yogī* who discovered the *yantra* of *sr̥ṣṭi*, which is a right-angled triangle, was residing at the hill top of Sunabeda plateau and probably to commemorate the memory of this great *siddha yogī*, a mountain under which Boden village exists, was named as Guru Ḍoṅger. Therefore, we have reason to believe that the *yantra* of *sr̥ṣṭi* (creation) was originated in the Boden Block area.

---

[1] N.K. Sahu (state ed.), *Gazetteer of India, Orissa, Bolangir*, Nilamani Senapati (chief ed.), Cuttack: 1968, p. 486.

[2] J.P. Singh Deo, "Study of Contribution of Boden Block Area to Yogic Tradition of Bharatvarsha", *Pātālgaṅgā (Souvenir)*, Pātālgaṅgā Utsav, 2006, Boden, p. 36.

The guru (Spiritual Master) who resided at Guru Ḍoṅger cave was a Śaiva, because the Śiva-liṅga worshipped by him is still there, near the opening of the natural cave on Guru Ḍoṅger. (Plate 4).

This guru may be identified as sage Kapila. The Vedic culture of Bhāratavarṣa consists mainly of four Vedas and six Darśana Śāstras.[3] Sage Kapila, the producer of Sāṁkhya Darśana, was the divine son of Devahūti, who was the daughter of the first Manu Svayambhuva, 1,900 million years ago.[4] Sāṁkhya Darśana calls *puruṣa* for the entire divine phenomena and *prakṛti* for the prime cosmic power *māyā* that evolves itself into the form of this universe with the help of *puruṣa* (God).[5]

So, it seems that while sage Kapila was meditating on the Guru Ḍoṅger, he got the revelation of Sāṁkhya Darśana. Sāṁkhya does not give any detail of the practice of meditation. It only emphasizes on intellectually understanding and meditating upon the understood truth and eliminating the attachment of the world. The practical side of Sāṁkhya meditation is the Yoga Darśana.[6]

Plate 4: "*Śivaliṅga* without Śākti", worshipped at the Natural Cave entrance of Guru Ḍoṅger, Dist. Nuāpāḍā, Orissa (courtesy: Samuel Dani).

---

3 His Divinity Dharm Chakravarti Swami Prakashanand Saraswati, *The True History and the Religion of India*, Delhi: Motilal Banarsidass, 2001, p. 555.

4 Ibid., p. 556.

5 Ibid., p. 560.

6 Ibid., p. 561.

The practical Sāṁkhya Darśana, in its *haṭha-yoga*, gave rise to the *yoga* of sexual transformation. Interaction between man and woman, Tantra wise, has three purposes — pleasure, proceation and *samādhi*.[7]

The earliest conception of Śakti and Śiva in union[8] has also been discovered in the Great Mahānadī Valley, in the form of stone sockets. These are in circular shape with a socket on the lower part and has components in the upper part which fit into the lower socket. The shape of this socket owes its origin to the rock-shelter painting of Yogīmaṭh Ḍoṅger. It can be interpreted as union of Śiva and Śakti, which represents the Yoga of sexual transformation. Later, it developed as *vajrolī* and *sahajolī mudrās* in the tāntric *haṭha-yoga* practice. Such a socket set was jointly collected by Baba Mishra and Pradeep Mohanty from the Kharligaṛh site of Bolaṅgīr district in Orissa and exhibited at the Manikyapur Musuem. Two such a stone socket sets were found in the ruins of the stone temple structure of eight-handed Mahi-ṣāsuramardinī, on the left bank of Udanti River, within Baṛgāon village of Sinapali Block in Nuāpāḍā district. One half of such a socket is found near the perennial water spring of Pātālgaṅgā site, within Boden Block area. Such an object had also been found from layer III (early historical phase) from Veerapuram in Andhra Pradesh, where it is interpreted as a votive *liṅga*.[9] The shape of such stone sockets had been utilized for the shape of Lord Buddha in the Amarāvatī crossbar railings, which show the presentation of Rāhula, in Sāñcī *stūpa* and Bharhut *stūpa*. Later, this shape evolved to be the image of Lord Jagannātha at Purī and the composite tāntric figure of Mahākāla and Mahākālī at Tala in Bilaspur district of Chhattisgarh, depicting all haṭha-yogic features throughout the body, relating to the *yoga* of sexual transformation.[10]

These archaeological findings of male and female principles in union in the Central Mahānadī Valley prove that this shape was also used to represent Lord Buddha.

With these new revelations, let us go back to the details of the Trikūṭa hill. According to *Purnachandra Ordia Bhashokosha*,[11] Trikūṭa means the imaginary point

[7] J.P. Singh Deo, *Tāntric Art of Orissa*, Delhi: Kalpaz Publications, 2001, p. 31.

[8] *THOMV*, 2004, pp. 31-32.

[9] Ibid.; T.V.G. Sastri, K.N. Bai and J.V.P. Rao, *Veerapuram*, Hyderabad: Bhavani Printers, 1984, *passim*.

[10] Ibid.; J.P. Singh Deo, "Composite Tāntric Yogic Figure of Mahākālā and Mahākālī", *Riddle of Indian Iconography* (*Zetetic on Rare Icon from Tala*), Delhi: Sharada Publishing House, 2000, pp. 127-34.

[11] Gopal Chandra Praharaj (comp.), *Pūrnachandra Ordiā Bhashākosha* (Oriya Lexicon), vol. III, 1933, p. 895.

— between the two eye-brows — in the human body on which attention is concentrated during the practice of *yoga*. So, the name of the hill itself proves that the locality is connected with *haṭha-yoga*, which believes in the thought that macrocosm is found in microcosm, i.e. *piṇḍa-Brahmāṇḍa* theory of the Nātha *yogīs*.

Traditionally, it is believed that once upon a time, there were 22 caves in the Trikūṭa hill. Among them Jagannātha Gumphā, Dhuli Gumphā and Rānī Gumphā may be mentioned. At the entrance of Mādhava Gumphā, a monolithic image of Lord Jagannātha is found. Hissing sound is always heard at the Dhuli Gumphā cave.[12]

This image of Lord Jagannātha may be represented as the image of Lord Buddha, which was worshipped by King Indrabhūti of Sambal.[13] According to Arjun Joshi:[14]

> It may be mentioned that Jagannātha as a deity being worshipped has been referred to by Rājā Indrabhūti of Sambal, who flourished in the eighth century CE. The tāntric literature, particularly the *Rudrayāmala Tantra, Brahmayāmala Tantra* as well as the *Tantrayāmala* and *Kalki Purāṇa,* mentions Jagannātha in Puruṣottama-Kṣetra. It appears that the synthesis between Jagannātha and Puruṣottama was worked out by the tāntric scholars prior to advent of Rāmānuja who converted Choḍagaṅga to Śrī Vaiṣṇava faith. It was because of the spiritual inspiration of Rāmānuja that Choḍagaṅga constructed the magnificent temple of Lord Jagannātha and Mahālakṣmī on the sea-shore.

Another monolithic Buddha image, in the shape of Lord Jagannātha, is found. The author[15] had earlier mentioned:

> In two sockets like shape of Buddha, two hands were added and such a shape is found in the monolithic figure, near the south-east slope of Mahendragiri mountain, which area comes under Andhra Pradesh province.

---

[12] *Sambad*, Oriya daily newspaper, 20 February 2007, *passim*.

Pabitra Mohan Barik, "Śrī Jagannātha Sanskruti Ku Abhibhakta Bolangir Jilla ra Abadana" (Oriya), *Souvenir*, Bolangir Loka Utsava, 2006, pp. 39-42.

[13] N.K. Sahu, *Buddhism in Orissa*, Cuttack: Utkal University, 1958, pp. 166-68.

[14] Arjun Joshi, *New Light on the Cultural Heritage of Orissa*, Cuttack: Baneeshree, 1980, pp. 77-78.

[15] J.P. Singh Deo, *Origin of Jagannāth Deity*, New Delhi: Gyan Publishing House, 2nd edn., enlarged edn., 2003, pp. 197-98.

The zone of Mahendragiri-Parlākhemuṇḍi has vast Buddhist remains.[16] One can also detect Buddhist remains in the vast archaeological wealth of the Gaṅga capital Kaliṅganagara.[17] The monolithic Buddha image of Mahendragiri-Parlākhemuṇḍi zone is misunderstood as Lord Jagannātha by S.N. Rajaguru.[18] There are many images of Lord Buddha at the Buddhist monastery of Laddakh (Jammu-Kashmir province) of north India, which resemble Lord Puruṣottama Jagannātha of Purī.

The new discoveries confirm that one of the images of Lord Buddha *alias* Puruṣottama Buddha Jagannātha evolved as Puruṣottama Jagannātha at Purī.

When worship of Lord Buddha, in the shape of present Jagannātha deity, was continuing in early medieval period, it is worth discussing the happening at Purī site in early historical period.

According to the new finding of His Divinity Dharm Chakravarti Swami Prakashanand Saraswati,[19] the period of Jagadguru Śaṅkarācārya was 509–477 BCE.

Regarding the installation of Puruṣottama Jagannāth, Satchidananda Mishra[20] states:

On a pillar of *jagamohana* of the temple of Jagannātha is a depiction of Śaṅkarācārya in painting. The significance of the painting is explained in a legend which is described in *Śrī Jagannātha Mandira,* written by Pandit Sadasiva Misra in Baṅgālī and published in CE 1911. Some Oriya books of late date also depict the legend. According to the legend: Before the present temple was built, Govardhana Maṭha of Śaṅkarācārya was located at the place where the present *jagamohana* is. The *ācārya*s of the *maṭha* were in-charge of the worship of Jagannātha. In those days the *āśrama* of the *saṁnyāsī*s was in Balisahi. To allow enough space for the construction of the massive temple (the earlier temple must have been a small one without *jagamohana*), Govardhana Maṭha was shifted to the *āśrama* in Balima-sahi. The legend

[16] J.P. Singh Deo, *Origin of Jagannāth Deity*, New Delhi: Gyan Publishing House, 2nd edn., enlarged edn., 2003, pp. 197-98; K.C. Dash, "Dantapura and Puspagiri", *The Journal of Orissan History*, vol. IX, June 1989, p. 9.

[17] Ibid.; N.S. Ramaswami, *Monograph on Temples of Mukhaliṅgam*, Hyderabad: Govt. of Andhra Pradesh, 1976, pp. 8-9.

[18] Ibid.; S.N. Rajaguru, *Śrī Puruṣottam-O-Śrī Mandira* (Oriya), Bhubaneswar: Orissa Sahitya Academy, 1996, pp. 35-52.

[19] *TTHATROI*, 2001, p. 502.

[20] Satchidananda Misra, "Installation of Puruṣottama Jagannātha", *Studies in the Cult of Jagannātha*, K.C. Mishra (ed.), Bhubaneswar: Institute of Orissan Culture, 1991, pp. 136-37.

further states that the painting of Śaṅkarācārya on a pillar of *jagamohana* was designed as a memento.

Basing on the legend it may be said that Śaṅkarācārya did initiate the worship of Jagannātha. Otherwise, how was his *maṭha* allowed space within the precincts of an already established temple? Why was the charge of the temple given to heads of the Govardhana Maṭha? As no king of Orissa is known to be a votary of the Smārtta faith, it is not probable that the *maṭha* was thrust into a functioning temple with royal patronage. The head of the *maṭha* could be in-charge of the temple only because the installation of the deity and the founding of the *maṭha* were done by the same person.

Doubtlessly, Jagannātha temple affairs were in charge of the heads of Govardhana Maṭha upto the middle of the eighteenth century CE when Orissa came under the Marāṭhā rule.

The statement of Satchidananda Misra confirms that Ādi Śaṅkarācārya had installed the shape of Lord Buddha as Jagannātha deity and had made it the male presiding deity of Govardhana Maṭha by defeating the Buddhists.

About Śaṅkarācārya, Satchidananda Misra[21] states:

Within his very short span of life Śaṅkara brought about several reforms and renovations in the Sanātana (Hindu) faith. His multifarious activities have left some permanent marks on the spiritual and cultural life of India. His life reveals that he has worked broadly on seven spheres as mentioned below:

1. One of India's renowned philosophers, he propounded the doctrines of "Advaita" and "Māyā". With a view to demonstrate how his doctrines rest on ancient authority, he wrote a gloss on *Viṣṇusahasranāma*, and scholastic commentaries on principal Upaniṣads, *Bhagavad-Gītā* and *Brahma-Sūtra*.

2. Śaṅkara created Daśanāmī Saṁnyāsī orders in order to organize persons following the fourth stage (*āśrama*) of life, perhaps taking the clue from the Buddhist Saṁgha. Further, he created the *nāgā saṁnyāsī* order, which was designed to function as a vigilant army of the domain of religion.

3. During Śaṅkarācārya's time, various religious sects (such as Pāśupata, Śaiva, Śākta, Tāntrika, Pañcarātra, Vaiṣṇava, Bhakta, Bhāgavata, Vaikhānasa, Saṅgata and Kṣapaṇaka) remaining within the confines

[21] Satchidananda Misra, "Installation of Puruṣottama Jagannātha", *Studies in the Cult of Jagannātha*, K.C. Mishra (ed.), Bhubaneswar: Institute of Orissan Culture, 1991, pp. 131-33.

of their sectarian faith often quarrelled with other sects. Śaṅkara propagated Smārtta faith with the joint worship of five principal deities basing on Vedic thought embodied in the *mantra*: *ekaṁ sad virpā bahudhā vadanti*. The non-sectarian principles found in the worship of Jagannātha may have its origin in the Smārtta faith.

4. Śaṅkarācārya has installed a number of images of different deities throughout India. Nārāyaṇa of Badrikāśrama, Kāmākṣī and Yogaliṅga of Kāñcī, Muktiliṅga of Kedāranātha, Varaliṅga of Nepal, Mokṣaliṅga of Chidambaram and Bhogaliṅga of Śṛṅgeri, etc. are known to have been installed by him.
5. Śaṅkarācārya was an accomplished poet and has a number of poetic compositions to his credit. His writings are as replete with religious emotion as with poetic lusture.
6. Śaṅkarācārya is remembered as the organizer of the largest of the religious concourses, the four Kumbha-Melās, where leaders and followers of all sects get together.
7. Before Śaṅkara there was no institution to organize and maintain Sanātana (Hindu) faith. Taking the Buddhist *vihāra*s as models he established several *maṭha*s. Principal among them are the four *maṭha*s located at the frontiers of the four directions of India. He put four of his disciples as *ācārya* of these *maṭha*s and divided his religious domain amongst them. As detailed in books like *Maṭhāmnāya* and *Maṭhetivṛttam*, territorial jurisdiction, religious sect, names of *saṁnyāsī*s and *brahmacārī*s, name and *gotra* of its first *ācārya* and Veda and *mahāvākya* of each of these *maṭha*s are distinct from each other. The sacred place, sacred waters and the male and female deities of each of these *maṭha*s are also distinct.

Direction	**East**	**South**	**West**	**North**
Maṭha	Govardhana	Śṛṅgeri	Śāradā	Jyotiḥ
Place	Puruṣottama	Rāmeśvara	Dwārakā	Badrikāśrama
Deity (male)	Jagannātha	Ādivarāha	Śiddheśvara	Nārāyaṇa
Deity (female)	Vimalā	Kāmākṣī	Bhadrakālī	Pūrṇagiri

Analysis of these data affords us an infallible clue to determine that at Puruṣottama Puri, Jagannātha was installed by Śaṅkarācārya. Because of this background, the author[22] had mentioned.

[22] J.P. Singh Deo, *Tāntric Art of Orissa*, Delhi: Kalpaz Publications, 2001, p. 112.

At Puruṣottama Purī, Śaṅkarācārya defeated the Buddhists and established one of the icons of Buddha as divinity of Govardhana Maṭha as Lord Viṣṇu Jagannātha, and his Śakti is Vimalā. It seems Jagannātha, established as the male deity of Govardhana Maṭha at Puruṣottama Purī by Śaṅkara, revolutionalized Jagannātha as a Vaiṣṇava deity. Further, Śaṅkara's commentary on the *Prasthānatrayī* added fuel to the fire of Puruṣottama cult and Jagannātha cult and made them synchronized as Puruṣottama Jagannātha. Lord Puruṣottama Jagannātha was made the presiding deity of Puruṣottama-Kṣetra during the period of Somavaṁśī King Mahāśivagupta Yayāti I in the early part of the tenth century CE.

This established fact of the author finds archaeological support from the new findings. The author[23] had stated:

> The Trinity conception of Jagannātha cult has also its origin from Yogīmaṭh rock art of Nuāpāḍā district. In the outskirts of Tentalkhunti village, situated on the right bank of Tel River, at a distance of about 40 km from district headquarters of Bolaṅgīr and 5 km from Tusra village, a huge mound of a fallen stone temple architecture exists.

In 2004, a Kondh tribe person named Trilochan Bhoi[24] had a dream and single-handedly dug out the temple, fallen stone and earth mound. Trilochan Bhoi dug out three images of Balabhadra, Subhadrā and Jagannātha. He also got some stone carved slabs, with the head of Dakṣiṇa Kālī and the lying Viṣṇu image. This discovery confirms the theory of construction of the oldest temple of Jagannātha Trinity by the Somavaṁśī King Yayāti Keśarī I in the ninth century CE as mentioned in *Mādalā Pāñjī*, the temple chronicle of Purī Jagannātha temple. The shapes of Balabhadra and Jagannātha excavated are made of stone, about 3′ each, without hands. The head of Dakṣiṇa Kālī made of stone was also dicovered from the same mound.

While writing the Introduction to the first edition of *Śilpa Prakāśa*, Alice Boner[25] had mentioned that we should like to add the remark that the tradition of considering

---

[23] J.P. Singh Deo, "Origin of the Shape of Lord Jagannātha Had Originated from Yogīmaṭh Rock Art of Nuapāḍā District, *Souvenir*, Swarnakshetra, Sunabeda, Sri Sri Jagannatha Seva Samiti, Sunabeda, 2006, pp. 10-11 (English Section).

[24] Sasanka Sekhar Panda, "Antiquities of Lord Jagannātha: An Amazing Finding", *The Youth World*, issue no. 27, January 2005, Arabinda Das (ed.), Bolangir, pp. 12-17; S.S. Panda, "Antiquities of Śrī Jagannātha: Amazing Finding", *Reference Orissa:* Century edition, A.N. Tiwari (ed.), Bhubaneswar: Enterprising Publishers, 3rd edn., 2005, pp. 72-77.

[25] Alice Boner, "Introduction", *Śilpa Prakāśa*, rev. 2nd edn., Bettina Bäumer, R.P. Das and S. Das (eds.), Delhi: Motilal Banarsidass, 2005, p. 7.

Lord Jagannātha as another form of Dakṣiṇa Kālikā, as he is invoked by the author of our text, goes back to the time of Śaṅkarācārya. It is said that when Śaṅkarācārya came to Purī, he found the temple broken and the sacred core of the image removed to Sonepur near Jajpur. He is said to have dug it out underneath a tree, where it was buried, to have brought it back to Purī, to have erected a shrine and to have established the tāntric worship of the divinity under the name of Dakṣiṇa Kālikā. According to the *Saudarśinī Vāmadeva Saṁhitā*, which might have been written by Padmapādācārya, a disciple of Śaṅkarācārya, Lord Jagannātha is the very self of Kālikā.

> *tarayantra pralambāgno subhadrā bhuvaneśvarī śyāmayantra mādhava ce dakṣiṇa kālikā svayam.*

In the *Mahānirvāṇa Tantra*, Jagannātha has been identified with Dakṣiṇa Kālikā and the *śloka* goes thus:

> *tara sākṣyāt śūlapāṇi*
> *subhadrā bhuvaneśvarī*
> *niladrou tu jagannātha*
> *sākṣyāt dakṣiṇa kālikā*

About the iconography of Dakṣiṇa Kālī, N.N. Bhattacharya[26] says:

> Of all these forms Dakṣiṇa Kālī or Śyāma is the most important. In her *dhyāna*, quoted in the *Tantra-Sāra*, she is described as having a terrible appearance, a fierce face, four hands, untied hair and a garland of several heads around her neck. In her lower and upper left hands she holds a freshly severed head and a sword, and in the lower and upper right hands she exhibits *abhaya* and *varada* poses. Naked, dark as dense cloud in complexion, her body is streamed with blood which oozes from the garland of severed heads that she wears. Two corpses serve as her ear-rings. Terrible in face and teeth, she has well developed breasts, her girdle is made of hands cut-off from the bodies of corpses. Her face is smiling but it is stained with blood falling from both corners of her mouth. She screams terribly. She lives at the cremation ground. She has three eyes resembling the orb of the rising sun. Her untied hair hang to the right. She stands on the chest of Śiva lying as a corpse. She is engaged in *vīparītarati* (inverted sexual intercourse, also called *puruṣayoto* with Mahākāla Śiva).

---

[26] N.N. Bhattacharya, *History of the Tāntric Religion*, New Delhi: Manohar, 1987, p. 340.

Monolithic Dakṣiṇa Kālī is found within the Ḍuṅguripali village of Nuāpāḍā district. There is a temple of Dakṣiṇa Kālikā at Purī also, where the *śloka* of *Mahānirvāṇa Tantra,* as quoted above, is chiselled on a marble slab. It means that the shape of Lord Jagannātha had originated from Yogīmaṭh rock art of Nuāpāḍā district and as such stone sockets, circular in shape, and components which fit into the sockets are very well found. As mentioned, they resemble the union of male and female principles, which are in true confirmation with the iconography of the Dakṣiṇa Kālī.

These archaeological findings also prove that the origin of the shape of Jagannātha deity, its trinity and Dakṣiṇa Kālī aspects had developed in the Central Mahānadī Valley.

This standing of the author is seconded by a rare finding in Sonepur district — a stone image of Jagannātha with square hands, measuring 3" each in length. The height of the image is 1' and width is 5". On the forehead a small half moon shape is chiselled.

The discovery of the stone image of Lord Jagannātha with square hands indicates the formative period. H.V. Stietencron[27] refers to *Mādalā Pāñjī*[28] and states:

> According to the chronicle, the images installed in the temple by king Yayāti were made of wood. The account states that 144 years before Yayāti, a conqueror named Raktabāhu invaded Purī. The priests, however, succeeded in carrying away in time . . . the God (who was entitled Parameśvara) and in burying him near Sonepur. For 144 years the God remained hidden and almost forgotten until Yayāti gave order to trace the place where the highest Lord had been buried. Nobody knew the exact spot but finally a sacred tree was pointed out, underneath which the God was supposed to lie. This tree was felled and people dug under its roots. The God was found. His images, however, were disfigured due to the long period they remained underground. Thereupon new images were made from the wood of the tree and installed in Purī.

This pass over information from generation to generation proves that the

---

27 H.V. Stietencron, "Early Temple of Jagannātha in Orissa: The Formative Phase", *The Cult of Jagannāth and the Regional Tradition of Orissa*, A. Eschmann, H. Kulke and G.C. Tripathi (eds.), New Delhi: Manohar, 1978, pp. 64-65.

28 Ibid.; *Mādalā Pāñjī* (Prachi edn.), A.B. Mohanty (ed.), Cuttack: Prachi Samiti, 1940, Bhubaneswar: Utkal University, 1969, pp. 4-5.

formation of Lord Jagannātha's shape took place originally in the Central Mahānadī Valley, the western Orissa. Trikūṭa hill near Koṭsamalai village of Sonepur district also had its own part to play in the development of the Puruṣottama Jagannātha cult.

8

Impact of Narasiṁha Cult on Orissan Culture

ACCORDING to H.V. Stietencron,[1] Vaiṣṇavism was the latest major Indian religion to reach central Orissa, the area where today Jagannātha dominates the religious scene. Nowhere in the whole region of Orissa and Kaliṅga was Vaiṣṇavism traceable prior to the Gupta period. It advanced towards Orissa from the south and from the west. But, its progress was slow and came to a stop outside the borders of Orissa in the post-Gupta period, when Śaivism and Śāktism rose to a prominent position. The absence of early traces of Vaiṣṇavism is all the more remarkable as the Vaiṣṇavas had crossed the Vindhya range and settled in the western Dekkanas as early as the first century BCE. They reached the Kṛṣṇā Valley in south-western Andhra Pradesh by the end of the second century CE. But, they do not seem to have been able to advance along the east coast. Of course, an argument *e silentio* cannot be conclusive. But, in view of the extraordinary wealth of archaeological remains in Kaliṅga and Orissa, the absence of early Vaiṣṇava remains is striking. It should be carefully registered before drawing conclusions which are based on other sources.

This view of Stietencron cann't be accepted by the author, because of two reasons: First, Indo-Aryans had spiritually and culturally taught and civilized the entire earth,[2] as dealt in Chapter 4 of this book. The distortion of ancient Indian history and culture had been done, because the English regime tried to destroy the culture and the religion of India by all means and, during that time, they deliberately produced such derogatory literatures in huge quantities that confused and misguided the whole world. The English people started demeaning the history

---

[1] H.V. Stietencron, "The Advent of Viṣṇuism in Orissa: An Outline of Its History According to Archaeological and Epigraphic Sources from the Gupta Period", *TCOJATRTTOO*, 1978, p. 5.

[2] V.K. Verma, *Missing Link of World Civilization, Indo-Aryan Colonization*, Delhi: Pratibha Prakashan, 2004, *passim*.

and the religion of India, misguiding the whole world and destroying and fabricating the historic records. These people could do anything and everything to prove their point. Therefore, the whole history and chronological dating of ancient history is perverted, mis-represented, twisted, put out of shape, turned aside from the true meaning and deformed.[3] Principal findings of recent research are that the English administrators had done, Politics of History, Spiritual Civilizations and Political Studies.[4]

The academics of India and the world follow the belittled political chronological chart, as bequeathed by the History and Archaeology Departments of British India. Therefore, Independent India is not yet free from its British yoke and is following the same British India's education policy, which is usually regarded as Macaulay policy.[5] Because of this reason, the author is following the chronology of history of Bhāratavarṣa as given in Appendix I.

In the Upper Mahānadī Valley, there is the site of Sabarinarayan *alias* Seorinarayan, situated at the confluence of the Mahānadī, Seonath and Jonk Rivers. At this site, Sabari had offered berries to Lord Rāma. It is the earliest site of Vaiṣṇava worship. The *Bilaspur District Gazetteer*[6] also records the legend of Sabarinarayan as follows:

> There is a story that once the place was a forest inhabited by an old Sawara or Saoner, who worshipped Jagannātha. The deity was afterwards removed to the temple of Jagannātha at Purī by a brāhmaṇa. But as a reward for the faithfulness of the old Sawara, Jagannātha wished that the name of the place of his concealment should contain the names of both the worshipper and the worshipped. Hence, the place came to be called Sawara-Narayan or Seorinarayan. Close to Mahānadī, there is a small tank, known as Rohiṇī-Kuṇḍa in which the bones of the dead are immersed.

Two, According to "The True History and Religion of India",[7] the period of Jagadguru Śaṅkarācārya was between 509–477 BCE. As dealt in Chapters 5 and 7, Ādi Śaṅkarācārya initiated the worship of Lord Viṣṇu Jagannātha. So, it is reasonable to believe that Viṣṇu worship originated in Orissa from the time of Ādi

[3] *TTHATROI*, 2001, pp. 31-32.

[4] Navaratna Rajaram, *The Politics of History*, New Delhi: Voice of India, 1995, *passim*.

[5] *THACOTIP*, vol. X, part II, 1991, pp. 42-88.

[6] *OOJD*, 2003, p. 37; *Madhya Pradesh District Gazetteers, Bilaspur*, Bhopal, 1978, pp. 524-25.

[7] *TTHATROI*, 2001, p. 502.

Śaṅkarācārya. Satchidananda Mishra,[8] while dealing on "Installation of Puruṣottama Jagannātha", claims that doubtlessly, Jagannātha temple affairs were managed by the heads of Govardhana Maṭha upto the middle of the eighteenth century CE when Orissa came under the Marāṭhā rule and gives seven arguments or explanations.

The author is interested to deal with arguments five and six of Satchidananda Mishra:

> Argument 5. Some books called "Karmāṅgīs", which describe the functions of temple servants, have recently come to light. Written probably in the eighteenth-century, "Karmāṅgīs" state regarding the functions of *ācārya*s of Govardhana Maṭha as follows: "Gurus are of three types. First, the *saṁnyāsī*s of Śaṅkarācārya's order. As head of the Govardhana Maṭha, he is also Śaṅkarācārya. He is the foremost Preceptor. He is to receive a pot of *mahāprasāda* and a plate of *khicaṛī* after offering is made to Goddess Vimalā. He has the right to sit within the sanctum of the temple. He is authorized to himself render any service to the deity. The priests of the temple enter service only when he permits them after examination. The priests are to daily serve his personal Narasiṁha. He is the original preceptor.
>
> Argument 6. The statement of "Karmāṅgīs" that the deity rituals of the Narasiṁha idol of Govardhana Maṭha was to be performed by the temple priests is also significant. Narasiṁha worship has close links with the worship of Jagannātha. The Narasiṁha temple adjoining *mukti maṇḍapa* is older than the present temple of Jagannātha. Scores of inscriptions of the time of Choḍagaṅgadeva, the builder of the temple of Jagannātha, on the walls of Narasiṁha temple indicate the prominence of Narasiṁha. That was the reason why in the gloss on *Bhāgavata Purāṇa,* written by Śrīdharasvāmī, a *saṁnyāsī* of Śaṅkarācārya's order, obedience is made first to Narasiṁha. The *māhātmya* books of Purī narrate how Narasiṁha was first installed and worshipped before Jagannātha was installed. These are pointers indicating close links of Govardhana Maṭha with the worship of Jagannātha.

Because of Ādi Śaṅkarācārya installing Puruṣottama Jagannātha deity as Vaiṣṇava deity, there are many links of Narasiṁha worship, related to the worship of Puruṣottama Jagannātha deity. This is the yogic and spiritual interpretation from intuitive aspect of knowledge. From educative vision of knowledge, Thomas Eugene Donaldson deals:

[8] Satchidananda Mishra, "Installation of Puruṣottama Jagannāth", *SITCOJ*, 1991, pp. 137-40.

In the *praśasti* sections of inscriptions, dealing with the genealogical background of a ruling family, kings are often favourably compared with various deities in respect to personal appearance, character, virtuous behaviour, wealth and munificence, administrative ability, battlefield prowess, etc. The Somavaṁśī kings (eleventh-twelfth centuries) of Orissa, for example, being primarily Śaivites, often compared themselves with Kāma, the God of Love, not only in respect to his handsome form and sexual prowess, considering themselves to be Kāma incarnate, but equally in respect to his valour and warrior aspects, championing him as the unequalled warrior, the conqueror of the otherwise invincible Śiva. In the ensuing Gaṅga period (thirteenth-fifteenth centuries), with the growing popularity of Vaiṣṇavism and the eventual adoption of Puruṣottama/Jagannātha as the state deity, it became particularly popular for the kings to be compared with Narasiṁha, the Lion *avatāra* of Viṣṇu. In the Cālleśvara Śiva temple inscription from the region of Anaṅgabhīmadeva III (CE 1211-38) for example, King Choḍagaṅga, the first of the Imperial Gaṅga rulers, is eulogized as follows:

> In the line of these sovereigns of renown, the radiant halo of the person of Narahari incarnated itself as King Choḍagaṅga, whose sword used to give deliverance to the hostile kings, when they turned, so to say, *saṁnyāsins* on the bank of the sacred river, which flowed from the oozings of the elephants in fury of war.

Narasiṁha is the furious of *ugra* aspect of Viṣṇu *par excellence*, as noted by Anncharlott Eschmann, yet he is one of the most complex of his incarnations, being equally associated with tribal worship and with Śaivism, and represented in aniconic (pillar), theriomorphic (animal) or anthropomorphic (human body with lion head) form. In tribal cultures of Orissa both his ferocious character and his association with wooden posts stressed with some traditions even suggesting that his strength to tear up Hiraṇyakaśipu was derived from Śakti residing within the post from which he sprung. Under the influence of Tantra and Śākta ideas, the concept of Narasiṁha as an incarnation of Viṣṇu became elevated to an independent deity with a furious character, in the manner of Bhairava, who not only destroys all the evils befalling his worshippers but in addition bestows upon them the benefits of virtue, wealth, love and salvation as mentioned in the *Brahma Purāṇa* (55.1.77). He plays a major role in the Hinduization of tribal deities and eventually becomes identified with the deity Puruṣottama and the cult of Jagannātha. The image of Narasiṁha was the original image in the Puruṣottama temple at Purī and

> he is still the guardian deity of the temple. All the performances beginning from cooking to *pūjā* are preceded by making offerings to him. In the *navakalevara* ritual, when the wooden figures of the Jagannātha trinity are renewed, they are addressed and treated as if they were Narasiṁha figures and all of the *mantras* used pertain to Narasiṁha. An image of Lakṣmī-Narasiṁha on the first pillar of the *jagamohana* when entering from the south is the *iṣṭa devatā* of the brāhmaṇa priests, suggesting the prior sanctity of Narasiṁha in the temple complex. His great popularity is evident by the fact that there are 105 Narasiṁha temples with land endowments in Orissa, in addition to many non-endowed temples of popular cults scattered throughout the countryside.

Donaldson[9] further details about the origin of various Lakṣmī–Narasiṁha images as: Sunakhala dated fourteenth century, Nuāpatna dated late thirteenth and early fourteenth century, Chadhaivar dated fourteenth-fifteenth century, images inside Varāha temple at Jājpur dated fourteenth-fifteenth century, Nārāyaṇa-Viṣṇu in *vajraparyaṅka* holding Śrī and Bhū dated fourteenth century and Hari-Hara seated in *vajraparyaṅka* with consorts Pārvatī on the right and Lakṣmī on the left, dated 15th century CE.

These Lakṣmī–Narasiṁha images owe their origin to *Śivalāṭa-mudrā*, which is a *haṭha-yoga* practice. Author[10] had earlier explained that the interaction between man and woman, Tantra wise, has three purposes — pleasure, procreation and *samādhi*. Before practising any of these purposes, the couple should sit down in *Śivalāṭa-mudrā*. Robert E. Svoboda[11] and his tāntric *guru* Vimalānanda, described it:

> When a man and a woman come together for *Śivalāṭa-mudrā*, the woman must sit on the man's left thigh and hold his penis with her right hand. He must cup her left breast with his left hand. Like a creeper she drapes herself around him, clinging tightly like a delicate vine, and he permits himself to be clung to, offering her support.
>
> There are three types of *Śivalāṭa-mudrā*: mundane, spiritual and one which is beyond both the mundane and the spiritual. The mundane gives

[9] T.E. Donaldson, "Iconography of the Lion Avatāra Narasiṁha and his Association with Kingship and Jagannātha in Orissan Sculptures", *Reference Orissa (An Indian State of Eastern Region)*, A.N. Tiwari (ed.), Bhubaneswar: Enterprising Publishers, 1999, pp. 123-44.

[10] J.P. Singh Deo, *Tāntric Art of Orissa*, Delhi: Kalpaz Publishers, 2001, p. 31.

[11] Robert E. Svoboda, *Aghora (at the Left Hand of God)*, New Delhi: Rupa and Co., 1993, pp. 271-72.

maximum sexual excitement; the spiritual is for *sādhanā*; and "beyond" is too advanced to be dealt with here. In all types the female counts *japa* with her left hand, the male with his right. The *mantra*s are specific for each type. He forgets who he is, and she forgets who she is. He thinks, "I am Lord Śiva in the form of Bhairava. (the Fearful Lord), and this is my Śakti, my Bhairavī." She thinks, "This is my Lord Śiva, and I am His Grand Consort, His Bhairavī (the fearful Goddess)."

If the couple is doing it for mundane purpose, they must concentrate on exciting each other. Without realizing it she will begin to breathe through her left nostril and will direct that Śakti to him. His right nostril will be working and that Śakti of his will be directed to her. Hypersecretion of all the glands will result, and at the moment of greatest excitation cessation of breathing occurs for a moment. Then the male mounts and discharges his semen convulsively. Because of hypersecretion he will now eject three teaspoonsful of semen as opposed to his normal one teaspoonful. Because the vagina and cervix have become utterly loose and dilated, the sperm will go directly to the mouth of the cervix. The result is a child, if this is done at the right time of the month. This is the *brahmacarya* appropriate to the ordinary householder because by such sex, satiation occurs for a month or more and *ojas* is not wasted by frequent orgasms.

The spiritual *Śivalāṭa-mudrā* is quite different. The Śiva must control his Śakti very carefully to ensure that she does not become sexually excited. The couple should be able to sit together for at least three hours without the least excitation, no twitching or oozing. The girl must understand that she will not get an ordinary orgasm this way. If she waits patiently she will eventually get a super orgasm which will make her forget sex for ever. If this *mudrā* is done properly she will go into *bhāva samādhi*: Her emotions will crescendo until her mind becomes totally one-pointed, directed towards Śiva, and she will partly forget her worldly existence for a while. Even *mahābhāva samādhi*, which I call emotional highlights, is possible — total immersion in Śiva but with retained awareness of the Bliss Wonderful.

The *lāṭa mudrā* had become very popular throughout the country during the medieval period. Therefore, lots of Umā-Maheśvara (Plate 5) images are found and K.S. Behera[12] mentions that beautiful images of Lakṣmī-Nārāyaṇa hail from

[12] K.S. Behera, "Traditions in Sculpture", *Art Traditions of Orissa*, Bhubaneswar: Orissa Sahitya Academy, 1983, p. 45.

Plate 5: "Umā-Maheśvara", flat-type sculptural art, prevalent in South Kosala region. Findspot: Amgura village, Dist. Nuāpāḍā, Orissa. It is kept as household deity and worshipped by Sanlal Herna of Amgura village. Early medieval period.

Liṅgarāja compound, Pratāpanagarī and Caurāsī. The magnificent image from Caurāsī shows the two deities together with their usual Vaiṣṇava emblems. Lakṣmī-Narasiṁha images occur at Konduli, Cuttack, Bhubaneswar (Liṅgarāja complex), Purī and other places. There was one Lakṣmī-Nārāyaṇa temple at Hariharpur, which was devastated by the Marāṭhās. The Marāṭhās took the fine image of Lakṣmī-Nārāyaṇa and left it at Remuna. Rani Sumitra Devi granted some land for building a temple and for the worship of the deity at Remuna.[13]

As *yoga* of sexual transformation had become very popular during medieval period, images of all cults developed the *lāṭa-mudrā*. Gaṇeśa with his consort is found at the Central Museum of Gwalior.[14]

From the daily ritual of Govardhana Maṭha, Narasiṁha worship has close links with the worship of Lord Jagannātha. The historical narration of Narasiṁha is

[13] P.K. Mishra, *Archaeology of Mayurbhanj*, New Delhi: D.K. Printworld, 1997, pp. 23-24.

[14] Shivakant Dwivedi, *Temple Sculptures of India*, Delhi: Agam Kala Prakashan, 1991, p. 99 and Plate 22.

found in the inscription of the Lakṣmaṇeśvara temple at Śrīpur (modern Sirpur) of Chhattisgarh. Hemant Kumar Panja[15] rightly mentions that the Somavaṁśī rulers were destined to play a significant role in upholding the cause of Vaiṣṇavism first and Śaivism next, and ultimately there was a fusion of Vaiṣṇavism and Śaivism under their patronage.

> Tīvaradeva, the Lord of the entire South Kosala, was the first great king of the Pāṇḍuvaṁśa who is known to have patronised the cause of Vaiṣṇavism. The seals of Tīvaradeva contain figures of Garuḍa, *cakra*, *Śaṅkha* and a flower device which are all Vaiṣṇavite emblems. In his Bonda plates, Rājim plates and Baloda plates, he calls himself Parama Vaiṣṇava. We learn from the Adhabhara copper-plate grant that Tīvaradeva and his son Mahā-Naññarāja, who declared himself Parama Vaiṣṇava, are known to have received the blessing of Bhagavāna-Nārāyaṇa Bhaṭṭāraka whom they had worshipped in many previous births. Under Tīvaradeva, Naññarāja, Candragupta and his son Harṣagupta, Vaiṣṇavism continued to receive royal patronage. In the Sirpur stone inscription of the time of Bālārjuna, Candragupta has been compared with Balarāma and Kṛṣṇa. In the same record it is mentioned that his son Harṣagupta, went after his death to the eternal abode of Lord Hari, where he lived in daily worship of Lord Acyuta or Viṣṇu. On the death of Harṣagupta, his widow queen Vasatā ruled for some time on behalf of her minor son Bālārjuna. His reign is important in the history of Vaiṣṇavism in South Kosala. For the first time in Orissan epigraphs the Sirpur stone inscription of Vasatā opens with invocations to Puruṣottama Viṣṇu (*oṁ namaḥ puruṣottamāya*). The first three invocatory verses of the said incription glorify Viṣṇu in his Narasiṁha incarnation. The widow queen herself is compared with the *Sata* (locks) of Narasiṁha. The same inscription further refers to Viṣṇu by various names such as Puruṣottama, Narasiṁha, Hari, Kṛṣna and Acyuta. The doorjambs of the Lakṣmī temple, where the inscription of Vasatā is found, contain figures of the *daśāvatāra*.
>
> Queen-mother Vasatā is known to have built some Vaiṣṇava temples in South Kosala during her regency. The Sirpur stone inscription itself refers to the construction of a temple resembling the abode of Vaikuṇṭha and dedicated to Lord Hari. She built the famous brick temple of Hari, now called Lakṣmī (Lakṣmaṇeśvara) temple at Sirpur in memory of her late husband.

[15] H.K. Panja, "Vaiṣṇavism in Orissa", *Religious History of Orissa*, N.R. Patnaik (ed.), Delhi: Indian Publishers' Distributors, 2004, pp. 131-32.

The author feels that the opinion of Prabodh Kumar Mishra[16] needs critical study. To quote him:

> Furthermore, it is interesting to note that the Narasiṁha incarnation of Viṣṇu has close links with the Jagannātha cult. Narasiṁha finds a place of eminence in the daily rituals beginning with the early morning *pūjā*. In this connection the story of Prahlād and Hiraṇyakaśipu appears quite relevant; Narasiṁha is known to have emanated from a wooden pillar and killed the demon. Similarly, Jagannātha, who is often represented as Narasiṁha and worshipped as such, is essentially a wooden deity. During *navakalevara*, *anavasara* and initiation of the temple priests, *mantra*s and ritual practices centre on Narasiṁha. In the epigraphs referring to Puruṣottama we often come across the mention of Narasiṁha as well. Puruṣottama and Narasiṁha are construed as identical.[17] This close link has led scholars to believe that the present Jagannātha figure evolved from the tribal deity made of wood through the process of Hinduization.[18] A close observation of the square head with round eyes of the image would bear testimony to the above hypothesis because there is a striking resemblance to the head of a lion with round eyes betraying the furious countenance of Narasiṁha. The account contained in Puruṣottama Māhātmya of the *Skanda Purāṇa* may be cited as corroborative evidence for the above theory. In this text, Brahmā called upon Indradyumna to worship Jagannātha with Narasiṁha *mantra* and explained its significance. Indradyumna saw the vision of *Yogī* Narasiṁha seated on a lotus with Lakṣmī on his lap and Balabhadra or *Śeṣa*, the serpent, holding his hoods over their heads like an umbrella. Such an amazing sight of Lord Puruṣottama gave Jagannātha triad. On the basis of the testimony of *Puruṣottama Māhātmya* and the prevailing practice of worshipping, the new image at the time of *navakalevara* with Narasiṁha *mantra*, it may be suggested that the present Jagannātha image evolved from the concept of Narasiṁha.[19]

Considering the Śaivite aspect of Jagannātha cult, another theory suggests that the triad evolved from the image of Ekapāda Bhairava, the *ugra*

---

16 P.K. Mishra, "Jagannātha Cult in Orissa", *Religious History of Orissa*, N.R. Patnaik (ed.), Delhi: Indian Publishers' Distributors, 2004, pp. 158-60.

17 Ibid.; K.C. Mishra, *The Cult of Jagannāth*, Calcutta: Firma K.L. Mukhopadhyay, 1971, p. 153.

18 Ibid.; *TCOJATRTOO*, pp. 196-97 and 116-17.

19 P.K. Mishra, "Jagannātha Cult in Orissa", *Religious History of Orissa*, N.R. Patnaik, (ed.), Delhi: Indian Publishers' Distributors, 2004, pp. 158-60; *TCOJATRTOO*, 1978, p. 104.

manifestation of Śiva. In fact, the close resemblance between the image of Ekapāda Bhairava and early image of Jagannātha as we see in the sculptures of Koṇārka prove this point convincingly. That Narasiṁha is also associated with Bhairava gives further credence to this theory.[20]

The view that the present Jagannātha image evolved from the concept of Narasiṁha cannot be accepted because with the latest findings (discussed in Chapters 5, 6 and 7) in the shape of Lord Jagannātha owes its origin to the union of *puruṣa* and *prakṛti*. Therefore, Lord Jagannātha is Dakṣiṇa Kālikā as mentioned in *Saudarśinī Vāmdeva Saṁhitā*, assigned to Padmapādācārya, *Mahānirvāṇa Tantra* and *Śilpa Prakāśa*, composed by Ramachandra Mahapatra Kaula Bhaṭṭāraka.[21]

The author of *Śilpa Prakāśa*[22] gives the following identification of himself within "First Prakāśa, śloka 565-69," thus:

> The river Musali, the daughter of the Bhārgavī, flows towards the ocean.
>
> On its shore there is a village, where I was born in a tāntric community, in a family of Udgātas, at present in Dhaumi Maṇḍala.
>
> All my forefathers were serving the kings. My father's name is Kuleśvara, and that of my mother is Sajñāmayī.
>
> I am Rāmacandra, among the best of brāhmaṇas devoted to Kulācāra. On the blue mountain (Nīlaśikhara), is the form of Dakṣiṇa Kālikā.
>
> My *iṣṭa mūrti* is Jagannātha, the giver of all perfections. By his grace alone the first part of this book, the description of the divine *mukhaśālā*, has been completed.

While giving historical note on the dating of *Śilpa Prakāśa* text, Rajendra Prasad Das[23] mentions:

> Vīravarma, the patron of the architect author Rāmacandra, was possibly a later minor ruler of a part of the old Airāvata Maṇḍala, who flourished after the Nandodbhavas whose last known record was dated CE 929. Since Vīravarma was ruling after CE 929 and before CE 1043 he belonged to a period around the middle of the tenth century CE or to the early eleventh century.

---

[20] P.K. Mishra, *OHRJ*, vol. III, p. 11.

[21] B. Bäumer, R.P. Das and S. Das (eds.), *Śilpa Prakāśa* (Medievel Orissan Sanskrit Text on Temple Architecture), Delhi: Motilal Banarsidass, 2nd rev. edn., 2005, *passim*.

[22] Ibid., p. 191.

[23] Ibid.; Vide Historical Note on the Dating of the Text by Rajendra Prashad Das.

As the author of this text mentions that he worshipped Jagannātha under the name of Dakṣiṇa Kālikā, it is sure that he knew that originally the shape of Lord Jagannātha represented the union of *puruṣa* and *prakṛti*. In due course of the development of the Jagannātha cult, it had embraced and included all cults and religions into its fold.

M.M. Mohapatra[24] has written about the Narasiṁha worship in Orissa:

oṁ ugravīram mahāvīram
jvalantam sarvato mukham
nṛsiṁham viṣṇam bhadram
mṛtyoḥ mūrtim namāmyaham.

Thus runs the invocatory verse in praise of Lord Narasiṁha, the most terrific form among all the incarnations of Lord Viṣṇu.

Although no dependable proof has so far been available with regard to the origin of Narasiṁha worship in Orissa, yet we get a glimpse of the worship of this popular deity from very ancient times from legendary and Dharmaśāstra sources, such as the *Paṇḍita Sarvasva, Gadādhara Paddhati, Haribhakti Vilāsa,* etc.

In *Atharvaveda*, there has been a mention that the Pippalāda section of brāhmaṇas, who were found only in ancient Orissa, were the worshippers of Lord Narasiṁha. In the Utkala Khaṇḍa of *Skanda Purāṇa* we come across a reference that King Indradyumna of Malava had performed a *yajña* near Śrī Gundhica Mandira worshipping Lord Yajña Narasiṁha before he saw Lord Jagannātha in that form.

In the Uttareśvara temple of Bhubaneswar, we come across two images of Narasiṁha, one on the outside wall and the other on the inside wall. From the iconographic features the outside image seems to be older than the inside one, probably dating to the sixth or seventh century CE and seventh or eighth century CE respectively. According to a tradition, many tāntricists who come here for tāntric worship become unsuccessful because of the influence of Lord Narasiṁha. The exhibition of the ferocious images of Lord Narasiṁha in the Gaurī temple and Vaitāl temple of Bhubaneswar points to the fact that there prevailed simultaneously the worship of Narasiṁha along with Tantra worship.

---

[24] M.M. Mohapatra, "Narasiṁha Worship in Orissa", *Glimpses of Orissan Culture*, Nihar Ranjan Patnaik (ed.), Cuttack: Kitab Mahal, 2004, pp. 376-79.

In the Mausima temple, Lord Narasiṁha along with Lordless Lakṣmī is worshipped outside the temple wall. In the premises of Liṅgarāja temple, there is a separate temple meant for Lakṣmī and Narasiṁha. The Narasiṁhanātha temple inscription of Vaijal Dev dated 17 March 1413 mentions the construction of a temple at Gandhamardana mountain dedicated to the worship of Lord Bidal Narasiṁha (Narasiṁha in the wild-cat form) there. One hundred cows and the revenue of the village Loasingi had been donated by the king for the worship of the deity.

As seven of the 27 kings ruling before Choḍagaṅgadeva bear the name Narasiṁha, it seems that they might be the devotees of Lord Narasiṁha. Anaṅgadeva II had donated revenue of a few acres of land for the worship of Bali Narasiṁha as evident from *Mādalā-Pāñjī*.

From Dasagoba copper-plate inscription of Rājarāja III of CE 1198, it is presumed that Lakṣmī-Narasiṁha were perhaps the tutelary deities of Gaṅga dynasty. There exists a Narasiṁha temple at Kenduli, the birthplace of Jayadeva who used to recite *Gīta-Govinda* before the deity every night. The existence of a large number of Narasiṁha images inside the Jagannātha temple of Śrī-Kṣetra facing different directions including that of Ādi Narasiṁha situated in the western side of *mukti maṇḍapa* points to the fact that perhaps Lord Jagannātha was worshipped earlier in the form of Lord Narasiṁha.

Lord Jagannātha is attired as Lord Narasiṁha on several festive occasions. During *Ratha-Yātrā*, an image of Lord Narasiṁha is first taken in procession to be placed on the "Tāla-dhvaja" *ratha* of "Baladeva" and then only Lord Jagannātha's Pahandi procession starts.

The image of Narasiṁha was the original image in the Puruṣottama temple at Purī and he is still the guardian deity of the temple. All of the performances, beginning from cooking to *pūjā*, are preceded by making offerings to him. In the *navakalevara* ritual, when the wooden figures of the Jagannātha trinity are renewed, they are addressed and treated as if they were Narasiṁha figures and all of the *mantra*s used pertain to Narasiṁha. An image of Lakṣmī-Narasiṁha on the first pillar of the *jagamohana* when entering from the south is the *iṣṭa devatā* of the brāhmaṇa priests, suggesting the prior sanctity of Narasiṁha in the temple complex. His great popularity is evident by the fact that there are 105 Narasiṁha temples of importance with land endowments in Orissa.

> Iconographically, the images of Narasiṁha are generally grouped into three forms, as in the *Viṣṇudharmottara Purāṇa*. They are the (i) *ālīḍha* pose; (ii) *sukhāsana* pose, and (iii) standing pose. We find Narasiṁha images at Turaṅga Tīrthamaṭha and Narasiṁhanātha in their *ālīḍha* pose, at Sunakhala, Nuāpatna, Chadheivara, Jajpur, Gandhamardana and Kenduli in their seating pose; and at Adasapur, Siṁhanātha temple and Viṣṇupur in their standing pose. We learn from various sources of two-armed, four-armed, eight-armed, ten-armed, three-faced and even five-faced Narasiṁha images.
>
> Lord Narasiṁha is the protector of the chariot Nandīghoṣa meant for Lord Jagannātha. In various monasteries of Kundheibenta Sahi, Matiapada Sahi, Bali Sahi and at Siddha Bakula Maṭha, Lord Narasiṁha is worshipped. In the several inscriptions of Kapilendradeva, we come across donations offered for the worship of Lord Narasiṁha in the various temples of Orissa.
>
> There is evidence in *Caitanya Caritāmṛta* that Caitanya had instructed his disciples first to offer prayers to Lord Narasiṁha before beholding Lord Jagannātha. The Gajapati kings of Orissa used to engrave the images of Lakṣmī-Narasiṁha in their royal seals. Bhoi ruler Mukundadeva had constructed a temple for Lakṣmī-Narasiṁha inside the premises of the Barabati Fort. We find special temples for Narasiṁha near Dayā River at Jasuapur, Nuasasan near Pipli and Oḍagāon of Nayagaṛh. In the Virañcinārāyaṇa temple of Buguḍa in the Gañjam district there is a statue of Lord Narasiṁha which is regularly worshipped.
>
> In the precincts of Sukunda Maṭha, a Narasiṁha temple is situated which is famous for its inner decorations. Lord Narasiṁha is worshipped in Erañca, Birabarpatna, Adaspur, Tirtol and Jagannāthapur of Cuttack district. In many places and private houses, *śāligrāma* stones are worshipped as the representatives of Lord Narasiṁha. Pudamari is famous for such kind of *śilā* worship. In the *Bedha-Parikramā*, a literary work of Jagannath Das, Lord Narasiṁha has been depicted as the protector of Śrī-Kṣetra. Similarly, in the *Narasiṁha Purāṇa* and *Narasiṁha Māhātmya*, the importance of this incarnation of Lord Viṣṇu has been described in detail. Almost in every part of Orissa, in the *Bhāgabata Gadis*, Lord Narasiṁha is worshipped in the form of *Bhāgavata Granthas*.

The Narasiṁha incarnation is the most violent form of Lord Viṣṇu (Plate 6). Originally, Purī was a place of Śiva worship. According to the Satchidananda Misra,[25] in some works it is mentioned that Purī was originally a seat of Śiva as

[25] Satchidananda Mishra, "Installation of Puruṣottama Jagannātha", *SITCOJ*, 1991, pp. 133-36.

Plate 6: "Narasiṁha", flat-type sculptural art, prevalent in South Kosala region. Findspot: Tank of Nilji village, Dist. Nuāpāḍā, Orissa. Early medieval period. Preserved at Khariar Branch Museum, now functioning at district headquarter, Nuāpāḍā.

Bhubaneswar was of Viṣṇu. In *Vāmadeva-Saṁhitā* (6.82), Śiva himself reveals this ancient knowledge to his consort.

> Hear, my dear lady, what I tell you has come down from earlier times. In ancient times this place (Purī) was of Śiva as Ekāmra was of Viṣṇu.
>
> The fact that Purī was originally a place of Śiva worship before Puruṣottama Jagannātha was installed therein was preserved for posterity in local legends.

One of the biographers of Ādi Śaṅkarācārya was Chidvilasa Swamy, who in his work *Śaṅkaravijaya* mentioned that Jagannātha has been installed by Śaṅkarācārya.[26] It was Śaṅkarācārya who initiated obedience and worship first to Lord Narasiṁha. Therefore, the Narasiṁha cult has a great impact on Orissan culture.

[26] Satchidananda Mishra, "Installation of Puruṣottama Jagannātha", *SITCOJ*, 1991, p. 131.

9

Syncretic Cultural History of Orissa Province, the Centre of Āgneya-Koṇa

Varāhamihira in his *Bṛhat Saṁhitā*, Kūrma Vibhāga 8, places a number of states of his period in Āgneya-Koṇa. From the grouping of these states, it is observed that present Orissa province is the centre of Āgneya-Koṇa.

Orissa province of India extends from 17° 49' N to 22° 34' N latitude and from 81° 29' E to 87° 29' E longitude on the eastern coast of India. It is bounded by the West Bengal on the north-east, Jharkhand on the north, Chhattisgarh on the west, Andhra Pradesh on the south and the Bay of Bengal on the east. Orissa province was created during British India on 1 April 1936. The Mahānadī River, which starts from Kanker district of Chhattisgarh, flows north and after meeting Seonāth River at Śabarinārāyaṇa site, immediately turns east and flows east to meet Bay of Bengal near Paradeep Port. This river is the major river of the Orissa province, while other streams and rivers flow in different directions.

In the opinion of Bichitrananda Sinha,[1] morphologically, Orissa can be divided into five parts: the coastal plains, the middle mountainous country, the rolling uplands, the river valleys and the subdued plateau.

Physical features, too, like the geographical existence, contributed much to Orissa's historical and cultural growths. The hill-tracts of Orissa were the abode of India's original tribal populations, who in their *silvan* isolation continued to maintain primordial cultural traits of much human significance. The major factor that helped the growth of the Orissan culture was her periodical political strength. Without political stability over a larger part of history and regular patronage from powerful rulers, there could not have been the development of Puruṣottama Jagannātha cult at Purī and there could not have been exuberant artistic and architectural creation over the length and breadth of Orissa through ages for which this land has earned

[1] B. Ṣinha, "Land and People of Orissa", *Sidelights on History and Culture of Orissa*, M.N. Das (ed.), Cuttack: Vidyapuri, 1977, pp. 3-5.

a special recognition. Orissa was the last great Hindu kingdom in India to succumb to foreign Muslim invasions. But, when that misfortune came, her cultural attainment had already reached its permanent shape.[2]

According to H.K. Mahatab:[3]

> Orissa, as it is today, consists of portions of three ancient regions, Kaliṅga, Utkala or Oḍra and Kosala, which in course of centuries under political, social and economic pressure jointed together in the twelfth century CE and developed to form the Oriya society as a distinct entity in the realm of India. Of all the regions, Kaliṅga was the most prominent and advanced in all respects. The original inhabitants of these regions belong to the Sabar tribe which had distinct civilization of its own. Thanks to the discoveries of archaeologists, it is now conclusively proved that pre-Aryan civilization was of a high order and it influenced the Aryan civilization in many ways. There was conflict between the two civilizations in the initial state as is found in *Ṛgveda,* the earliest of the Vedas. But in course of time by mutual give and take, there was mutual accommodation as is found in the later Vedas. Even then the shades of two civilizations remained prominent in various regions in India. The shades of Aryan civilization is distinguishable in north India whereas in the south that of pre-Aryan Draviḍian civilization is distinguishable. But Orissa is a region lying between the north and the south, the synthesis has been so complete that the shades of two civilizations are not distinguishable. Thus Orissa is the epitome of India, as its culture developed in course of centuries as a result of action and reaction of pre-Aryan and Aryan civilizations.

From the above quotation of Mahatab, it seems that he was not free from the imposition of the Aryan race theory which was imposed by British imperialistic historians. Further, the above-mentioned view — "of all the regions, Kaliṅga was the most prominent and advanced in all respects — is challenged by the author.[4]

Life-long explorations and surveys of the author have exposed that the shape of Lord Jagannātha had originated from pre-historic rock art of Yogīmaṭh Ḍoṅger, situated 8 km to the east of Khariar town in Nuāpāḍā district. The rock art was

---

[2] M.N. Das (ed.), *Sidelights on History and Culture of Orissa,* Cuttack: Vidyapuri, 1977, pp. i-iii.

[3] H.K. Mahatab, "Culture of Orissa", *OHRJ*, vol. XXX, nos. 2-4, 1984 (Golden Jubilee Volume), pp. 1-2.

[4] J.P. Singh Deo, *THOMV*, 2004, *passim.*

discovered by the author on 21 December 1970. There are three triple lines, painted in red tint *alias* ochre colour and three semi-circles resembling the Arabic numeral "8".

When iron came into use, the three semi-circles were carved in stones with two component parts, assembling the union of male and female principles. Such shapes of stone sockets were discovered at Mohangiri site of Kālāhāṇḍī district and Kharligaṛh site of Bolaṅgīr district. Now they are exhibited at the Manikyapur Museum of Bhawānīpatna. Two such stone sockets are found in the ruin of the stone fallen temple of Aṣṭabhuja Mahiṣāsuramardinī at Baṛgāon village, situated on the left bank of Udanti River and one half of such socket is found at the water spring of Pātālgaṅgā, near its pool, in Nuāpāḍā district. The stone sockets represent the union of male and female principles of nature. Jaṅghā Deva, representing the male principle and Jaṅghā Devī, representing the female principle, i.e. Śiva-Śakti are also worshipped by tribals at different places of Nuāpāḍā, Kālāhāṇḍī, Bolaṅgīr, Sonepur, Bargaṛh, Sambalpur, Deogaṛh, Jharsaguḍa and Sundargaṛh districts of western Orissa, which originally occupied the South Kosala region of ancient and medieval historical periods and forms the Central Mahānadī River Valley.

Comparative study shows that the shape of the above mentioned sockets in pair was first used to represent Lord Buddha in Sāñcī *stūpa*, Bharhut *stūpa* and Amarāvatī *stūpa*.

The critical study of the author, published in book form named *Origin of Jagannātha Deity*, which has already gone for two publications in 1991 and 2003, proves that Ādi Śaṅkarācārya had visited Purī, defeated the Buddhist scholars and established the socket shape of Lord Buddha into Puruṣottama Jagannātha deity and established Lord Jagannātha deity as the male presiding deity of Govardhana Maṭha, established by him at Purī. Ādi Śaṅkarācārya on his commentary of *Prasthānatrayī*,[5] established that Īśvara or the Puruṣottama stands for Akṣara. Akṣara is the *Para-Brahman*, the Supreme Being "He does not perish when all beings perish."[6] This Jagannātha as the deity of Govardhana Maṭha evolved into Puruṣottama Jagannātha as the presiding deity of Purī, during the rule of Somavaṁśī King Yayāti Keśarī I, in the tenth century CE.

---

[5] Phani Mohanti, *The Concept of Puruṣa and Puruṣottama in the Commentary of Śaṅkara on the Prasthānatrayī*, New Delhi: Gyan Publication, 1986, p. 49.

[6] Ibid., p. 55.

The Trinity conception of Jagannātha cult has also its origin from the Yogīmaṭh rock art. In the outskirts of Tentelkhunti village, situated on the right bank of Tel River, at a distance of about 40 km from the district headquarters at Bolaṅgīr and 5 km from Tusra village, a huge mound of fallen stone temple architecture exists. In 2004, Trilochan Bhoi, a Kondh tribal person,[7] had a dream and single-handedly dug out the temple, fallen stones and the earth mound. Trilochan Bhoi dug out three images of Balabhadra, *Subhadrā* and Jagannātha. Along with these, he got stone carved slabs with the head of Dakṣiṇa Kālī and lying Viṣṇu image in *anantaśayana*. This discovery confirms the theory of the construction of the oldest temple of Jagannātha Trinity by the Somavaṁśī King Yayāti Keśarī I, in the ninth century CE as mentioned in *Mādalā Pāñjī*, the temple chronical of Jagannātha temple at Purī. The images of Balabhadra and Jagannātha were made of stone of about 3' height, each without hands. The head of Dakṣiṇa Kālī made of stone was also discovered from the same mound.

According to the *Saudarśinī Vāmadeva Saṁhitā*, which might have been written by the disciple of Śaṅkarācārya, Padmapādācārya, Lord Jagannātha is the very self of Kālikā:[8]

tārā yantra pralambāgno subhadrā bhuvaneśvarī ।
śyāmayantra mādhava ce dakṣiṇa kālikā svayam ॥

In the *Mahānirvāṇa Tantra*, Jagannātha has been identified with Dakṣiṇa Kālikā and the *śloka* goes thus:

tārā sākṣyāt śūlapāṇi subhadrā bhuvaneśvarī ।
nīladrau tu jagannātha sākṣyāt dakṣiṇa kālikā ॥

About Dakṣiṇa Kālikā, tāntric scholar Prafulla Chandra Bhanja Deva[9] states:

> I now come to the contemplative description of the Goddess Dakṣiṇa Kālikā whose worship is the universal topic of most of the authentic Tantras of the

---

[7] S.S. Panda, "Antiquities of Lord Jagannātha: An Amazing Finding", The Youth World, Issue no. 27, January 2005, Arabinda Das (ed.), Bolangir, pp. 12-17; S.S. Panda, "Antiquities of Lord Jagannātha: An Amazing Finding", Reference Orissa, Century edition, A.N. Tiwari (ed.), Bhubaneswar: Enterprising Publishers, 3rd edn., 2005, pp. 72-77.

[8] B. Bäumer, S. Das and R.P. Das (eds.), *Śilpa Prakāśa* (*Medieval Orissan Sanskrit Text on Temple Architecture*), Delhi: Motilal Banarsidass, 2nd rev. edn., 2005, Introduction by Alice Boner, p. 7.

[9] J.P. Singh Deo (ed.), *A Tāntric Scholar and the British Wrath on Bastar State*, Kolkata: Punthi Pustak, 2007, pp. 124-26.

"Kadi" School. The *dhyāna* reads thus:

karālavaḍanāṅghorāmmuktakeśin caturbhujām ।
kālikādakṣiṇādivyāmmuṇḍamālā-vibhūṣitām ॥
sadyaścchinnaśiraṣkhaḍgam vāmordhvādhaḥkarāmbujām ।
abhayām varadāñcaiva lakṣinerdhāvapāṇikam ॥
mahāmeghprabhāṁ śyāmāntathaiva ca digambarām ।
kaṇṭhavaskata-muṇḍāligaladrudhira-carcitām ॥
karṇavataisatānitaśavayugmabhayānakām ।
ghoradaiṣṭrṅharālasyāmpinonnatapayodharām ॥
śavānāṅkara-saṁghātaiḥ-kr̥takiñcinihasanmukhim ।
sr̥kkadvayagaladrakta-dhāravispplūritānanām ॥
ghorarūpāmmahāraudrim śmaśānālaya-vāsinīm ।
danturāṇḍakṣinavyāpi-mukta-lambakacoccayām ॥
śivābhirghorarāvābhiścaturdikṣusamanvitām ।
mahākālena ca samaṁ viparītaralaturām ॥
sukhaprsannavadanām merānanasarerulām ।
evaṁ ancintayeddevim śmaśānālayavāsinim ॥

The literal and gross translation of this *dhyāna* is as follows:

> Thus should one meditate on the Goddess who makes the cremation ground her abode:
>
> She is fearful countenance and is terrible in majesty, with flowing locks and four arms. Her name is the divine Dakṣiṇa Kālikā or the deity appertaining to the propitious hour of the priestly fee calculated to make the flame of sacrifice Dakṣiṇa or Benign. She is adorned by a garland of heads. Her upper and lower left hands, resembling lotuses, carry the sword and a freshly severed head, while her upper and lower right hands depict the gestures of fearlessness and boon-bestowed respectively. Her hue is like unto a great nimbus cloud being dark-coloured and she is devoid of clothing having the directions for her garments. She is smeared like unguents with the blood dripping from the rows of heads that surround her neck like a garland. She inspires awe because of two dead bodies, dangling from her ear-lobes in the shape of ear-rings. She is displaying awful and cruel teeth and is endowed with large and prominent breasts (proclaiming eternal youth and motherhood) in appearance. Decorated by a girdle of severed

> hands, appertaining to dead-bodies. She smiles (to her devotees). Two streams of blood issue forth from the corners of her mouth. She is of terror-striking form, this mighty destructive energy (of God), who resides in the crematorium, which is her home.
>
> This prominent teethed Goddess had long untied locks spread out to her right. She is situated on the breast (the heart-lotus) of Mahādeva, the Great God, who is in the form of a corpse. Jackals, howling fearfully, surround her on all sides. She is united in the topsy-turvy union with Mahākāla, the all mighty time-spirit. Her face wears the expressions of felicity and satisfaction and is always smiling like a full blown lotus in a lake.

The iconograph of Dakṣiṇa Kālī is given by, N.N. Bhattacharyya explained in chapter 7.[10]

Such a monolithic figure of Dakṣiṇa Kālī *alias* Śyāmā Kālī is found chiselled on rock of Tandel donger, near a stream of Dungaripali village in Nuāpāḍā district, along with a monolithic six-handed Naṭarāja image, having Ūrdhva-liṅga (erected penis).

There is a temple of Dakṣiṇa Kālikā at Purī also, where the *śloka* of Mahānirvāṇa Tantra, as quoted above, is chislled on a marble slab, thereby proving that Dakṣiṇa Kālikā temple at Purī was built during modern period. All these prove that the shape of Lord Jagannātha had originated from the Yogīmaṭh rock art of Nuāpāḍā district. As mentioned earlier, they resemble the union of male and female principles, which are in true conformation with the iconography of Dakṣiṇa Kālī.

So, these archaeological findings prove that the origin of the shape of Jagannātha deity, its Trinity and Dakṣiṇa Kālī aspects had developed in the Central Mahānadī River Valley with its epicentre as Sunabeda plateau and its vicinity in Nuāpāḍā district of the modern Orissa province.

This discovery of the author is seconded by a rare finding in Sonepur district. It was reported in *Sambad*, Oriya daily newspaper dated 12 October 2005, that on 2 October 2005, Ghasiram Sahu, a resident of Pipilikani village within Ulunda Block area of Sonepur district, while digging to plant banana plants, by the side of his house, accidentally came across or dug out a stone Jagannātha image with square hands, measuring 3" each in length. The height of the image is 1' and its width is 5". On the forehead a small half moon shape is chiselled.

---

[10] N.N. Bhattacharyya, *History of the Tāntric Religion*, New Delhi: Manohar, 1987, p. 349.

These findings prove that the shape of Lord Jagannātha at Śrī-Kṣetra Purī had its origin from the rock art of Yogīmaṭh Ḍoṅger in Nuāpāḍā district and had its full development as Trinity in the Central Mahānadī River Valley. In *Jagannātha Caritāmṛta*, a work of post Pañcasakhā period, "Jagannātha" has been described as the Supreme Lord or *Pūrṇa Brahman*, whereas Kṛṣṇa, the son of Nanda, represents only a part of his glory.[11] As studied in the beginning, the union of male and female principles of nature has developed as the image of Jagannātha. Therefore, the shape of the deity, which finally evolved as Puruṣottama Jagannātha, represents *Pūrṇa Brahman alias* the Absolute. This finds its confirmation in the *Bhagavad-Gītā*: [12]

> प्रकृतिं पुरुषं चैव विद्धयानादी उभावपि ।
> विकारांश्च गुणांश्चैव विद्धि प्रकृतिसम्भवान् ॥
>
> *prakṛtim puruṣaṁ caiva vidhyānādi ubhāvapi* ।
> *vikārāṁśaca guṇāṁścaiva viddhi prakṛtisambhavān* ॥
>
> Know that both *puruṣa* and *prakṛti* are beginningless and know also that all modifications and qualities (*guṇa*s) are born of *prakṛti*.

This is a beautiful example of the manner of the great *yogī*s of the Central Mahānadī River Valley, who had given shape to infinite as finite Jagannātha deity, which evolved as Puruṣottama Jagannātha deity, the *Pūrṇa Brahman*.

In course of its development, the cult of Puruṣottama-Jagannātha embraced all divergent religious creeds and schools of philosophy that prevailed in India, at different periods of her long spiritual, yogic and cultural history. In the historic process of adjustments, Puruṣottama Jagannātha has assimilated strange contradictions in a manner that is most amazing in the history of religious thought. Hence, Nilakantha Das[13] stated:

> There is no discarding any in this religion of man and all the Gods and Goddesses attaching and appealing have found a place in the compound

---

[11] Durga Charan Kuanr (state ed.), *Gazetteer of India, Orissa, Purī*, Nilamani Senapati (chief ed.), Cuttack, 1977, p. 807.

Jagannātha Charitāmṛta, Cuttack: Union Printing Works, 1913, chapter XVIII, lines 29-30, p. 169 (Oriya).

[12] Sri Sri Paramahansa Yogananda, *God Talks with Arjuna: the Bhagavad Gītā*, Kolkata: Yogda Satsanga Society of India, 2nd impression, 2002, p. 889.

[13] Nilakantha Das, "The Cult of Jagannātha", *Orissa Review*, vol. XXVI, no. 12, Public Relations Dept., Govt. of Orissa, Bhubaneswar, p. 18.

of the temple. Puruṣottama Jagannātha has welcomed and embraced all, but been overwhelmed by none and has lost himself in none.

According to Niranjan Satapathy:[14]

> Thus the cult of Jagannātha incorporated in itself all faiths and all religions that flourished in Orissa by the end of the Gaṅga rule. The *mantra*[15] which is uttered at the time of the worship of Jagannātha at Purī sums up the findings of this work. It declares that Jagannātha is the same as the Supreme God of the Vaiṣṇavas, Śaivas, Śāktas, Jains and Bauddhas. He admits all interpretations with a broad smile. As a unique symbol of religious synthesis, he sits there majestically in the temple and confers his blessings on all people, irrespective of caste, colour and creed.

Ayodhya Prasad Sah[16] deals about religious eclecticism of Orissa during the period CE 600–1200 thus:

> Though diverse sects existed in Orissa during this period, the religious temper of the period was by no means sectarian. Wide and sympathetic toleration was the general characteristic of our age. There were a few persecutions here and there; in the *Caitanya Bhāgavata*, one of the Somavaṁśī kings is alleged to have killed six hundred and sixteen Buddhists and the colossal *liṅgam* now placed in the Bhāskareśvara temple at Bhubaneswar is said to have been a remnant of an Aśokan pillar as mentioned earlier. But cases of persecution were exceptional and did not represent the spirit of the age. Toleration was displayed by several Orissan rulers, who were followers of different religions.
>
> The Bhauma-Kara queen Tribhuvanamahādevī, though a Parama-Vaiṣṇavī, compared herself with Kātyāyanī, a Śākta deity. Further, she donated a village in Tamāla Khaṇḍa *viṣaya* in the Daṇḍabhukti *maṇḍala* of Uttara Toṣalī

---

[14] N. Satapathy, *Religious Life in Orissa* (*A Study of the Interrelation of Cults*), Kolkata: R.N. Bhattacharya, 2000, pp. 181-82.

[15] Ibid.

yogīnāmhaṁsatattvam hariharanāmitam śrīpatiḥ vaiṣṇavanām ।
śaivanāmbhairavākhyam pasapatiparamam śāktatattve ca śavitam ।
bauddhānām buddha sākṣāt rūpabhayād-iharo jaina siddhāntamūrtiḥ ॥

Quoted in D.C. Bhattacharyya, *Iconology of Composite Images*, New Delhi: Munshiram Manoharlal, 1980, p. 65.

[16] Ayodhya Prasad Sah, *Life in Medieval Orissa Circa CE 600–1200*, Varanasi: Chaukhambha Orientalia, 1976, pp. 203-05.

for perpetual offering of ablution, sandlepaste, etc., to the deity Umā-Maheśvara installed in the Nanneśvara temple constructed by Śasilekhā of the Virāṭa lineage. Śubhākara was a Buddhist king, but we find the figure of bull, the mount of Lord Śiva on his seal. The emblem of conch-shell, which is a representation of Viṣṇu, appears on the seals of the Śaivite Bhauma-Kara kings. The Śulki rulers such as Raṇastambha and Kulastambha were devout worshippers of Śiva, but at the same time they worshipped the goddess Stambheśvarī. The Tuṅga ruler Vinītatuṅga was a devotee of Śiva, but he was a patron of Buddhism also. The Bhañja kings such as Śatrubhañja and Raṇaka Raṇabhañja were Parama-Vaiṣṇavas or devout followers of Vaiṣṇavism, but they did not omit the customary verses in the honour of Śiva in their charters. The Śaiva symbols are also noticed on the seals of their grants. Again, though the Somavaṁśī kings were Śaivites, their seals bear the figure of the Gaja-Lakṣmī and their charters pay homage to various gods such as Āditya, Varuṇa, Viṣṇu, Brahmā, Soma, Hutāśana, etc. The Somavaṁśī King Mahāśivagupta Bālārjuna was a devout worshipper of Śiva, but he patronized Buddhism also. He was a symbol of religious toleration, as is indicated by the Mallar plates. Another Somavaṁśī king Mahāśivagupta Yayāti is said to have restored Jagannātha out of oblivion and constructed a temple for him. Thus we find the spirit of catholicity in the Somavaṁśī kings also.

Similarly, the eastern Gaṅgas were also catholic in their religious tastes. Like other early Gaṅga kings, the Gaṅga king Hastivarman was a great devotee of Śiva (Parama-Māheśvara), but he was tolerant of Vaiṣṇavism, as is evident from his donation to a Viṣṇu temple. The later Vaiṣṇavite Gaṅga kings continued to worship the Śiva God, Gokarṇeśvara and thus did not neglect their older Śaiva faith. The Śaiva temple of Megheśvara was built during their rule. Still more interesting are the instances in which a king openly declared his devotion to more than one religious faith. The illustrious Gaṅga king Anantavarma Choḍagaṅga Deva described himself both Parama-Māheśvara and Parama-Vaiṣṇava.

The sculptures of Orissan temples also display the spirit of toleration. Though the temple of Liṅgarāja is dedicated to Śiva, the choice of ornaments is by no means confined to emblems peculiar to the deity of the place. We find the Vaiṣṇavite symbols like *gadā*, *padma*, *śaṅkha* and *cakra* or mace, lotus, conch-shell and discus associated with the Śaiva cult. The figures of Harihara or

> personification of the two gods Śiva and Viṣṇu in one image in the Vaitāl temple (CE 775) of Bhubaneswar is another illustration of the same spirit. The front entrance of the Śaiva temple of Mukteśvara shows the image of Mahālakṣmī carved on the door sill.
>
> Further, we find members of the same royal family as votaries of different religious cults. From the Haṁseśvara temple incription it is learnt that Mādhavī, the queen of the Bhauma-Kara King Śubhākaradeva I, was a devotee of Śiva, although her husband is known from his own Neulpur plate as well as the records of his successors to have been a Buddhist. The Nanda ruler Devānanda II was a devout worshipper of Śiva, and another ruler named Dhruvānanda of the same dynasty was a Buddhist, as is known from their respective titles like Parama-Māheśvara and Parama-Saugata mentioned in their grants. Again, some Bhañja kings were Vaiṣṇavas and others were Śaivas. Śatrubhañja and Rāṇaka Raṇabhañja were Vaiṣṇavas, whereas Vidyādharabhañja and Neṭṭabhañja were Śaivas.
>
> It seems that there was no cultural difference between different religious sects, and that is why the rulers found it possible to support all sects.

More findings prove that Jagannātha cult assimilated the teachings of Christianity and Islamic religions also, which are basically Vedic in origin.

From the book, *The Unknown Life of Jesus Christ*, first published in 1880 and second reprint in 1981,[17] it is known that the noted Russian traveller Nicholas Notovitch discovered a manuscript, while convalescing in the Himis monastery in Laddakh. He started his journey to Tibet after the end of the Turko-Russian War in 1877-78. Notovitch has mentioned in the above-mentioned book that:

> When Issa had attained the age of thirteen, when an Israelite should take a wife, he left his father's house, went out of Jerusalem, and in company with some merchants, travelled towards Sindh. In the course of his fourteenth year, young Issa journeyed beyond Sindh and settled among the Aryas in the beloved country of God.

The noted archaeologist Prof. Roerich has also corroborated Notovitch in his despatch by observing that Jesus Christ travelled through India, and returned to Jerusalem when he was 29 years of age, and that it is proved by a manuscript,

---

[17] Nicolas Notovitch, *The Unknown Life of Jesus Christ*, Kolkata: Nababharat Publishers, 1981, Introduction, pp. vii-viii.

which he had the privilege to see for himself, in a Buddhist monastery, the Himis of Tibet. In the Epitome of the book, *The Unknown Life of Jesus Christ*, it has been mentioned that St. Luke has observed, "Jesus was about thirty years of age when he began to exercise his ministry". Here, again, Notovitch comes to our aid by observing, "Here the Evangelists again lost the thread of the terrestrial life of Jesus". St. Luke says: "He was in desert till the day of his showing into Israel", which conclusively proves that no one knew where the young man had gone to, to so suddenly reappear sixteen years later.

Swami Abhedananda was a direct disciple of Ramakrishna Paramahansa and a *guru-bhāī* of Swami Vivekananada. Swami Abhedananda, an apostle of Sri Ramakrishna, also saw the same manuscript on the life of Jesus in the Himis monastery, when he went to Kashmir and Tibet in 1922, after his return from the West, and has mentioned this fact in his Bengali book, *Kashmere-o-Tibbate*, giving a Beṅgālī translation of the portions which contain the *Unknown Life of Jesus* in India.

From the discovery of manuscript in the Himis monastery in Laddakh, by noted Russian traveller Notovitch and from the book of Swami Abhedananda it is known that Jesus Christ had visited Purī, where he was taught to read and understand the Vedas, to cure physical ills by means of prayers, to teach and to expound the sacred scriptures, to drive out evil desires from man and make him again in the likeness of God. It seems, the site of modern Purī had already become popular as a religious centre with its *vedī* (altar) during that period. The *vedī* at Purī finds first expression in the Vana-Parva of the *Mahābhārata*.

Muslim saints of later period — Salabega[18] and Ujeer Beg[19] — of Aul-Kanika areas in Orissa, have sung the spiritual glories of Puruṣottama Jagannātha. These prove that there has been syncretism, reconciliation and attempt to reconcile different systems of belief in the Orissa province.

There are ample scopes to study different aspects of the syncretic cultural history of Orissa province, whose main river is the great river Mahānadī, the centre of Āgneya-Koṇa. This study is an introduction to show the religious toleration in Orissa province and the uniqueness of Puruṣottama Jagannātha cult, which has

---

[18] Nilamani Mishra and Laxman Panda, *Salabega*, Cuttack: Rashtrabhasha Samavaya Prakashan, 1985, *passim*.

[19] Subhransu Bhushan Sutar, *Kanika* (Oriya), Kendrapara: Mally Ghar, Raj Kanika, 2000, pp. 83-86.

spread throughout the world by the International Society of Kṛṣṇa Consciousness and teaches all to live in harmony.

The cultural history of Orissa is at par with the great tradition of India,[20] i.e. the Vedic culture. Syncretism can be seen in temple architectures, sculptural arts and painting arts of the Orissa province.

[20] Swami Abhedananda Bharati, *Great Tradition and Little Traditions*, Varanasi: Chowkhamba Sanskrit Series Office, 1978, *passim*.

10

Yoni Tantra Traditions in the Central Mahānadī Valley and Kāmākhyā

One naturally formed female vulva or *yoni* of Mother Earth — as dealt in Chapter 1 — is found under a bamboo thicket, in the Pātālgaṅgā site, near Boden in Nuāpāḍā district and worshipped as *dvārsani*. It should be regarded as the earliest Śakti Pīṭha (site) of the Orissa province.[1] Comparative studies show that the primeval Śakti of the entire Āgneya-Koṇa of Bhāratavarṣa is this site, and *dvārsani* is worshipped at Sindhekela, Boṅgomuṇḍa, Bhawānīpatna, Veda Vyāsa site in Sundargaṛh district and many places in western Orissa. The author[2] had described it as the most important antediluvian finding, as it took the shape of female vulva or *yoni*, when the crust of the earth was under formation. Because of this reason, it should be accepted that *yoni* worship originated in the middle right Mahānadī Valley.[3]

Earliest trace of Yoga in India is also found in the Central Mahānadī Valley, as discussed in Chapter 2. Because of this reason, the most interesting feature of rock art of Orissa is that it depicts female genitals or *yoni*s as triangles pointed down.[4] In most of these painted triangles, a spot (*bindu*) in the centre is found. Triangles with spot (*bindu*) at the centre are *bhairavī-yantras*.[5]

According to Pushpendra Kumar:[6]

---

[1] J.P. Singh Deo, "Primal alias Ādi Śakti of Orissa Province Is Found in Nuāpāḍā District", *OHRJ*, vol. XLVII, no. 3, pp. 38-39.

[2] *THOMV*, p. 60.

[3] Ibid., pp. 71-74.

[4] Ibid., p. 20.

[5] David Frawley, *Tāntric Yoga and the Wisdom Goddesses*, Delhi: Motilal Banarsidass, 1996, p. 103.

[6] Pushpendra Kumar, *Śakti Cult in Ancient India*, Varanasi: Bharatiya Publishing House, 1974, p. 157.

> Bhairavī or Tripura-Bhairavī, the fifth Goddess of Daśa Mahāvidyās, is reddish like the morning sun. She is dressed in a silken cloth and wears a garland of heads on her neck. Her breast is annointed with *sindūra*. In her four hands she holds a rosary of beads, a book, and the poses of granting boons and assurances. She has a crescent on her forehead. Her three eyes are as beautiful as red lotuses, and there is a bejewelled crown over her head. A mild smile plays on her lips. As a Goddess she is Tripura Bhairavī, while as a Mahāvidyā she is designated as Bhairavī only. This is a benign manifestation of Śakti and is considered as the giver of knowledge.[7]

As Goddess Bhairavī is the giver of knowledge, the archaeological antiquities prove that the *yoni-yantra* of Goddess Bhairavī was well known to the spiritual heritage of the Mahānadī River Valley in remote days or during early civilization.[8] Further, *yoni-yantra* and Yoginī Tantra had originated in the central right Mahānadī River Valley,[9] and had migrated to Kāmākhyā during the early medieval period.

About the shrine of Kāmākhyā at present, Nihar Ranjan Mishra[10] mentions:

> The Kāmākhyā temple, which is situated atop the Nīlācala hill to the west of Guwahati (91° 41' E – 26° 10' N approximately), is at present an important part of a sacred complex. This complex not only houses many other temples but also a whole set of people connected with them. The main temple (Kāmākhyā temple) has the *pīṭha* of Goddess Kāmākhyā and two shrines of Lakṣmī and Sarasvatī nearby. Other major Devī temples in the complex belong to Goddesses like Kālī, Tārā, Bhuvaneśvari, Chinnamastā, Bagalā, Bhairavī and Dhūmāvatī. There are some minor temples of various Goddesses in this complex too. They are the Śītalā temple, the Lalitā-Kāntā temple, the Jaya-Durgā temple, the Vana-Durgā temple, the Rājarājeśvarī temple, the Śmaśānakālī temple, the Kālī temple of Abhayananda Dharmaśālā and the Śaṇkheśvarī temple. These temples are considered minor only from the point of view of comparatively less number of devotees going there. There are five temples of Lord Śiva in this complex. They belong to different manifestations of Lord Śiva like Kāmeśvara (Umānanda), Siddheśvara,

---

[7] Pushpendra Kumar, *Śakti Cult in Ancient India*, Varanasi: Bharatiya Publishing House, 1974, p. 157; *Śākta Pramoda*, Bombay: Sri Venkatesvara Press, 1951, *passim*.

[8] *THOMV*, p. 31.

[9] *THOMV*, pp. 115-22.

[10] N.R. Mishra, *Kāmākhyā: A Socio-Cultural Study*, New Delhi: D.K. Printworld, 2004, pp. 23-24.

> Amṛtokeśvara (Heruka), Aghora and Koṭiliṅga (Tatpuruṣa). Here a temple of Lord Viṣṇu as Kedāra (Kamaleśvara) is also situated near the northern side of the main temple. Another temple of Lord Viṣṇu known as Gādhara is found in north-western direction of the Kāmākhyā temple. A temple of Lord Viṣṇu Pāṇḍunātha is situated in the eastern foothills of Nīlācala which is known as Pāṇḍu. Lord Gaṇeśa, in his four different forms as Nandī, Bhṛngī, Mahākāla and Gaṇapati guards the four gates of this sacred complex. The complex is also dotted with a few sacred ponds (*kuṇḍas*) which are associated with various *pūjās* and rituals. These ponds are Saubhāgya-Kuṇḍa, Durgā-Kuṇḍa, Bhairavī-Kuṇḍa, Amṛtadhārā-Kuṇḍa, Ṛṇamocana-Kuṇḍa and Gayā-Kuṇḍa. The complex has a number of *āśramas* and *dharmaśālās* which are meant for saints and holy men. These are like Daśanāmī Akhāṛā, Abhayānanda Dharmaśālā, Kalipur Āśrama, Nigamānanda Āśrama, Satsaṅga Āśrama, Tapoban Āśrama and Bijay Krishna Āśrama.
>
> Various *pūjās* and festivals are performed in different temples round the year by both brāhmaṇa and non-brāhmaṇa personnel. These personnel have settled in this complex for generations. Their society is not only functionally integrated by itself but is also marked by its own peculiarities.
>
> This sacred complex, which is referred to as Kāmākhyā Dhāma or more simply Kāmākhyā attracts large number of devotees. They come not only from this region but also from different parts of this country. In fact, this temple of the north-east remains an integrating force not only among the people of this region but also serves as a major link with the peninsular mainland.

The major link of the Kāmākhyā area with the peninsular mainland is there, because originally the *yoni* and Yoginī Cults had migrated from the Central Mahānadī River Valley to that region.

The fire device with its spiritual yogic seven tongues had given birth or growth to the Sapta-Mātṛkā worship, which seems to have originated in Āgneya-Koṇa. According to Mahesh Prashad Dash,[11] the worship of female spirit in some form or the other can be traced to a very remote period — the Mother Goddess in the Indus Valley culture and the divine energy in the Ṛgvedic age.[12]

---

[11] M.P. Dash (comp.), *A Descriptive Catalogue of Sanskrit Manuscripts of Orissa*, vol. V (Tantra Manuscripts), Bhubaneswar: Orissa State Museum, 1965, pp. XXVII-XXVIII.

[12] Ibid.; "Devī Sūkta" of *Ṛgveda*, X.125.

According to a legend[13] described in *Īśānaśivagurudeva-Paddhati* (1.52.79 b), the Mātr̥kās were created to help Lord Śiva in his fight against Andhakāsura. When the Lord inflicted wounds on Andhaka, blood began to flow profusely from his body. Each drop which touched the ground assumed the shape of another Andhaka. Thus, there were innumerable *asuras* fighting against Śiva. To stop the falling of the blood Śiva created a Goddess called Yogeśvarī from the flames issuing out of his mouth. Brahmā, Viṣṇu, Maheśvara, Kumāra, Varāha, Indra and Yama also sent their Śaktis to follow Yogeśvarī in stopping the flow of blood. Thus, the Sapta-Mātr̥kās originated. They embody the seven female potentials of the important gods.

With this background, the tradition of seven tāntric maidens and *Śaśisenā Kāvya* developed in the Central Mahānadī Valley, comprising the present western portion of the Orissa province.

N.K. Sahu[14] states that Patnagarh was known as Kauori Patna or Kumārī Patna ever since the seven tāntric maidens who lived in this township for some time had practised the esoteric rites. These maidens were popularly known by their assumed names like Gaṅgī Gaudunī, Suā Telunī, Janānadei Malunī, Netai Dhobanī, Luhukuṭi Luhurunī, Sukūti Chamarunī and Patrapindhi Saharunī. There are popular tales and traditions in western Orissa, depicting the occult practices and tāntric activities of these maidens. They seem to be the followers of Lakṣmīkara, who propounded Sahajayāna Buddhism in western Orissa in the ninth century CE. As late as the sixteenth century CE, the Patna kingdom was known as Kaunri Patna after the name of the headquarters town of that name, as known from the *Nirguṇa Māhātmya* of the poet Caitanya Dāsa.

Author[15] had emphatically mentioned:

> N.K. Sahu considers the famous seven tāntric maidens of Patnagarh area to be the followers of Lakṣmīkara, who propounded Sahajayāna Buddhism. But this is not so, as it seems that the seven tāntric maidens of Patnagarh area continued the secret esoteric tāntric rituals of *yoga* of sexual transformation and of the Yoginīs which had originated earlier in the central right Mahānadī Valley. It seems that N.K. Sahu was ignorant of

[13] J.P. Singh Deo, *Tāntric Art of Orissa*, Delhi: Kalpaz Publications, 2001, pp. 51-57.

[14] N.K. Sahu (state ed.), *Gazetteer of India, Orissa, Bolangir*, Nilamani Senapati (gen. ed.), Cuttack, 1968, p. 489.

[15] *THOMV*, pp. 135-36.

the development of the *yoga* of sexual transformation or *yoga* which leads from sex to super-consciousness in this locality and its inclusion in Hinduism or Vedic culture, as expounded in the *Bṛhadāraṇyaka Upaniṣad* (VI.4.2-3) of the *Śukla Yajurveda*. This *yoga* of sexual transformation became very popular in the early medieval period, as revived by Mattamayūra Śaivism.[16]

Netai Dhobanī was the spiritual and tāntric *guru* (master) of the great Gaṅga King Choḍagaṅgadeva of Kaliṅga. This is mentioned in the *Mādalā-Pāñjī* and its archaeological evidences are the two images of Anantavarma Choḍagaṅgadeva, the Gaṅga Gajapati and Netai Dhobanī, in a small miniature temple in Chuḍanga Sai of Purī.[17]

While dealing on the the *Mādalā-Pāñjī*, Anirudha Das[18] states:

> Two images of stone, installed in a small miniature temple in Chuḍaṅga Sai (Purī), one of a male and another of a female, are of much significance. The beautiful male figure is seated on the throne and armed with bow and arrow. On both his sides are the figures of two attendants, one holding the royal umbrella and another a *cāmara*. On the pedestal, there is the image of a man with an elephant and another one with a horse. To this royal image, offerings stated above are made as the master's share and people till now believe that this is the image of Anantavarma Choḍagaṅga Deva, the builder of the great Jagannātha temple. During the past few months, the writer has visited some old temples and to his surprise he has seen some images which can be appropriately identified as the image of the kings who have built the temples.
>
> The image of this female figure by the side of this male figure is quite helpful to identify the male figure with reference to the accounts recorded in the *Mādalā-Pāñjī*. Seated on something like a stool, the figure appears to be busy with work on something which is called a Ud Khala or a wooden device commonly used for husking paddy. This also represents a tāntric or black-magic operation. This image is popularly known as Gāreḍi Suāi in the locality which means the lady practising witchcraft with reference to

---

16 *THOMV*, R.P. Mishra, "Mattamayūra Śaivism in Orissa", *Culture and Collections*, R.P. Mishra (ed.), Kolkata: Punthi Pustak, 1996, pp. 101-39.

17 Ibid.; *OHRJ*, vol. XIV, nos. 3 and 4, pp. 6-7.

18 Anirudha Das, "The Mādalā Pāñjī", *OHRJ*, vol. XIV, nos. 3 and 4, *passim*.

the episode of Choḍagaṅga Deva, as narrated in the *Mādalā-Pāñjī* and the offerings which used to be made on the 10th day of the bright fortnight of Āśvina. Can it not be identified as the Guru-Mā of Choḍagaṅga Deva? There appears to be legendary connection between the two images. It is known from the *Mādalā-Pāñjī* that due to the treachery of Vāsudeva brāhmaṇa, Choḍagaṅga Deva conquered Orissa. It has already been stated that Choḍagaṅga Deva learnt witchcraft from Netai Dhobanī to whom he was devoted as a disciple and a God-son. These two images are very old. People say that on the pedestal of this female figure, there was the figure of a male in the pose of learning something from the female figure, but due to the thick coating of vermillion (*chuā*) and sandal paste which was about half a inch thick, on both the images, it has been destroyed. With great difficulty the coating was removed by mild chiselling to enable to take a drawing of both the images.

It will not be out of place here to give a little introduction to Netai Dhobanī. The name Netai Dhobanī is well known in the folk tales, stories of witchcraft, etc., in many parts of Orissa. People still believe that many people and specially children are influenced by evil spirit as a result of which they are diseased and sometimes they die also. So, one adept in witchcraft is called and one recites, *nahebārā boli kāhāra ājñā, kitai mā, patra saurunī, netai dhobanī, sidha saurunī, ajñādei mālunī ra koṭi koṭi ājña*. So, in the names of all these ladies, such as Kitai Mā, Patra Sauruṇī, Netai Dhobanī, Sidha Saurunī and Ajñā Dei Mālunī, the person well versed with the *mantra* to cure possession of evil spirit cures the patient. In many parts of western Orissa, Netai Dhobanī is worshipped by certain classes of people. She has been described in the *Mādalā-Pāñjī* as the Nagara Devī or the deity of the capital. Considered from all angles, it is difficult to disbelieve that the image in question is not of Netai Dhobanī.

P.M. Nayak[19] states that Sonepur, too, was the ancient seat of Tantra, the abode of the seven tāntric sisters. The Sat-Bandha (seven tanks) of the town is traditionally associated with them. *Mantras* in which their names are invoked are chanted:

Go, disease go; for this the command of Kaunri Kāmacaṇḍī, Madana Malunī, Netai Dhobanī, Sukuti Chamarunī, Lohakuti Luhuranī, Gaṅgī

[19] P.M. Nayak, "A Fresh Look at Śaśisenā Kavya", *Confluence*, vol. I, P.M. Nayak (ed.), Registrar, Sambalpur University, Burla, 1992, p. 72.

fig. 10.1: Image of Anantavarma Choḍagaṅgadeva (now installed in a small temple in Chauḍaṅga Sai Purī). *Source*: *OHRJ*, vol. XIV, nos. 3 and 4.

> Gaudunī, Patrapindhi Sauranī, Sua Teluni Go, for Īśvara and Pārvatī order you a crore of time to go[20] (*fig*. 10.1).

Madana or Jñānadei Malunī and Netai Dhobanī are believed to be the inhabitants of Sonepur. Jagbandhu Singh[21] in *Prācīna Utkala*s tells the story of Choḍagaṅgadeva who saw Netai Dhobanī at Sonepur (*fig*. 10.2), on his way to coastal Orissa, cook with her one feet in the burning hearth and her child in the boiling cauldron. Even today in Sonepur the washerman worship Netai, the Mālīs worship Madana and the Lohāras worship Sukuti as their tutelary deities. Pandit

[20] P.M. Nayak, "A Fresh Look at Śaśisenā Kavya", *Confluence*, vol. I, Pratap Rai, *Śaśisenā Kavya*, Introduction, Sonepur edn.

[21] Ibid.; Jagabandhu Singh, *Prācīna Utkala* (Oriya), Purī, 1929, p. 101.

fig. 10.2: Image of Netai Dhobanī (now installed in a small temple in Chauḍaṅga Sai, Purī). *Source*: *OHRJ*, vol. XIV, nos. 3 and 4.

Gopinath Panigrahi quotes Ramchandra Panigrahi, an old brāhmaṇa of Sonepur, who used to locate the house of Madana and her flower garden close to the west of the present Palace. Thus, the topography of Sonepur, its flora and fauna, the visible remains of Śaśisenā story and the tāntric traditions correlate Sonepur with Kamantapur of the Kāvya.[22] The use of words and phrases here and there also betrays the nativity of the author, Pratap Rai, who in all probability was a resident of Raipali near Sonepur town.

The story of Śaśisenā is widely prevalent in the eastern states of India. It is there in Banmali Das's *Chata Ichhavati*, in Dhananjay Bhanja's *Ichhavati*,

[22] P.M. Nayak, "A Fresh Look at Śaśisenā Kavya", *Confluence*, vol. I, P.M. Nayak (ed.), Registrar, Sambalpur University, Burla, 1992, p. 72; S.C. Mullick, Odisa Itihasa (MS.), p. 22 (Oriya).

> and in one of the folk tales of Orissa known as *Chakulia Panda*.[23] It is there in Kavikarna's *Manohar Pasiara Pala* and *Maniman Sing Gitika*, of Bengal. Later Bipra Nilambar and Narasingha Dvija incorporated this episode in *Padma Purāṇa* (Chs. 6-10) and *Āsāṛh Māhātmya* (Chs. 22-26) respectively.

The author[24] had earlier mentioned that N.K. Sahu[25] while dealing about Sonepur states:

> A work called *Śaśisenā kāvya* written by Pratap Rai, describes Jñānadei Malunī, one of the seven tāntric maidens, as a resident of Sonepur. Śaśisenā was the daughter of some feudatory chief of western Orissa who fell in love with Ahimāṇikya, the son of Dīwān, when both of them were reading in the school. After their marriage which was secretly performed with the help of the teacher who officiated as priest, they came and lived at Sonepur, which was also then known by its second name Kamitapura. Jñānadei Malunī, also known as Madana Malunī the tāntric maiden, who was then living in Sonepur, was charmed by the beauty of Ahimāṇikya and so once when he went out alone to the bazar, she induced him to come to her place where he was transformed into a lamb by dint of her esoteric art. This tāntric maiden used to reconvert him into human form in the night, while at day time the unfortunate man remained as a lamb. In the meantime, Śaśisenā having lost her husband remained in the guise of a man, so that she could not be molested by malevolent persons and could search her husband everywhere in the town. She subsequently got an appointment under the *rājā* of Sonepur and became a soldier in the army. Very soon she earned reputation for her courage and heroism, particularly when she once killed a man-eater tiger at the risk of her life. The *rājā* being pleased with Śaśisenā desired to give his daughter in marriage to her. As Śaśisenā could not reveal her identity, she was forced by circumstances to marry the daughter of the *rājā*. She, however, described her misfortune to the newly-married girl and the latter, being full of sympathy for her, did not reveal anything about her identity. Both of them searched for Ahimāṇikya by all possible means. They excavated a tank at a place in the west of Sonepur town and constructed four temples on the four sides of the tank. A grand

23 P.M. Nayak (ed.), *Confluence*, vol. I; Surendra Mohanty, *Odia Sahitya-ra-Madhyaparva* (Oriya), 1992, p. 126.

24 *THOMV*, pp. 136-38.

25 Ibid.; N.K. Sahu (state ed.), op. cit., 1968, pp. 494-95.

festival took place on the day of consecration of the tank. Jñānadei Malunī came to see the festival at night with Ahimāṇikya who was then in human form. Ahimāṇikya could recognize Śaśisenā and not, being able to contact her, he wrote a few lines on the wall of one of the temples with a piece of chalk informing her that he had been taken captive and transformed into a lamb by the tāntric maiden Jñānadei Malunī. Śaśisenā came to know everything about her husband from the writing. She told the *rājā* that she would sacrifice some lambs before the Goddess Bhagvatī and that the lamb possessed by Jñānadei Malunī be brought for that purpose. The *rājā* at her request brought Ahimāṇikya, who was then in the form of lamb, from Jñānadei Malunī. It was then known that the lamb was no other than Ahimāṇikya and by the order of the *rājā*, Jñānadei Malunī brought him back to human form. Śaśisenā and Ahimāṇikya met together and on the desire of the *rājā* both his daughter and Śaśisenā became the wives of Ahimāṇikya.

This tradition is widely current in Sonepur even to this day. A place on the western part of Sonepur town where the reunion of Śaśisenā and Ahimāṇikya is believed to have taken place is now known as "Śaśisenā Tikra". A tank near about is also named as Śaśisenā Bandha. A temple without any opening has been constructed in the Śaśisenā Tikra by a former king of Sonepur and has been dedicated to the memory of Śaśisenā.

On the top of the Śaśisenā temple in Sonepur, lizards are designed, descending downwards from the *āmalaka śilā* of the temple. Lizard signifies the *nāsikāgra dṛṣṭi*, which is a haṭha-yogic practice involving gazing at the nose tip. This proves that the esoteric seven tāntric maidens were practising esoteric tāntric *haṭha-yoga*. Pratap Rai is the author of *Śaśisenā Kāvya*. The period of Pratap Rai is uncertain. The stories of seven tāntric maidens and Śaśisenā are popular in the folk tales of Assam. P.M. Nayak[26] asserts that the story of Śaśisenā is widely prevalent in the eastern states of India. These facts and the discussions show that the Yoni Tantra and the *yoga* of sexual transformation had shifted from the Central Mahānadī River Valley to the eastern states of India and especially to the Kāmākhyā and Assam areas.

Anthropologist, Gitanjali Nayak of Purī, had served as the principal of Keonjhar College. In 2003, she had camped at Khariar and had informed the author that in

[26] *THOMV*, pp. 136-38; P.M. Nayak, op. cit., 1992, pp. 69-76.

between Anandapur and Ghaṭagāon Tāriṇī villages of Keoñjhar district, a high school named "Patra Sauruni" exists. It seems that the occult teaching of "Patra Pindhi Sauruni" was popular in Keoñjhar district among some people. This high school seems to be the last remnant of the tradition of the seven tāntric maidens of the Central Mahānadī Valley before it went to the Assam region in eastern India.

The main factor[27] is Yoni Tantra was originated in the Central Right Mahānadī River Valley. On the original Yoni Tantra text itself, J.A. Schoterman[28] has done the critical edition of this text and states that the most important part in determining the origin of the text is Paṭala IV: "We are thus informed that in a country called Koca, near Yonigarta, on the *paścima* side of the river Ganges, a certain Mādhavī is known to exist whose *yoni* is unequalled on earth, it is an object of constant veneration for Mādhavī who is the narrator in this fourth Paṭala of the Yoni Tantra. The country called Koca is unmistakably modern Cooch Behar, north of Bangladesh. Thus, summarizing this section on the origin of the Yoni Tantra, he concludes that its origin is in the region of Cooch Behar near Yonigarta/Kāmarūpa centring around the cult of Mādhavī.

To this discussion of Schoterman, the author[29] had clarified thus:

> The country of Koca on the *paścima* (west) of Gaṅgā River, as mentioned in "Yoni Tantra", should have been Kosala country, i.e. South Kosala. It seems to be a spelling mistake or vague negligence of the unqualified writer of "Yoni Tantra", which was composed under the Vaiṣṇava influence, in the late medieval period. . . . The discussion proves that the central portion of Mahānadī River had contributed to the development of tāntric *haṭha-yoga* and the *yoga* of sexual transformation for the entire humanity, specially of the *Kaliyuga* (Kali age).

Because of this background or undercurrent of the Āgneya-Koṇa area, lots of erotic antiquities and sculptures are found in the western Orissa region, Chhattisgarh, Bengal and coastal Orissa.

Orissa State Museum has the most unique and large collection of palm-leaf inscriptions made by itching of iron stylus and paintings of which the most prominent ones are Jayadeva's *Gīta Govinda, Bidagdha Mādhava* of Rūpa Gosvāmī, *Amaru-Śataka*

---

[27] *THOMV*, pp. 115-16.

[28] Ibid.; J.A. Schoterman, *The Yoni Tantra*, New Delhi: Manohar, 1980, pp. 3-9.

[29] *THOMV*, pp. 121-22.

fig. 10.3: Rādhā-Kṛṣṇa in amorous love play. (*Source*: Subas Pani (ed.).

of Amaruka and *Uṣābilāsa* of Śiśu Śaṅkara Dās. The themes of these manuscripts are mostly love episodes of Rādhā and Kṛṣṇa as well as other mythical and legendary incidents. The paintings and drawings also present excellent scences of nature. In the *Gīta Govinda* of Jayadeva, Rādhā and Kṛṣṇa are seen in amorous love play also (*fig.* 10.3).[30]

In Sanskrit literature, with reference to Vātsyāyana's *Kāmasūtra*,[31] it can be mentioned that the description of sixty-four arts to be studied is given and the description of sixty-four sexual poses is not mentioned. It is for the first time that Kavi Samrāṭ Upendrabhañja of Orissa deals with sixty-four sexual poses in his composition *Pañcaśāyaka* in poetic Oriya language.[32] Gopal Bhañja, a scion of the Bhañja dynasty of Mayurbhañj, had also composed *Pañcaśāyaka* in Sanskrit language and about nineteen manuscripts of "Causaṭhī Rati Bandha" of him are available at manuscript section of the Orissa State Museum.[33] So, it can be claimed that sixty-four sexual poses, are the gift of Oriya literature to the oriental studies. Even now

[30] *Illustrated Palmleaf Manuscripts of Orissa* (*A Selection from the Orissa State Museum*), A Golden Jubilee Publication, Bhubaneswar, 1984, pp. 4-5 and 25.

[31] R. Burton and F.F. Arbuthnot (tr.), *Vātsyāyana's Kāmasūtra* (*A Classic of Love*), Delhi: Orient Paperbacks, rpt. 1982, pp. 30-34.

[32] *THOMV*, vide Appendix, pp. 255-70.

[33] *Illustrated Palmleaf Manuscripts of Orissa*, 1984, pp. 81-82 and 85.

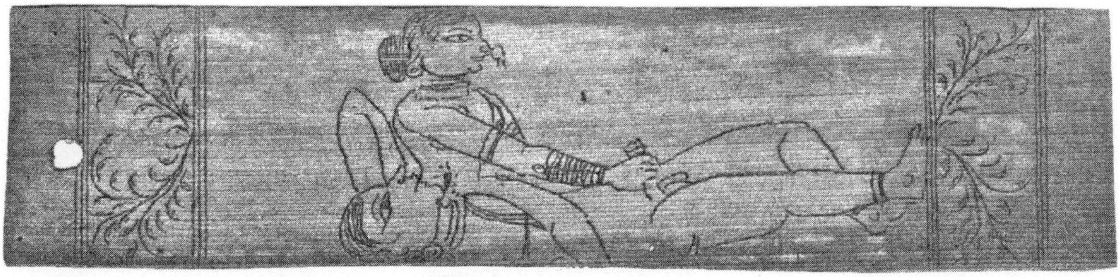

Pl. 7

Pl. 8

Pl. 9

Pl. 10

Pls. 7-70."Sixty-four sexual poses," found in palm-leaf etching of Orissa.

Pl. 11

Pl. 12

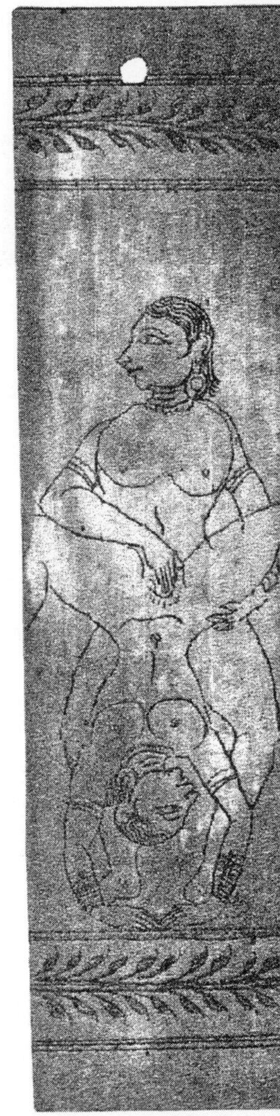

Pl. 13

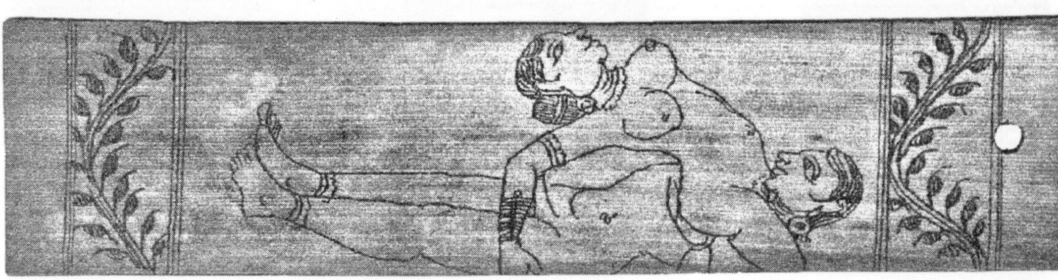

Pl. 14

Pls. 7-70."Sixty-four sexual poses," found in palm-leaf etching of Orissa.

Pl. 15

Pl. 16

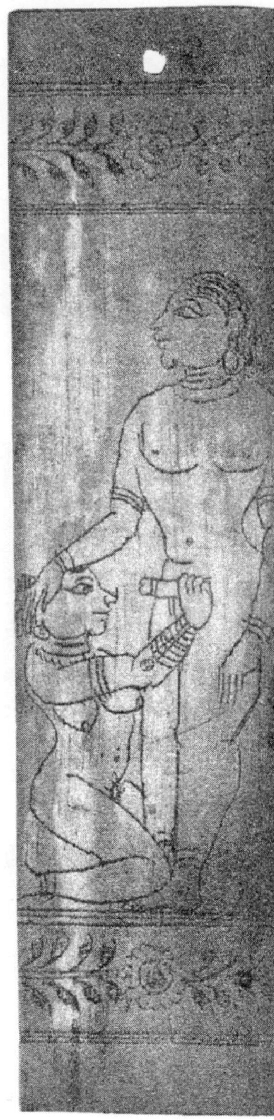

Pl. 17

Pl. 18

Pls. 7-70."Sixty-four sexual poses," found in palm-leaf etching of Orissa.

Pl. 19

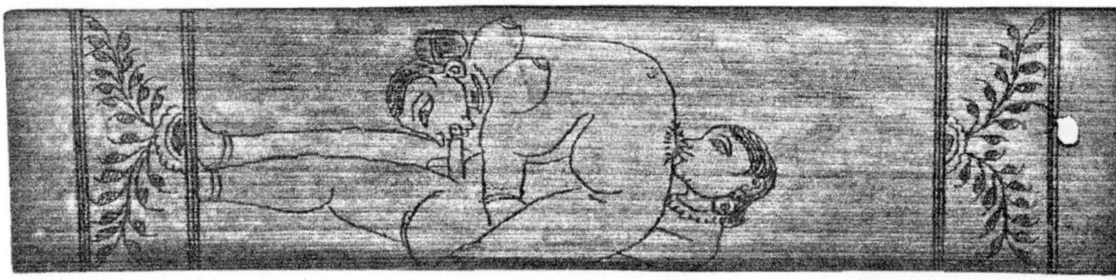

Pl. 20

Pl. 21

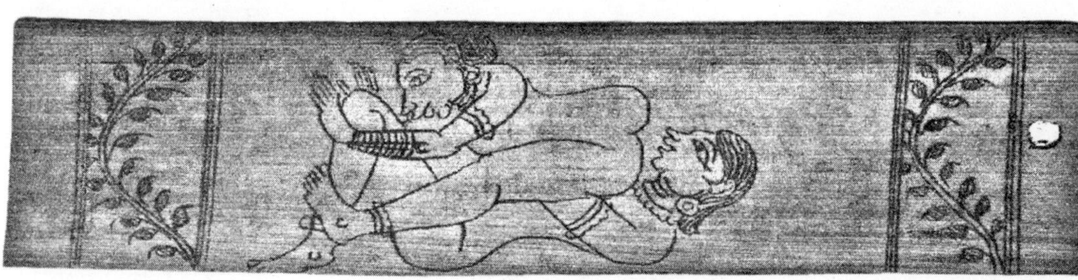

Pl. 22

Pls. 7-70."Sixty-four sexual poses," found in palm-leaf etching of Orissa.

Pl. 23

Pl. 24

Pl. 25

Pl. 26

Pls. 7-70."Sixty-four sexual poses," found in palm-leaf etching of Orissa.

Pl. 27

Pl. 28

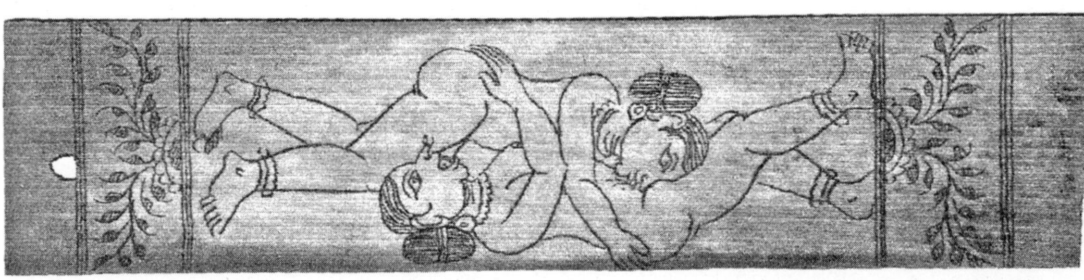

Pl. 29

Pl. 30

Pls. 7-70."Sixty-four sexual poses," found in palm-leaf etching of Orissa.

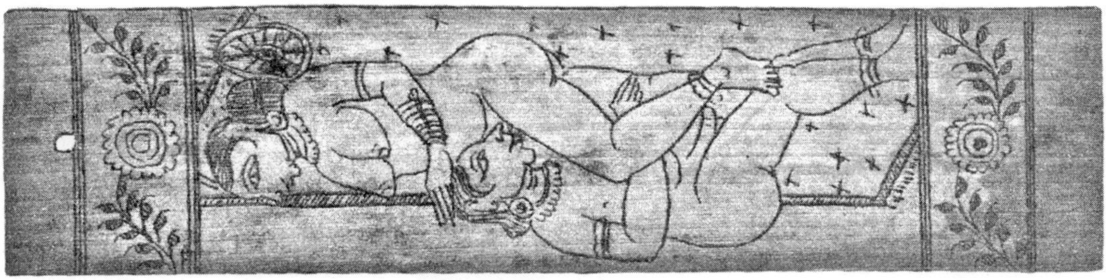

Pl. 31

Pl. 32

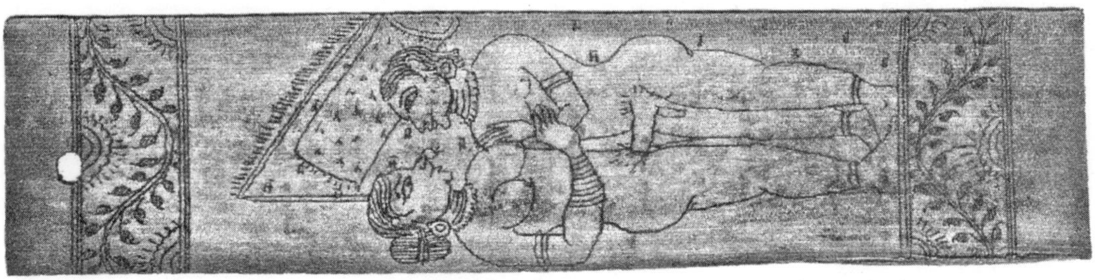

Pl. 33

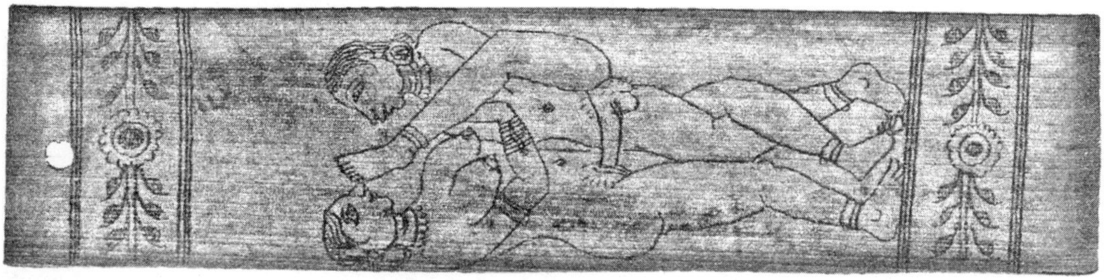

Pl. 34

Pls. 7-70."Sixty-four sexual poses," found in palm-leaf etching of Orissa.

Pl. 35

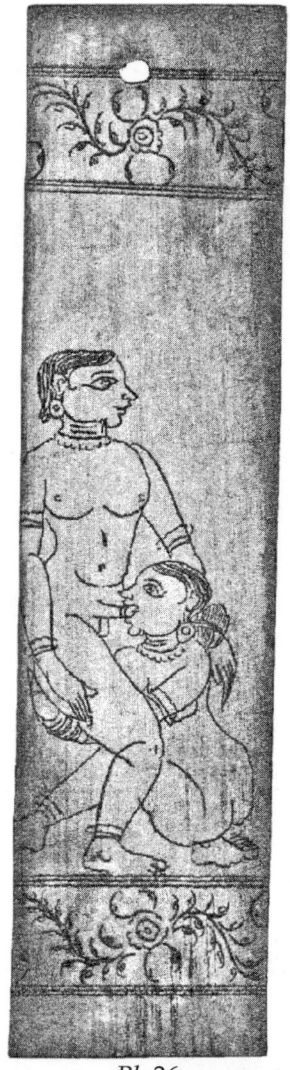

Pl. 36

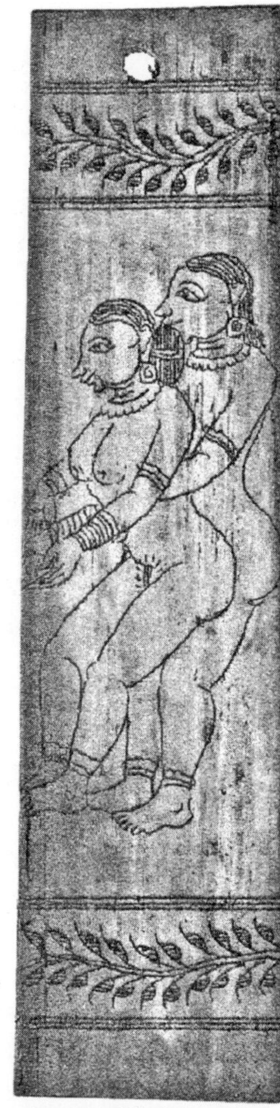

Pl. 37

Pl. 38

Pls. 7-70."Sixty-four sexual poses," found in palm-leaf etching of Orissa.

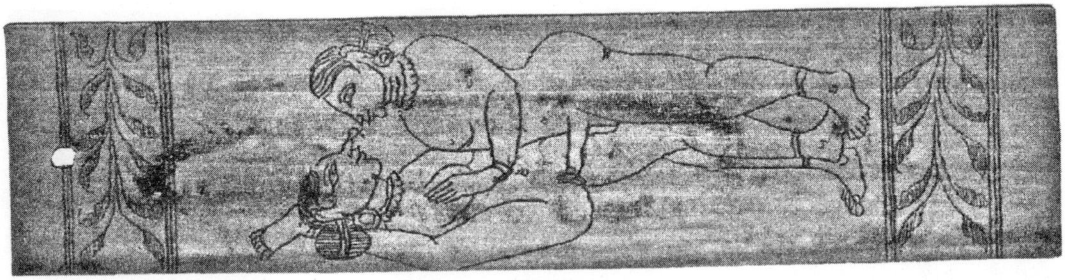

Pl. 39

Pl. 40

Pl. 41

Pl. 42

Pls. 7-70."Sixty-four sexual poses," found in palm-leaf etching of Orissa.

Pl. 43

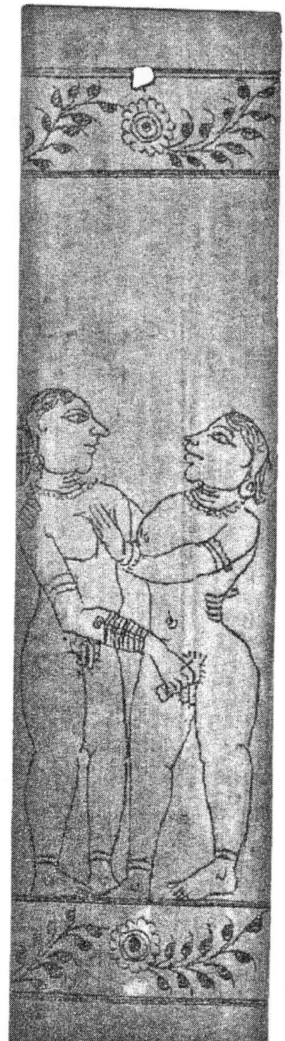

Pl. 44

Pl. 45

Pl. 46

Pls. 7-70."Sixty-four sexual poses," found in palm-leaf etching of Orissa.

Pl. 47

Pl. 48

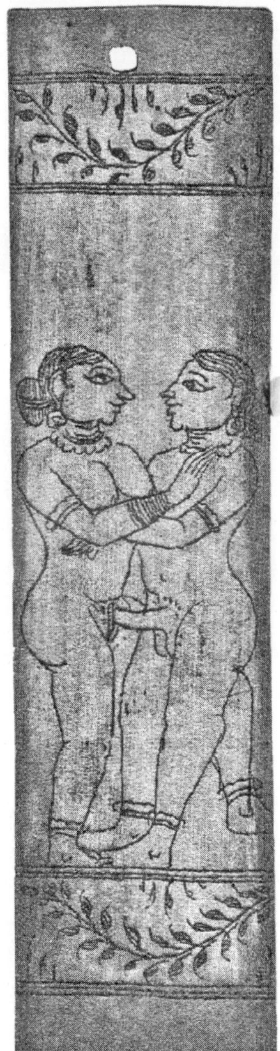

Pl. 49

Pl. 50

Pls. 7-70."Sixty-four sexual poses," found in palm-leaf etching of Orissa.

Pl. 51

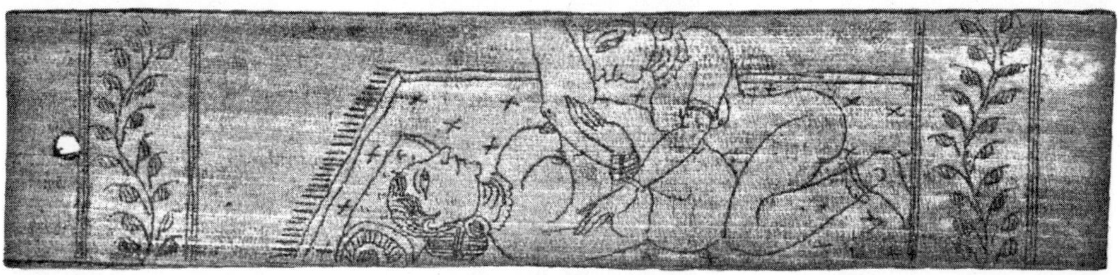

Pl. 52

Pl. 53

Pl. 54

Pls. 7-70."Sixty-four sexual poses," found in palm-leaf etching of Orissa.

Pl. 55

Pl. 56

Pl. 57

Pl. 58

Pls. 7-70."Sixty-four sexual poses," found in palm-leaf etching of Orissa.

Pl. 59

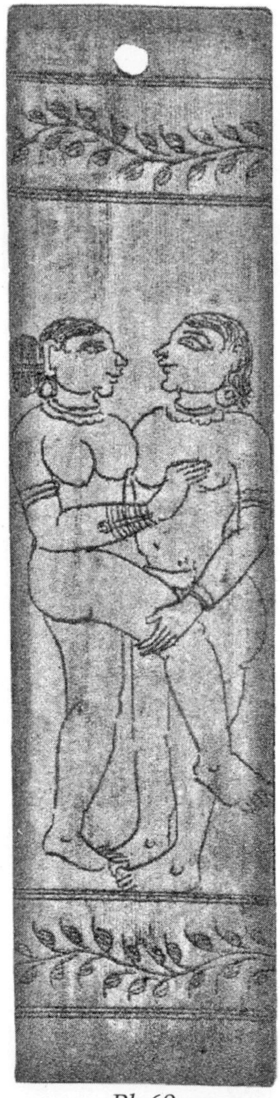

Pl. 60

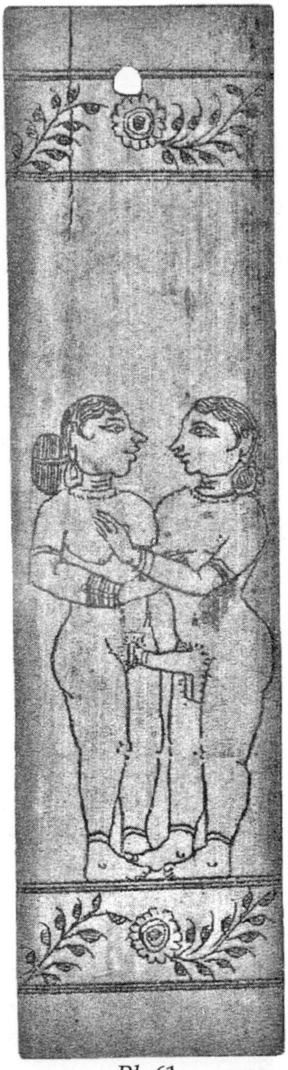

Pl. 61

Pl. 62

Pls. 7-70."Sixty-four sexual poses," found in palm-leaf etching of Orissa.

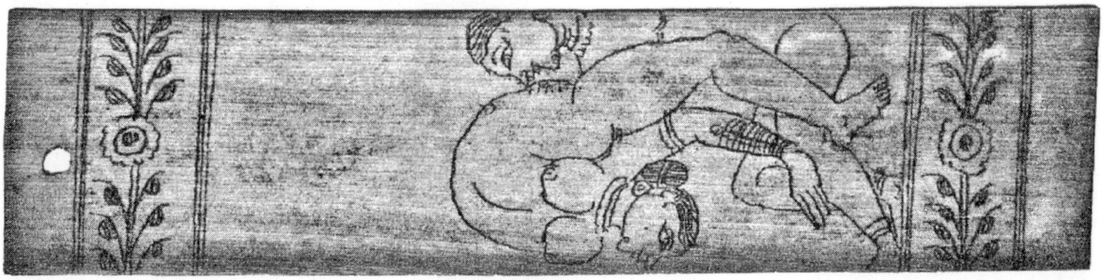

Pl. 63

Pl. 64

Pl. 65

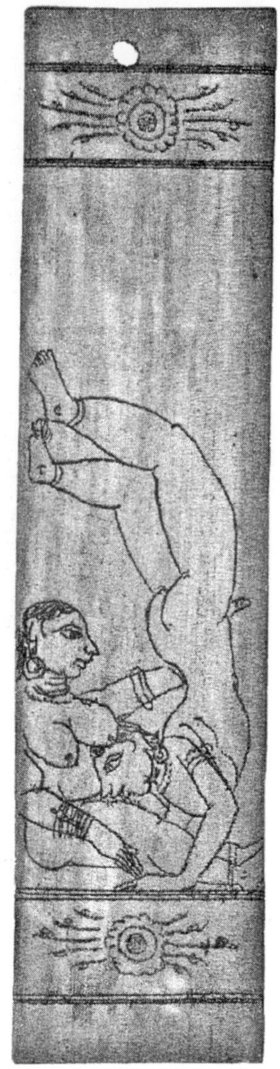

Pl. 66

Pls. 7-70."Sixty-four sexual poses," found in palm-leaf etching of Orissa.

Pl. 67

Pl. 68

Pl. 69

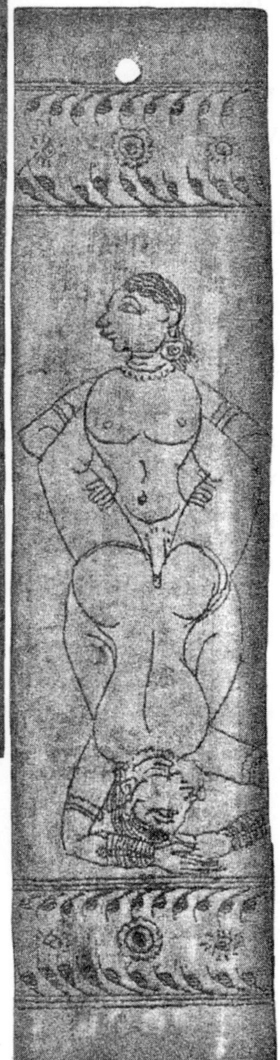

Pl. 70

Pls. 7-70."Sixty-four sexual poses," found in palm-leaf etching of Orissa.

the painting of sixty-four sexual poses in *paṭṭa-citra* paintings and palm-leaf etchings are continuing in the Orissa province (Plates 7-70). These are in great demand by the scholars and tourists who visit Purī, Koṇārka and Bhubaneswar.

Finally, *yoni* worship centred at Kāmākhyā, Puruṣottama Jagannātha *alias* Dakṣiṇa Kālī at Purī and the composite tāntric figure of Mahākāla and Mahākālī at Tala site[34] of Bilaspur district in Chhattisgarh province, i.e. the ancient South Kosala region.

The composite tāntric figure of Mahākāla and Mahākālī at Tala site is an indispensable composite sculptural art of Śiva-Śakti of Tantrism, in the Great Mahānadī River Valley. It requires explanation.

Kāla[35] means time, God of Death (death personified), all destroyer, an incarnation of Śiva, the Ananta form of Viṣṇu or the universal soul. Śiva, in his character of the destroyer of the universe, is called Mahākāla.[36] Mahākāla is the name of the phallic image of Śiva in Ujjain. The eternity personified is known as Mahākāla. Name of a class of attendants of Śiva is Mahākāla too.

Robert E. Svoboda[37] says that Śiva has a form, which means that his personality exists within nature, created from Ādya. Lord Śiva is not absolutely absolute because out of compassion he has taken on an attribute or two to enable us to comprehend him. These attributes, though, do give him certain limitations, very subtle ones, of course. So subtle that from our point of view they are no limitations at all. But they are sufficient to distinguish him from Mahākāla.

> Mahākāla has no limitation of any kind whatsoever, at least in the universe we know. He has no form at all, none. At least Śiva manifests a form we can concentrate on. Mahākāla is utterly formless, which means he can assume all forms at will.
>
> Mahākāla is the God of time. He is Satya Śrī Akāla: true, auspicious, beyond time. He is time: How can he be subject to it? Since time exists only for mortals,

[34] J.P. Singh Deo, "Composite Tāntric Figure of Mahākāla and Mahākālī", *Riddle of Indian Iconography* (*Zetetic or Rare Icon from Tala*), L.S. Nigam (ed.), Delhi: Sharada Publishing House, 2000, pp. 127-34;

THOMV, pp. 155-71.

[35] Gopal Chandra Praharaj (comp.), *Purnachandra Orḍiā Bhāshā Kosha* (*A Lexicon of the Oriya Language*), vol. II (Consonants, ka to ṅa), Cuttack, 1932, pp. 1546-47.

[36] Ibid., vol. V (Consonants, pha-ma), Cuttack, 1936, p. 6355.

[37] R.E. Svoboda, *Aghora* (*At the Left Hand of God*), New Delhi: Rupa & Co., 1993, pp. 85-86.

> Mahākāla must be immortal, which makes him true, because he is absolute, free of any taint or *māyā*. This makes him auspicious in the time sense of the world. Mahākāla is the only being of all possible beings in the universe who never falls prey to *māyā*. Even Lord Śiva, the same essence of Mahākāla in a different manifestation with a different job to do, fell once or twice. But Mahākāla never ever looks at *māyā*. No one can persuade him to. When he comes for you, no matter how hard you beg for five minutes just to put your affairs in order, "No" is the only answer you will get. When even Lord Kṛṣṇa himself could not induce death to wait for even a moment, how will you be able to do it?
>
> Why is this? Because Mahākāla is the pivot on which the entire universe turns. On the one hand, there is the *Saguṇa Brahman*, the *saṁsāra*, which is the infinity of forms, endless and on the other, the *Nirguṇa Brahman*, which is formless infinity, absolutely no form, zero as far as form is concerned. Between these two, connecting them together, is Mahākāla. He is the fulcrum, the tangent between infinity and zero.

The composite Mahākāla and Mahākālī image of Tala seems to be the full sculptural expression with aesthetics of the Śaiva and Śākta revolution of the whole Mahānadī River Valley, i.e. the centre of Āgneya-Koṇa, with all the *haṭha-yogic* features as components of the entire body.

Ādya[38] is the primeval energy of God. The union of male and female, i.e. Śiva-Śakti concept of Sāṁkhya Darśana, had evolved in Guru Ḍoṅger. Similarly, the nucleus of spiritual and yogic culture of the entire Āgneya-Koṇa was originated and developed in the Central Mahānadī River Valley.

As stated, Kāmākhyā temple is situated atop the Nīlācala hill to the west of Guwahati, in Kāmrūp district of Assam. It is a well-known fact that Purī site is also known as Nīlācala. K.C. Mishra[39] mentions that the names of Purī and Nīlācala were also used in ancient Jāvā and Bālī. In Bāli, the temple where images were worshipped was called Purī. This might have been due to our cultural contact with the far off islands.[40] So, it proves that there were spiritual, yogic, cultural, historical, commercial and trade contacts in early days.

---

[38] J.P. Singh Deo (ed.), *Tāntric Scholar and the British Wrath on Baster State*, Kolkata: Punthi Pustak, 2007, pp. 119-50.

[39] K.C. Mishra, *The Cult of Jagannātha*, Calcutta: Firma K.L. Mukhopadhyay, 1971, p. 85.

[40] Ibid.; Bicandet, *Legends of the Burmese Buddha*, vol. II, p. 96.

As there are syncretic cultural traces in Orissa, there are sculptures of a mother breast-feeding her baby, a woman apparently offering some drinks to a male partner who is already drunk, Veṇugopāla Kṛṣṇa in *tribhaṅga* posture, dreadful Goddess Cāmuṇḍā, Lord Gaṇeśa, scenes of four human figures engaged in music and dance, female engaged in dance, a sculpture of Agni and many others in Assam too. Their presence proves that Kāmākhyā temple complex is a rich storehouse of Assamese art and architecture.[41]

[41] Nihar Ranjan Mishra, op. cit., 2004, pp. 166-67.

11

Spiritual Relationship of Kālāhāṇḍī with Cāndīpur Tārā Pīṭha of Birbhum

WHILE making whirlwind tour to collect materials for starting a museum at Bhawānīpatna on 2 December 1992, the author had visited Mohangiri site of Kālāhāṇḍī district.

The *Gazetteer*[1] informs that Mohangiri (83° 40' E and 20° 20' N) is a village in the Madanpur-Rāmpur police station limit close to Bauḍh-Khoṇḍamal's district border in the north-east corner of the district. It is 35 km from Madanpur-Rāmpur. The village is near a hill stream, called Kālī Gaṅgā. A dilapidated Śiva temple stands on the bank of the stream. There are a few short epigraphical records on its walls and pillars.

This Śiva temple enshrines a big *Svayambhū Liṅga* of black chlorite stone and contains two small inscriptions — Spitacandra of Mudgala *kula* and Vyūha Bhairava.[2]

About the Mudgala rule in South Kosala, the author[3] was of the view that the Soro copper-plate[4] records the grant of Mahārāja Śambhujaśa, Mahārāja Bhānudatta and Mahāsandhiviṣahika Somadatta. The period of reign of the Mudgala dynasty in northern Toṣalī is not known definitely.[5] The Patiākela copper-plate[6] was the grant of Mahārāja Śambhujaśa, which speaks of his rule in southern Toṣalī. They were the ruling dynasty in the sixth century CE, probably.

> At the site of the dilapidated temple of Mohangiri, two small inscriptions are found. One is the Spitacandra who belonged to Mudgala *kula* and the

[1] D.C. Kuanr (state ed.), *Orissa District Gazetteers — Kālāhāṇḍī*, N. Senapati (chief ed.), Cuttack, 1980, pp. 453-54.

[2] Ibid., p. 41.

[3] J.P. Singh Deo, *Cultural Profile of South Kosala*, Delhi: Gyan Publishing House, 1987, p. 165.

[4] *EI*, vol. XXIII, p. 198.

[5] H.K. Mahatab, *The History of Orissa*, vol. I, Cuttack: Prajatantra Press, 1959, p. 77.

[6] S.N. Rajguru, *Inscriptions of Orissa*, vol. I, part II, Bhubaneswar, pp. 124-27.

other of Vyūha Bhairava, who was probably the presiding deity. Details about the Mudgala dynasty, who ruled the north-east portion of Orissa and how they shifted to the west, in the hilly and forest tract of Kālāhāṇḍī region in medieval period are not yet known.

It seems the Mudgalas were a business clan, because some Aggarwal families residing in Khariar Road (Jonk) township in Nuāpāḍā district are of Mudgala *gotra* (caste, tribe, clan, genus, family, race and lineage). Fresh discoveries and observations of this author, with the help of Dhudantadaman Singh Babu of Sargadi, has enlightened new light to the Mudgala migration, from north-east portion of Orissa province to the hilly area of Kālāhāṇḍī district.

The observation of Kedarnath Mahapatra cannot be overlooked. Mahapatra[7] remarked:

> The broken Śiva temple at Mohangiri in the north-east corner of this state bordering the Gañjam district and standing not very far from the famous Khingghāṭ is a noteworthy monument of this area. It belongs to the Paraśurāmeśvara type of temples at Bhubaneswar and is similar to the twin temples at Gandharāḍi of Bauḍh state on the bank of the Mahānadī. The place Mohangiri seems to have strategic importance in those days of yore as it was situated on the highway passing from Kaliṅga (Gañjam side) to Kosala (Kālāhāṇḍī-Patna side) and this temple was erected to serve the purpose of guide as well as a place of worship to the travellers passing on this way.

Palaeographically, the two small inscriptions of Mohangiri temple are dated to tenth century CE.

Fresh observations of the antiquities of the Mohangiri temple site gives more weight that the original temple at Mohangiri site was built by a Mudgala king, most probably Spitacandra, who belonged to the lineage of the Mudgala kings, who ruled north-eastern part of Orissa during sixth century CE or thereabout.

A modern temple is built over the *Svayambhū Liṅga* of Mohangiri, which was known as Vyūha Bhairava during tenth century CE and the modern temple is named as Dhabaleśvara Śiva temple. The original carved pillars of the *mukhaśālā* of the innate temple are still standing and the images and sculptures of the fallen structure are still existing there.

---

[7] K.N. Mahapatra, "History of the Kālāhāṇḍī State Before the Rise of the Gaṅga Powers", *The Journal of the Kaliṅga Historical Research Society*, vol. I, no. 4, March 1947, p. 268.

Originally, the temple was facing east and the same is the modern temple. The observation that came to the notice of the author is that the niches of the modern Dhabaleśvara Śiva temple have interesting old images *alias* sculptural arts. On the south niche, Lord Gaṇeśa is found, on the western niche, Lord Kārttikeya is found, and on the northern niche, a Goddess, breast-feeding an adult male, is found.

A Goddess breast-feeding a male, is a rare sculptural art. How could a Goddess breast feed a male adult? This question was perplexing the author. A revelation came like a boon, when Dhudantadaman Singh Babu of Saragadi village, informed the author about the original deity of Cāndīpur Tārā Pīṭha of Birbhum, in West Bengal.

Cāndīpur Tārā Pīṭha of Birbhum is a famous tāntric Tārā site. Before knowing about the Tārā deity of Cāndīpur Tārā Pīṭha, it is worth knowing about Goddess Tārā. The author's[8] view of Tārā is:

> The word "Tārā" means star. The name of this Goddess has similarity with the celebrated Mother Goddesses of Western Asia. In India, Tārā signifies protection and thereby saviour. In Buddhist tradition, she saves or protects her devotees from eight great fears (*aṣṭa-mahābhaya*). Her early history in India is a mystery, but from Subandha's work *Vāsavadattā*, it is believed that by sixth century CE her cult became popular in India. Goddess "Tārā" made her way into Buddhism and came to be known as Śakti or energy or Bodhisattva Avalokiteśvara.
>
> Tārā cult passed from India to Tibet and in various Goddess forms went to China within seventh and eighth centuries CE, corresponding with the female principle worshipped in Buddhism. In the Hindu pantheon, Tārā Ugratārā, Ekajaṭā and Mahā-Nīlasarasvatī Goddesses are found. The *dhyāna*s of these Goddesses, found in the Hindu Tantras, correspond to those found in the Buddhist Tantra *sādhanā*s.
>
> In the Buddhist pantheon, Tārā became the consort of Amoghasiddhi, who was destined to play a great role. Tārā's colour is green here and she is embodied of the element of air.
>
> Goddesses emanating from Akṣobhya consist of those belonging to the Tārā group. Foremost among these deities is Mahācīnatārā who is also known in Buddhist Tāntric literature Ugratārā. Tārā has been incorporated in the Hindu pantheon under the name of Tārā and is regarded as one of

[8] J.P. Singh Deo, *Tāntric Art of Orissa*, Delhi: Kalpaz Publications, 2001, pp. 67-69.

the Ten Mahāvidyā Goddesses (Tārā is a benign manifestation). It is interesting that the *dhyāna* of Tārā, as found in the *Tantrasāra* of Kṛṣṇānanda Āgamavāgīśa, is directly borrowed from the *Sādhanamālā*. Even the association of Akṣobhya with Tārā is maintained in the Śākta Tantras. Ekajaṭā is also a form of Tārā, whose cult is reported to have been brought to India by *siddha* Nāgārjuna from Bhoṭadeśa or Tibet.

Of all the Goddesses of the Vajrayāna pantheon of Tāntric Buddhism, Tārā became the most celebrated as the consort of Avalokiteśvara. Goddesses of the Tārā group in Buddhism are Khadiravāṇī Tārā, Mahāśrī Tārā, Ṣaḍbhuja Sīta Tārā, Dhanada Tārā and Sīta Tārā. Tārā is the common name applied to a large number of Goddesses such as Jāṅgalī, Parṇaśabarī, Mahācīnatārā, Ekajaṭā and others. Khadiravāṇī Tārā is also known as Śyāma Tārā because of her green colour. She is endowed with two hands and shows the *varada-mudrā* with the right and *utpala* in the left. This is the most common and most popular iconographical trait of Tārā. Khadiravāṇī can be recognized by the figures of the two attendant deities Aśokakāntā Māricī and Ekajaṭā. Māraśrī Tārā has two more attendants, Jāṅgulī and Mahāmayūrī, and she is also green. Vaśya Tārā, also known by the name of Ārya Tārā, looks exactly like Khadiravāṇī Tārā with the exception that she sits in *bhadrāsana* with both legs dangling. Tārā also has many-handed forms. Sīta Tārā is a white variety of Tārā with one face and four arms. Ṣaḍbhuja Sīta Tārā, as her name implies, is the six-armed form of white Tārā. Dhanada Tārā is one of the four-armed varieties of Tārā. The special features of the Goddess are that she rides an animal and, like Vajra Tārā, is surrounded by eight Goddesses.

Female emanations of Ratna-Sambhava also consist of two deities of the Tārā group — Vajra Tārā and Prasanna Tārā. The former is conceived of in the middle of the circle of eight mothers. She is eight-armed, four-faced and decked in all ornaments. She has numerous forms. Prasanna Tārā is of terrible appearance. She is yellow and has eight faces and sixteen arms.

There are Tārās of five colours in Tāntric Buddhism. In practice most of the Buddhist male deities of the later period came to be known as Avalokiteśvara or Lokeśvara and all of the female deities came under the general name Tārā. Different forms of this Goddess were classified from the viewpoint of her colour. To the red Tārā group belonged Kurukullā, to the blue group Ekajaṭā and Mahācīnatārā, to the yellow group, Vajratārā, Jāṅgulī, Parṇaśabarī and Bhṛkuṭi to the white group; Aṣṭamahābhaya Tārā, Mṛtyuvāñcana Tārā, Caturbhuja Tārā, Ṣaḍbhuja Sīta Tārā, Viśvamātā,

Kurukullā and Jāṅgulī, and to the green group Khadiravāṇī Tārā, Vaśya Tārā, Arva Tārā, Mahattarī Tārā, Varada Tārā, Durgottāriṇī Tārā, Dhanada Tārā, Jāṅgulī and Parṇaśabarī. It is definite that all the major Goddesses of Vajrayāna form of Tāntric Buddhism came to be known as Tārā.

Some Hindu deities such as Mahākāla, Gaṇapati, Gaṇapatihṛdaya, Sarasvatī, Indra, Yama, Varuṇa, Kubera, Īśāna, Agni, Nairṛti, Vāyu, Brahmā, Viṣṇu, Maheśvara, Kārttīkeya, Vārāhī and Cāmuṇḍā have been incorporated in the Vajrayāna pantheon of Tāntric Buddhism.

In one of the cells of a ruined Jaina monastery at Suai, situated in the road between Semiliguḍa and Nandapur in Korapūṭ district, one image of four-armed Tārā adorned with bangles up to the elbows, is found. Due to ravages of weather, the whole monastery is in a dilapidated condition.

Tārā cult became so much popular that in the Śākta Tantra, she has been given the position of the Supreme Being, as second Goddess of Daśamahāvidyās.

For the detailed information on the spiritual wisdom of Goddess Tārā, it is worth quoting Vedic scholar David Frawley[9]:

Tārā (The Saving Words)

The ruling lady of speech, like a wish-fulfilling vine around your devotee, you who grant all the accomplishment of all goals, everywhere adorned with all naturally perfect prose and poetry, you who grant realization.

You who are endowed with three eyes like a budding blue lotus, who are ocean of mercy, shower into our vision your grace with a rain of immortal blessedness.

EIGHT VERSES IN PRAISE OF TĀRĀ (TĀRĀṢṬAKAM) 2

Tārā is not only an important Hindu Goddess, she is also the most important of the Buddhist Goddesses. The Bodhisattva Tārā is the consort of the great Buddha Avalokiteśvara, the Lord who looks down with compassion on all living beings. In the Chinese Buddhist tradition, she is called Kwan Yin. Among the ten wisdom Goddesses, Tārā resembles Kālī and is her first transformation. Time and life (Kālī) are related to the sound current of divine word, which is Tārā. Tārā is the power of sound (*śabda śakti*),

[9] David Frawley, *Tāntric Yoga and the Wisdom Goddesses*, Delhi: Motilal Banarsidass, 1996, pp. 76-83.

corresponding to Kālī as the power of time and transformation. The word is the consciousness of time, whereas time is the movement of the word. The word is the intelligence of time, whereas time is the body of the word. The creative vibration or the divine word is the underlying energy of time.

THE SAVIOURESS

The term Tārā means the deliverer or saviour, from the Sanskrit root *tri*, meaning "to take across", as to take across a river, the ocean, a mountain, or any difficult situation. The Goddess Tārā is called upon the emergencies or at crossroads where we require guidance as to which way to turn. Tārā is the saving knowledge. She is the saviouress. The idea of the Goddess as saving wisdom is as old as the Vedas, and is a common idea in many spiritual traditions.

Second, the term Tārā means "a star", as the root *tri* also means "to scatter" (the stars being scattered in the heavens). Tārā is the star of our aspiration, the muse who guides us along the creative path.

TĀRĀ AS OṀ

The divine word in both Hindu and Buddhist systems relates to the *mantra* *OṀ* is the power of sound, called *praṇava* or the original vibration. Tārā (masculine, the deliverer) is the Vedic name for *OṀ* or the God Śiva, who in the Vedas is also known as Rudra or the resounder, relating to the transformative power of the divine word. *OṀ* is called Tārā or Tārāka, the deliverer because like a boat, it takes us across (*tarati*) the ocean of ignorance (*saṁsāra*). The main Sanskrit word for boat or ship (*nau*) also means the word (*nau*) and, as a feminine term, indicates Tārā. Tārā thus saves us from drawning or shipwreck, both literally and figuratively (being drowned by our emotional suffering in life).

As the power of deliverance Tārā is related to the Goddess Durgā, who similarly takes us across all difficulties (*durgāni*). Hence, she is also called Durgā-Tārā. Whereas, Durgā represents the power that overcomes or destroys obstacles and difficulties. Tārā is the power which takes us beyond them. While Durgā is more appropriate to call on in extreme danger wherein we need help against negative forces assailing us, Tārā has the additional power to lift us up in life generally. Tārā is the power to transcend all things. She not only lifts us beyond dangers but allows us to rise beyond our achievements and accomplishments to higher levels or realization. As the ultimate obstacle, we have to cross our own mind. Tārā provides the power to take us beyond the turbulent waves of our thought currents, which are nothing but a fragmentation of the sound current or divine word.

Tārā is the feminine form of *OṀ* or *OṀ* personified as a Goddess. Tārā is the unmanifest sound that exists in the ether of consciousness, through which we can go beyond the entire manifestation. Tārā is *OṀ* that has the appearance of the ether and which pervades the ether as its underlying vibratory support, but also transcends it. *OṀ* is the unmanifest field behind creation, which is the destroyer as well as the Creator of the Universe.

OṀ AS THE TEACHER OR GURU

OṀ is the sound that reveals all other words and their different meanings. *OṀ* or the primal sound is the original ether behind all creation, but it is a little different than ether in the ordinary sense. Ether in the ordinary sense is just a medium. *OṀ* also has a luminous nature and reveals things.

According to Patañjali's *Yoga-Sūtras*, *OṀ* is the voice of Īśvara, the Lord, the primal world-*guru*. All his instructions come forth through *OṀ*. Hence, we must first contact the power of *OṀ* for other *mantra*s to work and for their specific meanings to be known. We must first contact *OṀ* to know the *guru* or divine guiding power within us. Different *mantra*s are only valuable as various means of integrating us back into the primal unitary sound vibration which is *OṀ*. Hence, *OṀ* precedes all other *mantra*s. Only through their connection with *OṀ* can other *mantra*s be effective or be understood in their specific nature. As such, Tārā contains within herself all *mantra*s, and only through her grace can we come to understand and use them properly. Tārā is perhaps the most important Goddess of mantric knowledge, the very personification of *mantra* Śakti.

The same divine sound or primal root meaning enters into manifest sounds and affords them their particular meanings. Tārā gives poetic and oratory powers to her devotees, and should be worshipped by those who seek these capacities. One devoted to Tārā, it is said, can never be defeated in debate or in the display of literary talents.

SOUND AND BREATH

Tārā is the purifying force of the vital breaths. Sound that manifests in the ether is the same as the *prāṇa* (life-force) that manifests in the ether. Breath is the primal sound of life, and the sound of the original, spontaneous and unuttered *mantra* (*so 'ham*). Both mind and *prāṇa*, as word and vibration, have their root in sound. Hence, the use of sound or *mantra* purifies and energizes the mind.

TĀRĀ AS KNOWLEDGE

Tārā is the radiance of knowledge that arises from the differentiation of meaning through sound. Different sounds serve as vehicles whereby different ideas or meanings flash forth. *OṀ* is the underlying light that illumines these different sounds and allows meaning to flow through them. All meanings exist to reintegrate us into the ocean of meaning that is pure consciousness itself.

Tārā is thus of the nature of knowledge and inquiry into crossing over *saṁsāra* or the waters of darkness. All knowledge is a striving towards the infinite and the eternal, an attempt to link us back to some greater reality. This inherent aspiration of Tārā hidden in our speech and our thought is ever seeking to move us beyond the realm of the known.

Tārā relates specifically to the third of the four stages of speech, *paśyantī*, the state of seeing, the perceptive or illumined word. She is sound that perceives or reveals the truth. Knowledge and perception are thus not different than subtle sound. For the perfection of true knowledge, Tārā should be worshipped. Tārā is the Goddess of consciousness itself.

TĀRĀ AS SPEECH

In her manifest form, Tārā is consort (Śakti) of Bṛhaspati or Jupiter, the Vedic Lord of Wisdom, who is the Lord manifest sound.

As the abode of speech, Tārā relates to the tongue. In Sanskrit, tongue (*jihvā*) is a feminine term. On a mystic level the tongues are the tongues of fire (Agni) or the speech powers of the Cosmic Being (*puruṣa*). Tārā is not only the power of speech but the ability to discern the taste or flavour of things, the esthetic mind. She allows us to perceive the essence in all things, which is a perfect delight (*ānanda*). She helps the Soma or immortal nectar flow into us. As such she is connected with Soma or the Moon and with the esoteric (yogic), as opposed to the exoteric (ritualistic) path (represented by Jupiter).

In Pūraṇic mythology, Tārā (the stars) is the wife of Jupiter, but also has a secret love affair with the Moon. Tārā, thus, has a dual nature, both supporting knowledge (Jupiter) and ecstasy (the Moon). From her relationship with the Moon, she gives birth to a son, who is Mercury, the planet of speech and intelligence.

TĀRĀ AND GAURĪ

Tārā, as a form of Kālī, is another form of the consort of Lord Śiva. As such Tārā is called Gaurī, who is the wife of Śiva in her beneficent form. Gaurī represents the Divine Mother in her nurturing capacity, which is her capacity to increase spiritual knowledge within us. She represents pure light and knowledge standing beyond all ignorance and duality. Tārā takes us back to Gaurī, the Divine Mother who stands behind all the worlds.

UGRA TĀRĀ/NĪLA SARASVATĪ

Tārā has a wrathful or terrible form, which is called Ugra or fierce Tārā. In this capacity she is dark blue in colour and is also called Nīla (dark blue) Sarasvatī or the Goddess of Speech. The wrathful form of Tārā is thus also the wrathful form of Sarasvatī, which is the protective and destructive power of speech. Ugra Sarasvatī gives us victory in all debates and contests of knowledge, but for this we must be devoted to truth, not merely to our own opinions.

LOCATION IN THE BODY

"Tārā relates primarily to the navel *cakra*, which is the centre for the third or illumined stage of speech (*paśyantī*). Her other centre is the tongue. Yet because she is the rising sound current that leaps upward from the naval centre, she is not limited to this location. As *OM* or the *guru* she relates to the Third Eye or *ājñā cakra*. She is, thus, the rising current from the navel *cakra* to the head.

MEDITATION FORM

Tārā's meditation form is described as follows:

Mother, dark blue Sarasvatī, who grant all that is auspicious to those who surrender to you, who sit with your left leg extended, you who are the heart of Śiva, with a smiling lotus face.

Who have three eyes like budding lotus, the creatrix, who carry a severed head, a lotus, and a sword, I take refuge in you, the Supreme Lady of the worlds.

— Tārāṣṭakam 1

Tārā, like Kālī, is deep blue in colour. She has matted hair, wears a garland of human heads and has eight serpents for her ornaments. She is dancing on a corpse, has four arms and carries in her four hands a sword or head choppe, a scissors, a severed head and a lotus.

Tārā, like Kālī, is dark blue (Nīla) according to her tāmasic nature. *Tamas* (darkness) is the nature of the unmanifest. As Kālī is unmanifest time, Tārā, is unmanifest sound, from illumining the unitary nature of sound vibration (*nāda*). She has matted hair. Her eight serpents relate to the eight *siddhi*s (magic powers which give us the ability to assume any size and shape and to fulfil any desire we might have). Her scissors relates to her ability to cut-off all attachments. Her carrying a lotus flower symbolizes her open heart.

Tārā is also portrayed as white, particularly as relating to Gaurī, referring to her transcendent immaculate form. She is dark blue in her descent into creation. She is multicoloured in action in the outer world. In Buddhist thought, there are additional colours of Tārā according to her different functions as the Cosmic Mother (white, blue, yellow, red and green). These resemble not only Kālī but also Lakṣmī and Sarasvatī, the Hindu Goddesses of beauty and wisdom.

MANTRA

Tārā's main *mantra*, her *bīja* or seed-syllable, is *OṀ*. She can be worshipped simply by chanting *OṀ*. She possesses a longer five-syllable *mantra*:

oṁ hrīṁ strīṁ hūṁ phaṭ

OṀ is the *mantra* of deliverance (*Tāraka mantra*), *hrīṁ* is a *mantra* of purification and transformation. *Strīṁ* is the feminine nature (*strī*) and provides the power to give birth and sustenance. *Hūṁ* is the *mantra* of divine wrath and protection, as well as knowledge and perceptive power. *Phaṭ* also gives protection and destroys obstacles.

This *mantra* has two variations. Either the initial *OṀ* can be dropped — *hrīṁ strīṁ hūṁ phaṭ* — or both the initial *OṀ* and the concluding *phaṭ* can be dropped — *hrīṁ strīṁ hūṁ*. The three forms of the *mantra* relate to the three aspects of the Mother as pure consciousness, as the cosmic ruler, and as the *kuṇḍalinī* or serpent power. Sometimes, the second syllable is presented as *trīṁ*, which relates specifically to deliverance. Particularly in her wrathful role, Tārā can be worshipped simply by the *mantra hūṁ*, which is a significant part of all variations on her *mantra*. The *Tārā-Yantra* can be used along with the *mantra*.

The seer of Tārā's *mantra* is the Ṛṣi Akṣobhya. Akṣobhya means without disturbance and he represents the aspect of Lord Śiva that transcends all agitation. He is also one of the five *dhyānī* or meditation *buddhas* in the Buddhist tradition and symbolizes the mirror-like wisdom that reflects everything with detachment and which nothing can disturb. Only when the mind is free of agitation we can chant the *mantra* and gain its full power.

All people are entitled to use *OṀ*, which is called the Tārā-Vidyā or knowledge relating to Tārā. *OṀ* is not only for renunciates or for the initiated. It is the most universal and, therefore, most motherly of all *mantras*. It does not recognize any special outer requirements of class or age, nor any inner requirements of initiation, discipline or knowledge. It is the beginning and end of all the teachings and, hence, can be freely used by eveyone according to their aspirations.

MEDITATION APPROACHES

Tārā's main meditational approach is through *mantra*, particularly repeating *OṀ*, which be chanted along with the breath. While repeating *mantras* to Tārā, one should also call upon divine grace to save and deliver all beings, and thereby become Tārā oneself.

Another way to worship Tārā is to let the mind abide in the interval of silence between manifest sound — to try to hear the silence between sounds. The unmanifest sound *OṀ* exists in the interval between manifest sounds, but owing to our attachment to manifest sounds we fail to hear it. While repeating *OṀ*, one should trace the root of thought, following the sound current back to its source in silence. All thought is a kind of sound vibration. At the root of all thought is *OṀ* or Tārā, which takes us to our inner self (*ātman*) that is pure silence. If we do this we will find the energy of our awareness naturally arising and ascending, lifting us effortlessly beyond all obstacles, dangers and attachments.

In *Daibi Śakti* (an Oriya magazine),[10] edited by Haradhan Banarjee, the author came across the full description of Cāndīpur Tārā Pīṭha and the iconography of the original Goddess Tārā, which is always kept in disguise. The original Tārā

[10] "Nigamananda Sadhana Piṭha Āśrama, Kolkata (Courtesy), *Daibi Śakti* (Oriya Spiritual monthly magazine), Hardhan Banarjee (ed.), Sirlonabagram, Raghunathpur, Cuttack, September 1995, pp. 9-39.

fig. 11.1: *Tārā-Yantra.*

deity of Tārā Pīṭha is conceded of its identity because the iconographical shape of the deity is of unusual character — Goddess Tārā is breast feeding, her left breast to Lord Śiva, her own husband.

The myth of Cāndīpur Tārāpīṭha is very popular. The myth is that Vasiṣṭha (not to be confused with Vedic Ṛṣi Vasiṣṭha) was a great devotee of Goddess Tārā. To get more knowledge of Tārā worship, he visited Mahācīna. There he found that the left hand devotees were worshipping Goddess Tārā with wine and goat sacrifice. He became bewildered of the exciting worship and told them that even they worship in this manner for one thousand years, they will not get or receive any spiritual advancement. Thereby the worshippers of Goddess Tārā at Mahācīna got angry and cursed him. At last Vasiṣṭha came back and expired or left his mortal body at Candranātha.

In the next birth, Vasiṣṭha went to Cīna for spiritual austerity and received revelation by worshipping Lord Buddha that he will get divine grace and boon, if he meditated and worshipped Goddess Tārā. Who resides at the bank of north flowing Dwārakā River in Birbhum. Accordingly, Vasiṣṭha came back and worshipped with great austerities. While practising severe austerities, a desire developed in Vasiṣṭha's mind, within rigorous worship and he asked the boon that he desired to have the vision of Goddess Tārā breast feeding Lord Śiva. Goddess Tārā replied that it couldn't be, because Lord Śiva was her husband and asked Vasiṣṭha to close his eyes for a moment. When Vasiṣṭha opened his eyes, he witnessed a sculptural image of Goddess Tārā breast feeding Lord Śiva, installed in the front.

So, this is the real original iconographical image of Goddess Tārā at Cāndīpur Tārā Pīṭha of Birbhum district, West Bengal. When such sculptural image is found fixed on the north niche of the modern Dhabaleśvara temple at Mohangiri. It can be supposed that this idea or spiritual tāntric vision was brought by the Mudgala kings to this hinterland of Kālāhāṇḍī, as they originally ruled, the north-eastern Orissa, bordering Bengal.

A great devotee *alias* intoxicated mystic, *Yogī* Bāmā Khepa[11] of Mā Tārā at Tārā Pīṭha had a *darśana* (vision) of Mā Tārā. He entered *mahāsamādhi* in CE 1911.

---

[11] Elizabeth U. Harding, *Kālī: The Black Goddess of Dakshineswar*, Delhi: Motilal Banarsidass, 1998, pp. 274-81.

12

Jyoti Darśana of Prafulla Chandra Bhanja Deva and the Archaeological Discoveries

RAJKUMAR Prafulla Chandra Bhanja Deva was the scion of the ruling Bhañja dynasty of Mayūrbhañj state, now in the Orissa province and had married the Mahārānī Prafulla Kumari Devi of Bastar state, now in the Chhattisgarh province.[1] He was authoritative as a theorist and practitioner, being the favourite disciple of Sadguru Paramahaṁsa Nigamānanda Sarasvatī, who, in turn, was the disciple of Bāmā Khepa, one of India's greatest tāntric.[2] After *guru*'s *samādhi*, the departured prince, in his wanderlust, met famous Tārā Khepa at Tārāpīṭha and became the disciple of Yukteśvaragiri — Guru of Yogānanda, the celebrated author of *An Autobiography of a Yogi*, wherein Prafulla appears:[3]

> Master, so far as I know, was never at close quarters with a leopard or tiger. But a deadly cobra once confronted him, only to be conquered by his love. The encounter took place in Purī, where my *guru* had a sea-side hermitage. Prafulla, a young disciple of Śrī Yukteśvara's later years, was with master on this occasion.
>
>> "We were seated outdoors near the *āśrama*", Prafulla told me. A cobra appeared nearby, a four-foot length of sheer terror. Its hood was angrily expanded as it raced towards us. Master gave a welcoming chuckle, as though to a child. I was filled with consternation to see Śrī Yukteśvarajī engage in a rhythmical clapping of hands. (The cobra swiftly strikes at any moving object within its range. In most cases complete immobility is one's sole hope of safety.)

---

1 *ATSATBWOBS*, 2007, p. 3.

2 Juga Bhanu Singh Deo, *A Man Called Prafulla Chandra Bhanja Deva*, Bhubaneswar: the Author, 2005, p. 7.

3 Ibid., 2005, vide Back Cover page, extracts from *Autobiography of a Yogi*, by Yogananda, Bombay: Jaico, 1946, *passim*.

> He was entertaining the dreaded visitor: I remained completely quiet, inwardly ejaculating fervent prayers. The serpent very close to the master, was motionless, seemingly magnetized by his caressing attitude. The frightful hood gradually contracted, the snake slithered between Śrī Yukteśvarajī's feet and disappeared into the bushes. "Why the master would move his hands and why the cobra would not strike them were inexplicable to me then." Prafulla concluded, "I have since come to realize that our divine *guru* is beyond fear of hurt from any creature" (p. 110).
>
> It is interesting to observe that the master has merely to clap his hands and, before finishing, he is attended by some small disciple. Incidentally, I am much attracted to one of them — a thin lad, named Prafulla, with black hair falling to his shoulders, a penetrating pair of sparkling black eyes, a heavenly smile: his eyes twinkle, as the corners of his mouth rise, like the stars and the crescent moon appearing at twilight. Prafulla was the lad who was present with the master when a cobra approached (p. 372).

Before dealing about mystique tāntric scholar Prafulla Chandra Bhanja Deva, it is worth knowing the life of Bāmā Khepa.

Bāmā Khepa, Mā Tārā's God-Intoxicated Saint

Elizabeth U. Harding[4] deals about Mā Kālī's God-intoxicated mystics and gives a narration about Bāmā Khepa:

> Although Bāmā Khepa is not particularly known for worshipping Kālī, he was such a great mother worshipper and contemporary of Śrī Ramakrishna that he should be mentioned in this book. Bāmā Khepa worshipped mother in the form of Tārā and became a famous tāntric saint practising *sādhanā* at the Tārāpīṭha cremation ground. Tārāpīṭha in West Bengal is difficult to get to and therefore only a few Westerners have visited this ancient spiritual centre. Tārāpīṭha is situated in the district of Birbhum, home of the Bauls and birthplace of famous Vaiṣṇava and Śākta saints.
>
> Bāmā Khepa was born in 1837 — one year after Śrī Ramakrishna near Tārāpīṭha in the village of Atla. Although his parents were poor brāhmaṇas, Bāmā Khepa's father Sarvananda Chatterjee, was well known and respected for his piety and so was Bāmā Khepa's mother, Rājkumārī. His name was actually Bāmā, but since he showed absolutely no interest in worldly matters even

[4] Elizabeth U. Harding, *Kālī: The Black Goddess of Dakshineswar*, Delhi: Motilal Banarasidass, 1998, pp. 274-81.

from early youth, people called him mad and added "Khepa" (mad) to his name. Khepa is a term used mostly by tāntrics and Bauls and is not an ordinary madness. One who is called Khepa is generally considered a great soul.

As a young boy, Bāmā Khepa had a peculiar habit. At the dead of night, he liked to steal into his neighbours' houses, take their images of Gods and Goddesses and carry them to a river bank some distance away. There he worshipped the images all night long. When, in the morning, the villagers couldn't find their family deities they would make a big scene. Bāmā Khepa was discovered as the culprit but no matter how severely his parents scolded him, they could not prevent him from taking the images.

Bāmā Khepa's education never went beyond the simple village school he attended. There was not enough money in the family to send the boy away for higher education and study of the scriptures. His father died when Bāmā Khepa was very young, and, therefore, his mother and widowed elder sister were the first ones who gave him any kind of spiritual instructions. They told the boy ancient Hindu stories from the *Rāmāyaṇa* and *Mahābhārata*, and it was due to their efforts that Bāmā Khepa developed a spiritual sentiment early in life. He enjoyed singing devotional songs which he became rather good at it to the delight of his mother and elder sister.

Financial troubles worsened, and Bāmā Khepa's mother had sent him and his brother to live at an uncle's house. The uncle made an effort to make the boys active parts of his family and dispatched them to look after his cows. But when he found Bāmā Khepa unfit to take care of even this simple task, he sent him back home to his mother.

Bāmā Khepa proved incompetent to perform any kind of work. All he wanted to do was worship Mother Tārā. When he saw a red hibiscus flower, he thought of Mā Tārā. When he uttered Mā Tārā, he became unconscious of his surroundings. Even his mother was convinced her son was mad and, in order to keep him out of harm's way, she put him under house arrest. But at an opportune moment, Bāmā Khepa broke out, swam across the river Dwārakā and walked all the way to holy Tārāpīṭha.

He had heard about Kailāsapati Bābā, the well-known tāntric who was believed to be a realized soul. Bāmā Khepa went straight to his cottage. Recognizing Bāmā Khepa's potential for spiritual realization, the Bābā accepted him as his disciple. Bāmā Khepa began to practise serious tāntric *sādhanā* under the guidance of Kailāsapati Bābā.

Meanwhile, Bāmā Khepa's mother was worried about her son and, after a long search found him in Kailāsapati Bābā's cottage. When she realized that she couldn't persuade him to come with her, she asked one of her family members who was a prominent man in town to help him. This uncle, by the name of Durga Charan Sarkar, was an agent of the Mahārāja of Natore and using his influence in Tārāpīṭha, he procured Bāmā Khepa a job of collecting flowers for the service at the Tārāpīṭha temple.

But Bāmā Khepa was not meant for work, and couldn't perform this task. Instead of picking flowers, he sat absorbed in thoughts of the divine mother. Forgetful of his physical comforts, he was unaware if it was day or night, hot or cold, rain or sunshine. Smoking hemp, he lived in the Tārāpīṭha cremation ground surrounded by snakes, dogs, cats and jackals.

Although Bāmā Khepa seemed to have caused nothing but trouble to his mother, and he had not contacted her for a long time, he had great love and reverence of her. When news reached Tārāpīṭha that she had died and that her body could not be brought to the Tārāpīṭha cremation ground due to excessive flooding, Bāmā Khepa swam across the flood-swollen river. With his mother's dead body in his arms, he returned to Tārāpīṭha and asked his brother Ramcharan to perform the funeral rites. How could this poor family afford to pay for the funeral? By divine providence, as it were, money and food came to feed all the guests. People in Tārāpīṭha still tell the story about the dark clouds that appeared in the sky as the body of Bāmā Khepa's mother was burnt. Though all the Tārāpīṭha was flooded by the sudden heavy downpour, not a single drop fell on the funeral gathering.

Bāmā Khepa was in the habit of moving around completely naked. One day someone asked him "why are you naked?" Bāmā Khepa replied, "My father (Śiva) is naked, my Mother (Tārā) is also naked. So, I am practising that. Moreover I don't live in Society. I live in the cremation ground with my mother. So, I have no shame or fear!

Under the guidance of his Guru Kailāsapati Bābā and the tāntric master Mokṣānanda, Bāmā Khepa completed all the major tāntric rites and *sādhanā* in accordance with the Śāstras. It is interesting that Bāmā Khepa, like Śrī Ramakrishna, practised Tantra while remaining absolutely celibate. Just as Śrī Ramakrishna, Bāmā Khepa also looked upon women as mother. One day a beautiful, young woman tried to tempt Bāmā Khepa by offering herself to him as his Bhairavī. No matter how much she tried, she could find no "male sign" in him. Suddenly, Bāmā Khepa cried out "Mā Tārā" and bit the woman's breast. Blood oozed from her breast and she fell down, unconscious.

When Bāmā Khepa's spiritual guides saw that their disciple had attained perfection, Kailāsapati Bābā and Mokṣānanda installed him as the spiritual leader of Tārāpīṭha and left. Yet nothing, not even thigh high honour, could bind Bāmā Khepa. He neglected to follow temple regulations and did not obey social rules. Sometimes, he sat with stray dogs, sharing his food with them, and sometimes he answered calls of nature within the holy temple terrain. He was not concerned, and the thought of purity or impurity did not enter his mind. He had practised same-sightedness for so long.

One day the temple priests caught Bāmā Khepa eating the temple food before it was offered to Mā Tārā. They were so angry with him that they stopped supplying him with food. Four days after this incident the Mahārānī of Natore had a strange dream. Mā Tārā appeared to her and said. "I am thinking of leaving this place. I asked my favourite son Bāmā Khepa to eat, and the priests have beaten him and taken away food. If my son does not eat first, how can I, his mother?" When she woke up, the Mahārānī ordered that, henceforth, Bāmā Khepa should be fed before Mā Tārā. After that, nobody dared to obstruct Bāmā Khepa.

The mad saint of Tārāpīṭha became famous for his yogic powers and even people from far away came to see him. Some sought nothing but his blessings, while others asked to be headed or helped in distress.

Bāmā Khepa healed many sick people with his psychic powers. Once a dying man came to Tārāpīṭha and asked Bāmā Khepa for *prasāda*. Bāmā Khepa took pity on him and fed him with his own hand. Soon after, the man miraculously recovered and walked home. There was a leper in Tārāpīṭha by the name of Nanda Handi, who belonged to the untouchable caste. Nanda often brought Bāmā Khepa food and, although he was a brāhmaṇa of the highest caste, Bāmā Khepa accepted Nanda's food. In return for the favour, he gave Nanda some mud one day and asked him to rub it on his sores. Nanda did as told and the terrible leprosy left his body.

A man from Belagram by the name of Nimai suffered terribly from hernia problems. He had so much pain that he was unable to maintain his family. Thinking he was of no use to anybody, not even to himself, he resolved to commit suicide. Rope in hand, he came to Tārāpīṭha one dark night with the intention to hang himself. Suddenly, he heard a terrible voice. It was

Bāmā Khepa calling upon Mā Tārā. Nimai was too scared to commit suicide and, not knowing what to do with himself, he remained in Tārāpīṭha near Bāmā Khepa. One day Nimai, enraged Bāmā Khepa because he lit his pipe on Bāmā Khepa's holy *dhūnī* fire. The angry saint kicked the hernia patient in the lower part of his abdomen and Nimai fell down unconscious. But to his great surprise, when Nimai got up some time later, he was completely cured of his hernia afflictions.

Another story about Bāmā Khepa tells of a dying tuberculosis patient who was brought to the saint on a stretcher for final blessings. Instead of blessing the man, Bāmā Khepa caught him by the neck. Furiously choking and shaking the man Bāmā Khepa shouted, "Now, will you commit anymore sin?" Strangely enough, after Bāmā Khepa's rough treatment, the man got off the stretcher, asked for some food and drink and then walked home healthier and wiser.

But not all people who approached Bāmā Khepa were so lucky. When a couple of snobbish young men made fun of Bāmā Khepa because he shared his food with stray dogs, Bāmā Khepa suddenly touched them. To their horror, they saw that Bāmā Khepa and the dogs had turned into Gods while they had turned into hideous bats.

Having heard about Bāmā Khepa's healing powers, a priest by the name of Nagen Panda brought a dying man to Tārāpīṭha. The sick man was very rich, and Nagen Panda thought that he would be richly rewarded if he could get Bāmā Khepa to cure him. But contrary to Nagen Panda's expectation, Bāmā Khepa did nothing of the sort. He just uttered the word *phaṭ*, and the man died immediately. Furious, Nagen Panda accused Bāmā Khepa of killing the man. "I am not responsible," said Bāmā Khepa, "for it was the mother who spoke through me."

Bāmā Khepa was not learned but the mother revealed everything to him, as he used to say. The saint of Tārāpīṭha lived a long life and through his holy presence sanctified the place and the people who came in contact with him. He entered *mahāsamādhi* in 1911.

Mysterious are the ways of creation. As stated, Prafulla Chandra Bhanja Deva was the favourite disciple of Sadguru Paramahaṁsa Nigamānanda Sarasvatī whose head *maṭha* is now at Halisahar, near Kalyani, West Bengal.[5] It is worth of knowing

[5] *ATSATBWOBS*, 2007, p. 13.

about him, because his "Jyoti Darśana" narration as given in Appendix II solves the obscure yogic spiritualities, which developed in Āgneya-Koṇa.

Rajnath Singh[6] mentions that the central feature of the cosmogony of the Tantras is the female principle, the male principle having only a secondary position. This female dominated world-view is in substantial agreement with that of the Sāṁkhya, according to which the material *prakr̥ti*, conceived as a female principle, is the cause of the universe and the *puruṣa* or the male principle is nothing but a passive spectator. There is reason to believe that the Sāṁkhya philosophy was originally a development of the primitive proto-materialism which formed the sub-stratum of Tantrism itself.[7] The anomalous position of the male principle of the Sāṁkhya and the Tantra philosophy can presumably be traced to the anomalous position of the males in the primitive female-dominated societies, in which the male had something to do in the matter of procreation but in the family he is insignificant and a passive spectator, exactly like the *puruṣa* of the Sāṁkhya philosophy.

As dealt in Chapters 1, 2, 5 and 7 of this book, *sr̥ṣṭi-yantra* (*yantra* of creation) has been discovered from the Boden Block area. This was originated from the Sāṁkhya Yoga and influenced the growth of *yoga* of sexual transformation, shape of Lord Jagannātha and its cult, Kosali style of Rekha temple architecture, Kosali styles of Khakhāra temple architecture, Kaliṅga style of temple architecture, erotic sculptural art and the Sixty-four Yoginī cult. The whole of Sāṁkhya Darśana, in its all *yantra* aspects, was experienced during Jyoti Darśana, by a tāntric scholar of twentieth century CE in the Orissa province.

Rajkumar Prafulla Chandra Bhanja Deva*

"Lal Saheb",[8] Prafulla Chandra Bhanja Deva was born on 23 May 1909 at Baripāḍā,

* MA, Cantab., FRAS, Fellow of Utkal University, former prince of Mayūrbhañj, consort of mahārānī of Bastar State, former President of Ganatantra Parishad Party and former Member of Parliament (Rajya Sabha).

6 Rajnāth Singh, *Religious Tāntricism*, vol. 2, New Delhi: Dominant Publishers and Distributors, 2001, p. 260.

7 Ibid., Debiprasad Chhattopadhayaya, *Lokayata*, New Delhi, 1968, p. 360ff.

8 "Lal Saheb" is an honorific title given to a princely order, whose nomenclature differs from place to place, in Orissa. In this case, being the scion and first cousin of the then Mahārāja, Prafulla comes under the category of Raj Kumar, R.K., etc.

Here the first brother was Mahārāja Shree Ram Candra Bhanja Deva, whose achievements and

→

House of the Bhañja of Mayūrbhañj

Dāmodara Bhañja
(ruled CE 1761-96)

1st wife Sumitrā
(ruled 1796-1810)

2nd wife Jamunā
(d/o Abhiram Singh of Seraikella. Had two sons who died premature (ruled 1810-13)

Tri Bikram Bhañja
(adopted from Keoñjhar, s/o Balabhadra Bhañja)
(ruled 1813-22)

Rājā Jadunāth Bhañja
(ruled 1822-63)

Śrī Rāmcandra Bhañja Deva
(b. 17.12.1871
d. 22.2.1912)
(ruled 1892–1912)
Minor ascended *gaddī* in 1892

Chotrai Śrī Shyam Candra
(by adoption went to become as Śrī Śyāma Candra Mardarāj Rājā of Nilgiri State 1885 (d. 1913)

Rasala Mañjarī Devī,
married to Rājā Narpat Singh of Porahat Chakradharpur

Routrai Śrī Dam Candra
(d. 6.2.1946)
married to Ramesh Priyā Devī from Seraikella state

1st wife
Lakṣmī Kumārī Devī gd/o Mahārāja Nīlamaṇi Singh of Chota Nagpur in 1896 (d. 1902)

2nd wife
Suchari Devī
d/o. Keśava Candra Sen, founder of Naba Bidhan Brahma Samaj
married in 1904

Dhubendra Son
d. 2.8.1942
(R.A.F. Pilot
d. in W.W. II)

Daughter
Jyoti (Jayati Mañjarī)
became Rānī of Nandgāon

Son Pūrṇa
(b. 07.8.1899)
(d. 21.4.1928)
ascended *gaddī* on 13.11.1920
married to Takhat Kunwar Ba (d/o Mahārāja Omar Singh of Kathiawada) on 27.01.1917

Daughter
Sripat Mañjarī

Son Pratap
(b. 18.2.1901)
(d. 15.7.1968)
ascended *gaddī* on 23.4.1928
married to Prem Kumārī Devī, Princess of Sahapura 25.11.1925

Son Prafulla
(b. 23.5.1909)
(d. 05.3.1959)

the capital of Mayūrbhañj state, the biggest state in the Orissa province. He was the only child of his father Routrai Saheb Śrī Dām Candra Bhañja Deva,[9] uncle of the ruler, the Mahārāja of Mayūrbhañj, and mother Ramesh Priyā Devī,[10] a princess from Seraikella.

Routrai Saheb was the virtual head of the Mayūrbhañj state who ruled as the regent, because both his nephews — Pūrṇa and Pratāpa — were minors. Pratāpa was eight years older to Prafulla. Routrai Saheb was held in great veneration by the people, his subjects for the nobility of his character and loftiness of his views.

The story goes that Routrai Saheb had the habit of going around Baripāḍā, the capital of Mayūrbhañj state, on elephant back, keeping abreast with the affairs of the kingdom. One day, on the outskirt of the town the elephant's leg got struck, in the marsh near a stream that joins, at a short distance, the main river, Budha Bolaṅga. The elephant started trumpeting. He ordered the *mahout* (elephant-driver) to get down and inspect the leg to check if the pachyderm might have trampled on a thorn or some sharp object. He also got down from the mount *howdah*, and started giving a helping-hand to the *mahout*. To his utter amazement, he could fork-out a *Śivaliṅgam* from the depths of its marshy water. On that day Lord Śiva came in his dream and Routrai begged him with a request to grant him a child. Śiva gave blessings, assuring fulfilment of Routrai's long wait, provided Routrai constructs a beautiful temple at a spot he found him. For long many years after marriage Routrai Saheb and his wife remained without a child. However, with this Divine blessing and propitiation, she conceived and gave birth to Prafulla — their only child. Right on the day of the prince's birth, the construction of Pañca-Ratna-Mukhī five-headed temple started in honour of Śiva to propitiate the Lord and, on completion, Baruneśvara Mahādeva (another name of Śiva because he emerged from the water) was consecrated and

---

→ contribution to the well-being of Orissa are written in golden letters. His biography is treated as a textbook in Orissa School Curricula till the present day. Orissa's oldest, foremost and the best medical college at Cuttack was donated by him and named after him as "Shree Ram Candra Bhanja Deva Medical College and Hospital", in short "S.C.B. Medical College".

The second brother, carrying the title of "Chotrai Saheb", Shree Shyam Candra Bhañja Deva, went to become the Rājā of Nilgiri, by adoption for the continuance of Bhañja family/lineage as *Mardarāj*.

[9] The third brother of the ruler is addressed as Routrai Saheb.

[10] Ramesh Priya Devi d/o Devi Dutt Singh, gd/o Ram Mohan Singh and ggd/o Raja Ajambar Singh of Seraikella — thereby a cousin of Tikayet Nruparaj Singh.

pūjā performed. The temple still exists and is the cynosure of the town specially during the annual Śiva-Rātri — night of Śiva celebrations.[11]

Young Prafulla could not speak for five years. When he started talking he got his primary education at home since he was not sent to a formal school. His father had kept the best of private tutors — Maithilī brāhmaṇa Budhi Nath Pandit teaching Vedānta and Narayan Tripathy, having perfected Tārā Mantra at Bhusandpur Ugratara — when he showed his steak of brilliance at an early age. However, in order to inculcate discipline, he was made to cycle down 15 km to attend Krushna Chandra Mission School, which he did for quite some time. He had the best exposure to all good things around him.

The prince joined Raj Kumar College, Raipur, in 1919 and stayed there for three years to obtain his diploma. He surprised everybody with his exceptional brilliance by topping the all India list of successful candidates.[12] It is of particular significance that in the "Character Certificate", the principal found it necessary to remark that "Prafulla could be led, but not driven".

The British found out, when he was 14, that Prafulla was the right person to finally get married to the princess (minor) Prafulla Kumārī Devī of Bastar — destined to become the Mahārānī of Bastar.[13] He was given special training in administration to conduct himself as the designated "would-be-consort, to the Mahārānī of Bastar" — somewhat like Prince Philip, the Duke of Edinborough, is to the Queen Elizabeth II of England.

Finally the marriage between Lalsaheb Kumar Prafulla Chandra Bhanja Deva and Prafulla Kumārī, the Mahārānī of Bastar, took place on 20 January 1927 at Jagdalpur, the capital of the Bastar state.

Their's was a happy marriage and the young couple were supremely happy with each other and acted in all matters in one accord. Even both their names begin with Prafulla: one Candra, other Kumārī. The extended honeymoon, lasted

---

[11] As of now, the temple, since constructed, has suck in by 20 inches. Nearby is the cremation ground with the temple of Goddess "Tārā".

[12] Kumar Donger Singh of Suarmer Zamindari (Komakhan), later his colleague in Cambridge, was the "Joint-First" with Prafulla in Diploma Examinations.

[13] The historical truth:

It was Pratap, who, at first, was considered for the marriage with Prafulla Kumārī of Bastar. As Pūrṇa was issueless — being impotent — he stopped Pratap going elsewhere because Mayūrbhañj *gaddī*, would therefore have remained vacant and the question of resultant succession. Hence, the decision by Hobson's choice that Prafulla would marry her.

five months in Kashmir. Prafulla became the darling of his wife and they bore four children: two sons and two daughters.[14] He also became the darling of the Bastar subjects, having felt they had found the man for the dynastic continuity. He moved from Baripāḍā (Mayūrbhañj) to Jagdalpur (Bastar) — to the dislike of the British much later, who viewed him as a "nosy-parkar".

This naturally won him tremendous influence amongst the people and proportionately also proved an eye-sore to the government and its agents. They started deprecating and discouraging the devotion that he was showing to his religious-cum-spiritual preceptor, Sadguru Nigamānanda, who was also his wife's *guru*.

Prafulla and His First Wife

However, Prafulla wholeheartedly devoted his time to judicial work and studied the customs and traditions of the Bastar House to foster and augment, which was the chief aim in his life. Noting the religious trend of the public, he ardently devoted himself to the study and practice of "Śakti" philosophy, which won him religious "head-ship" of the State — one of the prerogatives of the ruler.

In search of a *guru*, Prafulla came in contact with a naked *aghorī* (renunciate) Keśavānanda on the bank of the river Narmadā at village Sainkheda, who used to beat his disciples with a broom-stick — a form of blessing. He was sitting surrounded by dogs and advised Prafulla that his *guru* was waiting for him in Calcutta. Meanwhile, surprisingly, there was a letter from another adept, Pragyānanda Mahārāja of Kokila Maṭha (in reply to his request, made one-and-half years back) forwarding a book *Tāntric Guru* written by Nigamānanda,[15] mentioning Nigamānanda was staying in Calcutta at the residence of his disciple Phani Bhusan Mitra, advocate, at 203 Panchanan Tola Road, Howrah.

In December 1927, Prafulla took Mahārānī to Calcutta for the delivery of their first child, daughter Kamalā, born on 2 February 1928. Next day he met his "*guru-*

[14] Children:

Children:	First	Daughter, Bod Moni Kamla (b. 2.2.1928 at Calcutta; m. in Bijwa, U.P.; d. in 1954)
	Second	Son, Pravīr (b. 12.3.1929 at Calcutta; m. in Patan, Rajasthan; d. 25.3.1966)
	Third	Daughter, San Moni Gita (b. 29-10-1930 at Shillong; m. in Bonai, Orissa; d. 17-12-2002)
	Fourth	Son, Vijay (b. 4-3-1934 in London; m. in Sayala, Gujarat; d. 12-4-1970)

[15] Nigamananda wrote, among others, four famous books: 1. *Yogi Guru*, 2. *Gyani Guru*, 3. *Tantrik Guru* and 4. *Premik Guru*.

to-be" smoking *hukkā* and Nigamānanda asked, "What do you want?" Prafulla described all his experiences and desires, right from his childhood. Then after hearing him Nigamānanda smiled and said, "My child, I have been waiting for you all along; I have relation with you from the previous birth; you are lucky — you have got *Tārā mantra* — this is also my tutelary *mantra*". On 4 February 1928, Nigamānanda came over to Prafulla's house to bless his wife and daughter.

The *dīkṣā* (acceptance) by Sadguru Nigamānanda took place on the auspicious day of Śrāvaṇa Śuklāṣṭamī at Purī Nīlācala Sārasvat Āśrama Kuṭīra in the night, as per the same tāntric rites which he had received from his Guru, Bāmā Khepa.

During the Daśaharā of 1928, during 18-31 October, Nigamānanda visited Jagdalpur, the capital of Bastar, to give *dīkṣā* to Mahārānī, which was carried out with great devotion and fanfare. Daśaharā in Bastar focuses principally on the Goddess Danteśvarī, a form of Durgā. The entire festival is a riot of colour, and is a wonderful amalgam of local religious belief, mingling individual village divinities with ancient ritual and tribal customs. Although the chariot-ride of the royal couple was the "piece-de-resistance" (of the Daśaharā festival ending with the ceremonial *durbār*), the visiting Swāmījī became the centre of attraction. The Administrator Griegson met Nigamānanda on 31 October, and also to ascertain if he was taking the couple on *sādhanā patha*, i.e. *vairāgya* (renunciation of worldly duties). Guru replied, "Whilst remaining *gṛhastha* (married), mind can remain in spiritual path and that is what he preaches." Hearing this, Griegson returned satisfied.

In December 1928 Prafulla attended the Sarasvat Convention at Dacca and went around visiting great tāntric *pīṭhas* — starting with the most sacred Kāmākhyā Devī at Guwahati, Assam, and including Tārāpīṭha, made famous by Bāmā Khepa.

In due course, Prafulla became one of the most developed and gifted disciples of Nigamānanda, and the foremost in Orissa. He was probably the only disciple whom Nigamānanda found fit and eligible to meet Ek Jataṁba (*alias* Basanti Divya from Nāgā community — Guru Mā) — the reclusive Bhairavī Sādhikā of Bāmā Khepa — who inspired and infused in him the ultimate realm of Tantra Śāsana. Many felt he was a unique but a rare combination of "Lakṣmī and Sarasvatī" — i.e. spirituality, prosperity and wisdom.

Although an undeveloped state, Bastar is rich in deposits of iron-ore in southern Baila Dila range, timber and other natural resources. The Nizam of Hyderabad had always cast covetous eyes on it and had suggested to the British overlords for a treaty of perpetual friendship between the two states, which would eventually bring Bastar within its grasp. The prince was all against it and advised the Mahārānī against signing the treaty. He was offered bribes, estates and titles but he rejected all these and replied:

> If I am convinced that the treaty is in the best interests of the state and the people, I shall be the first person to ask the Mahārānī to sign it, otherwise no power on earth can force me to do so. After all I am the son-in-law of Bastar and not the Owner.

The prince stood undaunted — a young man at the tender age of 19 was above all temptations. He carried on with his reform movements, thanks to his wife who stood by him. The British did not like it. They wanted the Mahārānī to be the "puppet" in her governance; most of the decisions to be taken by the political agent. Small bickerings ensued, and the British started telling the Mahārānī that her husband was hob-nobbing in the affairs of running and ruling the Bastar state.

The Mahārānī made suggestions for a "joint-rulership" in the state, with her husband as the president in the Council of Regency. The main consideration for this was her ill-health due to early child births. Then, after the birth of the third child Gītā, she contracted infection, necessitating her to consult the famous doctor Bidhan Chandra Roy, who later became the chief minister of West Bengal. Besides, she wanted clarity from the government to safeguard and strengthen the succession, to obviate further Court-of-Wards rule, and give the state a real chance for self-expression under an active ruler, in view of the government's deliberate neglect of her administrative training. It was her hope that the government would consider her request with favour — especially as the succession of "consorts" and "son-in-laws" was not precedented in Hindu history. Her appeal and concern was for the sake of the state, her dynasty, her happiness, the future of her children and the undefined status of her husband — should anything happen to her!

All attempts were made futile as the political department would listen to no rights and logic except those that suited and pleased them. They did not wish to loosen their grip, and as the Bastar state was continuously under Court-of-Wards, for over 50 years, there could not be a situation of greater convenience than a woman ruler, untrained in governance, could be effectively bullied, dictated to and manipulated along with the undefined status of her husband, the consort.

It was around this time the proposal was brought forward to take the Mahārānī to England for treatment. It was a God sent opportunity to suggest that the entire family should go for broadening the outlook and upbringing of the children abroad.

The Mayūrbhañj people, chiefly Prafulla's cousin, the Mahārāja, were jealous of his growing popularity. Also he had a rift with his father — Routrai Saheb — due to his attachment and Mahārānī's religious preceptor, Guru Nigamānanda. Needless to say, Routrai Saheb had developed a soft corner for "Brahmo Samāj" movement, not to the liking of Prafulla. All heads put together, it was decided that Prafulla with Mahārānī and family be sailed for England in April 1931. (For detailed life, consult the works of Jugabhanu Singh Deo[16] and the author[17]).

Prafulla Chandra Bhanja Deva

(s/o Routrai Saheb Shree Dam Candra Bhanja Deva of Mayūrbhañj state)

(b. 23-5-1909) (d. 5-3-1959)

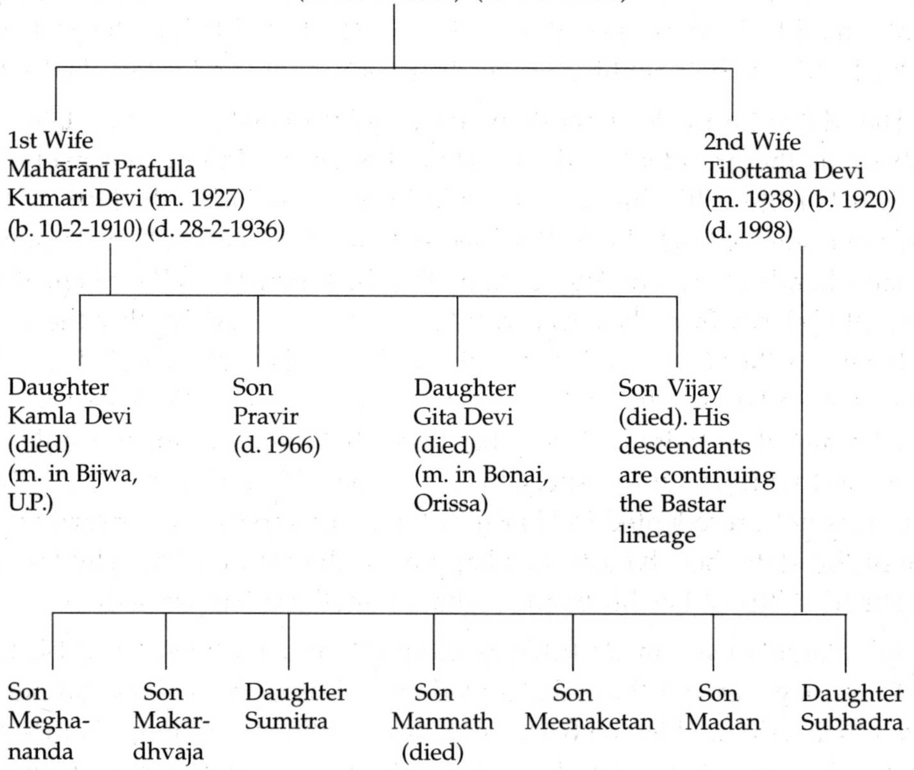

[16] Juga Bhanu Singh Deo, op cit., p. 166.

[17] *ATSATBWOBS*, 2007, *passim*.

In 1933, the Government of India recognized his wife, as the first Mahārānī of Bastar state and conferred on her successors the title of "Mahārāja".

In June 1935, the prince graduated with a high second class Honours and obtained his MA degree from the Cambridge University. He took archaeology and anthropology in his last year, due to the fact that there existed vast scope of research in these subjects in Bastar. He narrowly missed the first class in the final examination as he could put in only four months of study. Their spiritual Sadguru Nigamānanda Sarasvatī passed away on 29 November 1935 and Mahārānī Prafulla Kumari Devi of Bastar died on 28 February 1936 after nine years of their marriage. The circumstances in which Mahārānī of Bastar expired is descriptively dealt in author's book.[18]

Prafulla and His Second Wife

He moved to Cambridge after his first wife's death, bought a house, got married to the beautiful Tilottama Devi in 1938, who became his second wife. Pandit Jawaharlal Nehru was his contemporary in Cambridge. Sarvepalli Radhakrishnan had taught him philosophy there. George Bernard Shaw wrote about him, "I am yet to come across an Indian prince so highly qualified. I recommend him for any job under the sun."

From his second wife, he had seven children, five sons and two daughters (except the last two born in India), all were eligible to become "British citizens", to which none became so.

Prafulla's Life After the Independence

India got its freedom on 15 August 1947. A "Free India" meant to the prince as the end of his internment. He became a freeman. No more hounding by the prying eyes of the British sleuths simply overwhelmed him by gaining this freedom — the call of India, the expectation of his people back home, became his passion.

In 1948, after a total stay of fifteen years in England and leaving "the bed of roses" and friends, he boarded a warship, that took him three months via the Cape of Good Hope, to return home for good. He had to sell his house in England at Cambridge to defray the cost of clearing all past dues, compounded by war ravages, and as the price of leaving the shores of England with a large family.

On arrival in Bombay, Lal Saheb and his family stayed for a month at Taj Mahal Hotel. Then he moved to Orissa, whilst putting up his family in Banaras (Varanasi)

---

18 *ATSATBWOBS*, 2007, *passim*.

— considered to be the oldest city in the world, like Jerusalem — and decided to bring up his children in true Hindu tradition. He felt like transforming them, from the onslaught of foreign environment and culture to total Indianization — to imbibe the ethos of our *paramparā*. He put two elder sons in a school there.

In 1948, he went to Jagdalpur, where two lakh people gathered to usher him by constructing thirty gates and arches to welcome the "Mahārāja-Pitā" (Father of Mahārāja).

He was appalled, being an ardent nationalist and true Indian, to see disrespect shown to India's tri-colour by his son Pravīr, Mahārāja of Bastar. He used to write articles in the *New Statesman, Nation and United India*. Many of his research papers were published in different journals and papers of the world and can be found in many libraries of Europe and USA. Devastated, he decided to leave Jagdalpur forthwith, without a fuss. He found his other children, from the first wife, spoiled and neglected under the British care, indoctrinated with pro-British habits and anti-Indian sentiments. The children were deprived of their parent's love.

He left Jagdalpur (Bastar) and came to Baripāḍā (Mayūrbhañj), where he built a house for permanent establishment of his headquarter and shifted his wife Tilottama Devi and children from Calcutta in 1949. While constructing his new house at Baripāḍā, he used to live in a big tent, because he was not allowed to stay in the palace of Baripāḍā. His new house was named "Bhagavati Bhavan", the area now is known as Prafulla Nagar at Baripāḍā. It faces across the rivulet at Takhatpur — now renamed Sree Ram Vihar, the campus of the latest North Orissa University.

Hare Krushna Mahatab, the then prime minister of Orissa — invited him to utilize his services, to which Prafulla obliged to do it free, as he wanted to serve the people, serve the country to the best of his ability. He took up an honorary job with the Orissa Government as special officer for backward classes. He brought out a paper on problems faced by the *ādivāsīs*. There was police firing on them in Mayūrbhañj, for their aspiration for a separate autonomous body — as the Mayūrbhañj state got merged into the Union Territory on 1 January 1948, six months later than the Princely States. He did not like this, the functioning of government *apparitor*, got dissatisfied and resigned after a year of joining. During this period he brought a house at Gopalpur-on-Sea and the family lived there for quite some time.

He had started rice mills in Mayūrbhañj area. He was senate member of Utkal University. He joined the political party "Ganatantra Parishad", in 1950, started by

Mahārāja Rajendra Narayan Singh Deo of Patna and Mahārāja Pratap Keshari Deo of Kālāhāṇḍī, thus forming a *"Triloka"*. In two years of joining, and doing commendable work in the district of Mayūrbhañj, he not only became the president of the party in March, 1952 by winning 39 seats, out of 140 in the Orissa Legislative Assembly and five Lok Sabha (Lower House) and two Rajya Sabha (Upper House), but by sheer grit, determination and dedication was nominated by the party to be the Member of Parliament in the Rajya Sabha.

In 1952, when the "Jan Sangh" party was formed in Kanpur, R.N. Singh Deo (MP, Lok Sabha) and P.C. Bhanja Deo (MP, Rajya Sabha) represented Ganatantra Parishad to bless the formation of All-India Rightist Party, based on Indian tradition and nationalism. Atal Behari Vajpayee was then the secretary of Shyama Prashad Mukherjee — its founder.

He became a staunch critic of the government and threw challenges to the Congress government, as a member of the Opposition benches in the Upper House of the Parliament, on issues of political importance. He made solid contribution towards amelioration of the conditions of his people. Besides, his debates were of the highest order, significantly contributing to areas relating to finance, economics, agriculture, natural resources, people and population, foreign affairs, defence, etc.

He was twice elected to the Rajya Sabha.

(i) For the period 1952–1954 on 27 March 1952.

(ii) For the period 1954–1960 on 27 March 1954.

The Discovery of Deva Kuṇḍa and Jyoti Darśana

The author's cousin dada (elder brother) Juga Bhanu Singh Deo[19] of Seraikella has married Subhadrā Devī, the youngest daughter of Lal Saheb Prafulla Chandra Bhanja Deva, from his second wife Lal Saheb Tilottama Devi. He describes "Deva Kuṇḍa" (*Deva* — God, *Kuṇḍa* — pond = the celestial pond). The first of the five ponds or pools of water — with four above — the cascading "Devī" mountain-stream, connecting each other with cataracts, and descending down with a 50' waterfall into it — lies on the south-eastern slope of Meghasani mountain range of Simlipal Bio-sphere Reserve (SBR) and Tiger Project — National Park — in the Mayūrbhañj district of northern Orissa, forming a part of the Eastern Ghāṭs of India. Deeply forested and impregnable, it is the home of elephants, tigers (world

[19] *AMCPCBD*, 2005, pp. 78-88.

famous for Khairi), sambars with record-size antlers, teeming with rich flora and fauna of every hue. The peculiarities are: singing Myna, *Śyāma pakṣī* (a bird whose chirping sounds like *OṀ*) and flying squirrels — they let out a bizarre sound as they fly from one tree to another. The present census records, besides others, 500 elephants and 100 tigers.

Lal Saheb had stumbled upon this spot, exactly 50 years back, in 1954 — shrouded in mystery — due to the occurrence of some supernatural events, which became his "Tapo-bhūmi" (penance ground) for the rest of his life in pursuit of his *sādhanā* (deed of spiritual involvement in Tantra) with the sifting of "Jyoti Darśana" connected with "Pañca Sāgara Tīrtha" (pilgrimage to five oceans), and leading to his discovery of 51st Tantra Mātā Pīṭha of Śakti. His own version — pursuant his personal experience — in Oriya (translated into English by Juga Bhanu Singh Deo), appears in the end [vide Appendix II] who has married his second daughter Subhadrā Devī, born from his second Wife, Lal Saheb Tilottamā Devī.

"Deva Kuṇḍa", nestling amidst natural sylvan surroundings, has become famous as a "Tantra Pīṭha", and already made a mark in eco-tourism, where "Makar Melā" is fervently celebrated in every January. It is 10 km away from prince's "Khamar", farm-house at village Śrī Dam Chandrapur, 27 km from town Udala and 55 km from Baripāḍā.

Mercury, according to Hindu belief based on the Śāstras, is the *amṛta* alias *śukra* (semen) of Śiva (Bhairava). Deva Kuṇḍa and its vicinity is one of the very few places in India where mercury is found, though not commercially exploited. The recurrence of mercury itself shows its effect on *sphoṭika*s for the formation of rare crystals and availability of the other minerals.

Lal Saheb had found the spot where drops of mercury used to trickle-down on the rocky surface and get collected in a tri-angular receptacle, Amṛteśvarī — the "Guhya Mūrti" of Ambikā — which esoterically meant the *yoni* (vagina) of Śakti (Bhairavī).

Śiva, all over the world, is worshipped as the "phallus" symbol of *liṅgam* with *yoni*. This spiritual concept of the eternal cosmic union of male and female principles — as against physical manifestation of the same in the body and shape, as depicted in stone, mural, painting art, cloth, etc. — is wrongly understood in the mundane world as eroticism. It is the arousal of psychic energy Śakti (Kuṇḍalinī) from the *kuṇḍa* at the base of the body *mūlādhāra* (*mūla* — base; *ādhāra* — support), to traverse through the *suṣumṇā* nerve inside the back-bone and to meet with the "mystic-union" with Śiva in *sahasrāra* located at the crown of the head. This process is the attainment of permanent bliss, *sat-cit-ānanda*, the Supreme reach of human soul, the bed-rock of Tantra, for our body (a part micro) is the microcosm of the cosmos (whole-macro) macrocosm.

Lal Saheb was an adept and he had reached new heights in search for it. He realized what he found at Deva Kuṇḍa, was the culmination of his insatiable search for the truth. He constructed the temple there, commemorating Goddess "Devī Ambikā" erected the "Pañca-Muṇḍī-Āsana"[20] and sitting on this sacrosanct *siddha* seat did his *sādhanā*. Till today no one dare to sit on it, for fear of calamity befalling him.

Hindu mythology says at the beginning of the Vedic Age, prior to the Purāṇas, Devī committed suicide *satī* — unable to bear the insult thrown at her mendicant husband Śiva — by jumping into the *kuṇḍa* pit of religious fire invoked at the *yajña* being celebrated by her father, Dakṣa Prajāpati. On her death Śiva got so enraged that he went into frenzy, carrying the dead body of his wife — the corpse of Devī — on his shoulder danced awe-inspiring *tāṇḍava* which shook the three worlds and spelt doom for total annihilation. All, including the gods, requested Viṣṇu — the Preserver — to save them from extinction. So, Viṣṇu in order to diminish the wrath of Śiva, guided his weapon *sudarśana cakra* that cut Devī's dead body into pieces. There were 52 of them which fell in different parts of India and where they fell, each became famous in various names as "Mahā Pīṭhas of Śakti" (energy) for tāntric worship; holiest of them being at Kamrup Kāmākhyā (Guwahati, Assam) where her *yoni*, "Devī kuṇḍa" is considered to be the penultimate 51, where the fingers of her (Ambikā) left foot fell.

During *Mahābhārata* the entire tract was Ajñāta Vanavāsa of the Pāṇḍavas wherein five of them had to move incognito to serve the sentence-term inflicted on them by the Kauravas. After many thousand years, we find here their names in numerous places — of temples and ruins, either existing or non-existing — indicating the strong presence and activities of Pāṇḍavas during the *Mahābhārata* days. Let us name a few (in ex-Udala):

[20] Made of skulls of five dead people who died accidentally or due to unnatural causes. As per tāntric mysticism — they are Vetāl (spirits), whose "Pre-tā-tmā" (unrealized souls) are hovering around in the atmosphere without reaching salvation.

"Āsana" (seat) denotes the exaltiveness of *pañca muṇḍa* (5 heads) of Brahmā, the Creator.

1. Virāṭ Gaṛh — 6 km (south) — the capital of Virāṭ Kingdom.
2. Paṇḍara Village — named after the Pāṇḍavas: Śiva Pīṭha (north-east flows the river Subarnarekhā).
3. Arjun Dorah — 12 km (off village Poda Diha — flows the river Kālī). Dorah or Depth is a particular place in the river. Arjuna had moved around the place, following a curse, as Bṛhannalā (eunuch).
4. Bhīma Jukti — where Bhīma killed the demon Kīcaka.
5. Bhīma Pada — "Jāgṛt" Devī of Kanaka Durgā.
6. Bhīma Kuṇḍa — 40 km near Bangriposi of the river Baitaranī.
7. Bhīma Bharab Devī — 14 km village Pod-Gadi.
8. Pañca Liṅgeśvara — Panch Liṅgeśvara is located in Mayūrbhañj district of Orissa (previously Baripāḍā).
9. Som Vṛkṣa — 1000' high, beautifully shaped solid rock standing rounded at the top with crevices in its upper reaches — which can accommodate about 100 persons. Linked with the Pāṇḍavas, it is believed that Soma Latā (the celestial plant) was found here which oozed milk from its roots.

   It would be worthwhile for the *aficionados*, archaeologists, historians, discoverers and even laymen, deeply interested in the subject and area, to dig deep into its hoary past and unearth the richness of this beautiful tract of mountains, forests, rivers — as history is both hidden and strewn all over — and very little is done by any. It is still a virgin land.

Death of Lal Saheb Prafulla Chandra Bhanja Deva

On 4 March 1959, Prafulla Chandra Bhanja Deva complained of chest pain in the afternoon and so he left the Parliament House at 2 p.m. to retire to his MP quarter at 77, North Avenue, 1 km away from the Parliament. Invariably, he used to walk down to attend the Parliament, but not this time. He was admitted to the Willington Hospital at 9.30 p.m.

On 5 March 1959 morning, he passed away at 4.50 a.m., the day he was to speak on the budget in the Parliament. The House adjourned for the day as a mark of respect to the departed leader.

The Vice-President of India, S. Radhakrishnan, as the Chairman of Rajya Sabha (Upper House of Parliament), said:

Prime Minister Pandit Jawaharlal Nehru, his colleague in Cambridge, personally looked after the details of Prafulla's cremation, which took place at Nigambodh Ghāṭ on 7.3.1959, with Lal Bahadur Shastri being one of the pall-bearers and Bed Kumar Pratap Ganga Deb, MP, of Bamra gave the *mukhāgni* (the final send-off-rite). In Delhi circle he became famous as the "Mystique with a Red Ṭīkā". He was fair in complexion, of average height, slightly oval face with the trade-mark "Tilak of Rakta Candana" and his customary black cap, wore white *dhotī* with crumbled border (like the bellow of an accordion) and had an overpowering image of religiosity.

The then prime minister Jawaharlal Nehru, Lal Bahadur Shastri and others offered floral tributes to the departed Prafulla, at his North Avenue residence, New Delhi, before his body was taken for cremation at Nigambodh Ghāṭ.

The study of the life-story of Lal Saheb Prafulla Chandra Bhanja Deva is a saga of romance and courage, who faced the Britishers most doggedly and did what he felt was right — so sure of himself that he stood like a rock, in each and every step he took in life, and achieved mastery over what he cherished most. No other Indian prince could ever raise his head against the mite of mighty British Empire whose "sun never used to set on the earth".

A rare breed, a shining gem, he scaled new heights — as the leader likes to tread the untrodden path fearless, unique in style and action, is prepared to bend but not break.

It is impossible to emulate him, even we strive to achieve for it; for he was of a different period, of different generation, of a different zone, but very much one of us. An amiable person, he behaved like a commoner, mellowed with the passage of time — as a sacrifice for his persecution against heavy odds that he faced in life — but remained very Indian, a true patriot.

Prafulla's premature death — he was not even 50 — ended a brilliant personality, India lost an able son but the indomitable spirit of this man carries on . . .

Jyoti Darśana of Lal Saheb Prafulla Chandra Bhanja Deva

Tāntric scholar Prafulla Chandra Bhanja Deva had a Jyoti Darśana, i.e. he witnessed the Divine Jyoti (Divine Light) for half-an-hour at Deva Kuṇḍa, site, the then Mayūrbhañj state, now Mayūrbhañj district, as he confesses in his own Oriya writing on 23 January 1954. He had maintained detailed diary and noted in detail his experiences in a paper written, after four years later, in 1958. Thanks, that he wrote and acknowledged in writing, otherwise his experiences would have gone to oblivion and the ancient celestial glory of Āgneya-Koṇa would have become obscure.

Juga Bhanu Singh Deo[21] has done verbatim English translation of his Oriya writing, which is given in Appendix II.

This verbatim translation of Jyoti Darśana of Prafulla Chandra Bhanja Deva solves the mystery of the spiritual, yogic and cultural background of Āgneya-Koṇa region, whose centre is the Greater Mahānadī River Valley, comprising the modern provinces of Chhattisgarh and Orissa. This area was once Uḍḍiyāna Pīṭha in the ancient period. These aspects are described in earlier chapters of this book.

It is known from Makardhvaja Bhanja Deo, his second son from his second wife, Prafulla Chandra Bhanja Deva had a dream, while staying in England of Ambikā Devī, who revealed that she will give her Darśana, (i.e. reveal herself) to him, after the death of one of his children. It so happened that Prafulla Chandra Bhanja Deva[22] writes:

> Third Day's happening (23.1.1954) — Sitting on a stone inside *nadī* stream, after a bath for my evening prayers, suddenly my forehead was filled with infra-red light of the rising Sun. Now not knowing what to do, and thinking it must be something to do with the setting sun, I opened my eyes — there was no sign of the sun or any glow in the sky of the impending dusk, as it was fully covered with clouds. Again I closed my eyes — and then again that luminous object started pounding on my forehead. Somehow in the midst of this experience I could manage to complete my evening prayers.
>
> Some time elapsed thinking about the above. A courier came from Baripāḍā, bringing my "Dak" (mails), the news of passing away of my eldest daughter (Kamalā) of Bastar. The enactment of life and death, as well as showering of nectar by the bounteous Devī Bhagavatī, prompted me to proceed to the "Kuṇḍa" for "Darśana" and completion of my evening prayers. On completion, during the dinner time my chief aide, Shri Padma Lochan Jena, was by my side looking after me. He was heading west, to bring water for washing my hands, when he shouted aloud, "By father, what a big glow over Deva Kuṇḍa", saying this he got down from a rock and started running towards the Kuṇḍa (pond). We all ran behind him and stood still

[21] *AMCPCBD*, Bhubaneswar, 2005, pp. 196-216.

[22] Ibid., pp. 197-200.

— believers and non-believers — some chanting religious rhymes, others doing salutations and others with closed eyes offering prayers. The reflection of Divine Light — "Jyoti Darśana" — from Deva Kuṇḍa waters stretched towards us, all remained transfixed for about half-an-hour.

Everybody stunned looking at this strange appearance moving towards Deva Kuṇḍa. Surrounding me and my three children in the centre, my colleagues moved ahead and collected themselves at the edge of the pond. All were astonished to watch two powerful luminous objects, originating from the mountain opposite to us, were heading towards the waterfall. Whilst one in transit got diffused in the forest, but the other one came near the waterfall and stood before us. The colour of Jyoti — Fire Ball — was golden, superimposed are two squares and within the squares was *'AUṀ'* — inside two topsy-turvy inverted triangles having six-pointed ends.

At the end Padma Lochan Jena requested to make an "offering". Someone collected jungle fruits and after cleaning them in the pond come to me. I asked with what *mantra* should I make the offering? All said, "Whichever comes out straight from your heart — today, because of you we were fortunate for 'Jyoti Darśana'." I raised my hands, holding in my palms "Footy & Tarbhuj" fruit and focusing on my *iṣṭa devatā* recited (Sanskrit *śloka*):

suleno pahino devi khaḍgeno cāmbike
ghaṇṭa sva-neno-naḥ pahi-ca padyane
sva-neno-ca.

After recital of this *mantra,* I offered the "offerings" into the "Kuṇḍa".

After about fifteen minutes the Fire Ball slowly retracted, and got diffused in the forest. *Ādivāsīs*-workers, frightened to the core wanted to leave "Deva Kuṇḍa" that very night. However, after lots of persuasion for an hour, they were pacified to stay back for a couple of days.

Explanation of the Tāntric Interpretation on Jyoti Darśana (Fire Ball)

The Jyoti Darśana which was like a fire ball, experienced by the tāntric scholar Prafulla Chandra Bhanja Deva has much tāntric esoteric significance, which may be illustrated and explained thus:

> Jyoti (fire ball) was golden, superimposed are two squares and within the squares was *AUṀ* — inside two topsy-turvy inverted triangles having six-pointed ends.

fig. 12.1: Jyoti (Divine Light), as signed by tāntric scholar Lal Saheb Prafulla Chandra Bhanja Deo, at Deva-Kuṇḍa site of Mayūrbhañj district, Orissa, for fifteen minutes, on 23 January 1954.

This Divine Light experience is to be analyzed with its *yantra* manifestations. The *mantra, tantra* and *yantra*, each is a separate part of occult science and has its importance at its own place. *Yantra* means an instrument, appratus, talisman or mystical diagram. The use of mystical designs and magical diagrams, known as *yantra*, is of great antiquity, not only in India but in all countries. Among the early archaeological findings are included specimens of such designs and diagrams, which were neither strictly utilitarian nor solely decorative in function.[23]

According to S.K. Ramachandra Rao:[24]

> The possible *yantra*s are indeed innumerable. The combinations of the primary geometrical forms (triangles, circles and four sides figures) can be myriad, and the association of *mantra*s with the designs render the number of these

[23] Jyotis Shiromani L.S. Chawdhri, *Practical of Yantras*, New Delhi: Sagar Publications, 1984, pp. ix-x.

S.K. Ramachandra Rao, *Yantras*, Delhi: Sri Satguru Publication, 1988, p. 1.

[24] S.K. Ramachandra Rao, op. cit., 1988, p. 14.

combinations really huge. There is a Sanskrit text, comparatively recent, which enumerates as many as 10,000 *yantras*! The name of this text is *Yantroddhāra-Sarvasva,* and the author (anonymous) claims that he obtained all these *yantras* from *Atharvaveda,* not, however, explaining how. The largest well-known collection, however, is to be found as the supplementary section to *Saundaryalaharī,* ascribed to the great Śaṅkara: it contains 103 *yantras* with details concerning their use known as *prayoga*: Another text *Yantra-Cintāmaṇi* contains about eighty *yantras*; *Mantra-Mahodadhi* describes about seventy, *Prapañca-Sāra-Saṁgraha* about sixty, *Prayoga-Kaumudī* about fifty, *Mantra-Yantra-Mahārṇava* about the same number. Other texts like *Kāma-Ratna, Maṇi-Mantra-Koṣa, Devatā-Pūjana-Vidhi, Yantra-Prakāśa, Yantra-Pratiṣṭhā* and *Yantra-Pūjana-Prakāra* also contain numerous illustrations of *yantras.*

The two squares are interesecting each other and thereby making eight-pointed star is kāmakalā-yantra.[25] This kāmakalā-yantra is the plan of "Kosala style of Rekha temple style", which is found at: (i) Būḍhī Komnā site of Nuāpāḍā district, Orissa, (ii) Dhobanī site of Raipur district, Chhattisgarh, (iii) a temple in ruin at Adabhara site, near Kharsia in Bilaspur district, Chhattisgarh, and (iv) a temple ruin at Kansil village area in Rānīpur-Jharial complex site, known as Cheliā temple of Bolaṅgīr disctrict of Orissa province. This kāmakalā-yantra plan of "Kosali Rekha temple style" is studied to have influenced the development of temple architecture, throughout India.

Therefore, the author[26] had earlier mentioned that the "Kosali style of temple architecture" developed in South Kosala, during early Somavaṁśī ruling period had influenced the neighbouring territories. Thus, they influenced the Muketeśvara Temple of Bhubaneswar, the temple within the Nurpur fort and Thousand Pillar Temple of Warangal.[27] It seems, the "Kosali style of temple architecture" had influenced the Lakṣmaṇa temple at Sirpur and Indralāṭh temple at Rānīpur-Jharial, to some extent, as these temples also consist of the sanctum proper (in *pañcaratha* plans) and *maṇḍapa* in front, with an antechamber (*antarāla*) connecting the two. The *kumbha*-shaped moulding of "Kosali style of temples", connecting the *maṇḍapa* and the *antarāla* of these two temples, is practically the same. The pillared *maṇḍapa* of Indralāṭh temple at Rānīpur-Jharial complex has fallen since long. The scattered stone pillars are now utilized as seats by the Orissa State Archaeology department.

[25] *THOMV*, 2004, pp. 185-210.

[26] J.P. Singh Deo, "Kosali Style of Temple Architecture", *OHRJ*, vols. XXIV–XXVI, pp. 175-76.

[27] Ibid.; *Caravan*, English magazine, June (First), 1977, no. 60, p. 52.

Some influence is also noticeable between the "Kosali style of temples" and of *pañcaratha* plan, when the sharp edges of early Kosali style, rounded up in later years. Nīlakaṇṭheśvara temple of Dadpur, in the district of Kālāhāṇḍī is a stone structure and seems to be a late medieval structure, with the influence of "Kosali style of temple architecture", in its plan. Here, it will be interesting to know the view of K.S. Behera, on the Brāhmanical temples of Orissa, under the Somavaṁśīs. While giving the account, Behera[28] mentions that the Somavaṁśīs, who succeeded the Bhauma-Karas, came from South Kosala but they did not introduce any unfamiliar line of development in art and architecture. The pillared *maṇḍapa* of the Kosaleśvara temple at Baidyanath (district Bolaṅgīr, now district Sonepur), with lateral transepts and large sculptures in the interior, seems to suggest that when the Somavaṁśīs were ruling in the Upper Mahānadī Valley, there was some central Indian influence of the temple architecture but as they proceeded towards the coastal region, they strengthened the traditional temple style. Here, it is to be noted that there was influence of the "Kosali style of Rekha temple", architecture.

> The number of interesting squares developed particularly in the Cāḷukyan monuments of the eleventh–twelfth century CE in Gujarat. Even in the Hoysala temples of Mysore (now Karnataka province) the star-shaped plan becomes the usual fashion.[29] The maturity of structure, influence each other and developed into such extent that Cāḷukya-Hoysala school of architecture gradually developed in eleventh, twelfth and thirteenth centuries CE. This shows the plan of intersecting two squares of Kosali style of early phase to have prevalence over these styles of architecture later.

With the squares, Lal Saheb Prafulla Chanda Bhanja Deva saw the vision of *AUṀ*. According to Swami Chinmayananda,[30] the sound of *OṀ* is also *praṇava*, meaning that it is something that pervades life, or through *prāṇa* or breath.

It may now be asked as to why this particular word *OṀ* should be chosen as the word representative of the "thought", out of which the universe has become manifested. And the answer can be found in Swami Vivekananda's own words:

> This *OṀ* is the only possible symbol which covers the whole ground, and there is none other like it. The *sphoṭa* is the material of all words, yet it is not

[28] *Orissa Review: Mountain Special*, January 1976, p. 60.

[29] *THACOTIP, The Struggle for Empire*, vol. V, 2nd edn., 1966, p. 24.

[30] Swami Chinmayananda, *Vedanta the Science of Life*, part III, Bangalore: The Chinmaya Vigyana Mandir, 1982, pp. 1040-41.

> any definite word in its fully formed state. That is to say, if all the particularities which distinguish one word from another be removed then what remains will be the *sphoṭa*. Therefore, the *sphoṭa* is called the *Nāda-Brahman*, the sound-*Brahman*. Now, every Word-Symbol intended to express the inexpressible *sphoṭa*, will be so particularize it that it will no longer be the *sphoṭa*. That which particularize it the least and at the same time most approximately expresses its nature, will be the truest symbol thereof; and this is the *OṀ*, and the *OṀ* only; because, these three letters *A, U, Ṁ*, pronounced in combination as *OṀ*, can alone be the generalized symbol of all sounds. The letter *A* is the least differentiate of all sounds. Again, all articulate sounds are produced in the space within the mouth — beginning with the root of the tongue and ending at the lips — the throat — sound is *A* and *Ṁ* is the last lip-sound; and *U* exactly represents the rolling forward of the impulse which begins at the root of the tongue, continuing till it ends in the lips.
>
> If properly pronounced, this *OṀ* will represent in itself the whole phenomenon of sound production, and no other word can do this; and this, therefore, is the fittest symbol of the *sphoṭa*, which is the real meaning of the *OṀ*. And as the symbol can never be separated from the thing signified, the *OṀ* and the *sphoṭa* are one. And, as the *sphoṭa*, being the finer side of the manifested universe, its nearer to God, and is indeed the first manifestation of Divine Wisdom, this *OṀ* is Truly Symbolic of God.
>
> *OṀ* thus represents the entire manifested world and the unmanifest, and also that which lies beyond both the manifest and the unmanifest — the *Brahman*, which is the changeless substratum for changing objects of the world of experiences.

Lal Saheb Prafulla Chanda Bhanja Deva could see or had the faculty of sight of two topsy-turvy inverted triangles having six-pointed-ends. The triangle pointed down is the *yoni-yantra* and the triangle pointed up is the *liṅga-yantra*. So, two triangles intersecting each other is the symbol of cosmic union of male and female principles, which represents Śiva and Śakti.

The opinion and writing of Paramahansa Satyananda Saraswati[31] on unity of Śiva and Śakti solves many mundane mysteries. Hence, the author thinks it proper to quote him:

---

[31] *ASCITATTOYAK*, 1989, pp. 329-32.

UNITY OF ŚIVA AND ŚAKTI

In the following discussion we are specifically talking about the Śākta and Śaivite sects, with the emphasis on the Śāktas.

Śiva represents the unmanifest and Śakti the manifest. Śiva is the formless and Śakti is the formed. Śiva is consciousness and Śakti as energy, not only in the cosmos as a whole, but in each and every individual. Śiva is the Supreme Consciousness pervading each individual and Śakti is the power that manifests the potential contained within the consciousness in different manifested centres within man and the universe. The roots of Śakti are in Śiva. Though one of manifested and the other unmanifested, they are in the ultimate sense one and the same. One is the principle of changelessness and the other is the principle of change. Śakti is change within changelessness and Śiva is changelessness as the root of change. This relationship seems contradictory in logical terms, yet the experience of perfect oneness and unity of the changeless and the changeable, the dissolution of duality, is the aim of Tantra as well as Yoga. There is ultimately no difference between Śiva and Śakti, but this not realizable except in states of higher awareness. And this realization transforms life into a source of wonder and joy.

Everything that you see around you, everything that is physical, psychic, mental or whatever is Śakti both individually and collectively. This includes your mind and body. It includes every tree, every dog, every stone, the sun. Śakti is everything. All these manifestations have came from the underlying substratum, Śiva. The aim of Tantra is to retread, in a sense, the path of manifestation, so that Śakti is the vehicle to reunite the individual with Śiva and know the supreme experience. *Samādhi*, *nirvāṇa* or whatever you want to call it. Tantra aims to lead you on the path back to union of Śiva and Śakti, union of the individual being (*jīva*) with the *paramātman* (supreme).

Tantra says that Śakti or the power of creating separate centres of manifestation (i.e. objects, individuals, etc.) is in essence consciousness itself (Śiva). However, the power of the phenomenal world around us veils itself (through *māyā*) and it is not obvious at ordinary states if awareness that it is indeed consciousness. Each and everything in the created universe is no more than manifested consciousness. But strange though it seems, there is no change in the nature or content of consciousness, even though everything comes from it. In the *Īśavāsya Upaniṣad* it says:

> That is full, this is full.
> From full, the full is taken,
> the full has come.
> If you take out the full
> from the full, the full
> alone remains.

The great ancient sage of Europe, Plotinus said exactly the same thing:

The one is everything and also not everything. It is not everything because it is the source of everything. It is transcendentally everything because there everything is . . . , or, more exactly, is not yet but is to be.

These two quotations are the essence of Tantra and every religion. Don't worry if you don't understand their meanings, for what they are trying to convey defies intellectual speculation.

Consciousness is an inexhaustible source of everything in the universe, yet ever transcending the things which come out of it. Consciousness never ceases to be what it was, is, and will be. From Śiva comes the universe as a whole and everything individually through the power of Śakti . . . yet Śiva remains ever the same. At the same time, Śiva and Śakti, in the highest sense, are one and the same. This is the eternal mystery, the eternal wonder, whichever defies description. It is far better to count every stone on the beaches of the world than try to attempt to describe the impossible.

Tantra regards the material universe as the form, pattern, or expression of the totality. According to Tantra, both the manifested and unmanifested, the background and the projection, the film and the screen are real. In fact, to tell a person that the things around him are unreal is nonsensical for his personal experience in normal levels of awareness tells him otherwise. Also from the point of view of tāntric, yogic or any other spiritual practice, the world must be regarded as real. One must use the body, the mind and other aspects of the world to know that which is beyond. If one regards the mind and body as unreal, as do some systems, then how can one practise spiritual techniques, how can one practise with things that are unreal? Of course, this is a ridiculous point of view in normal levels of experience. Many other systems regard the universe as unreal because it changes. Though it is really no more than a matter of definition, Tantra says that everything, whether it changes (Śakti) or is changeless (Śiva) is actually real. Both are no more than two different aspects of the totality.

Śiva is father (*pitā*) of all that moves and is motionless: He is said to be naked — clothed in open space (*digambara* — clothed in everything in the universe). Nowadays, he is usually depicted wearing a tiger skin and portrayed as holding a trident which represents the three qualities of nature — *tamas* (inertia and darkness), *rajas* (activity) and *sattva* (light and harmony) of which he is the eternal master. He is said to ride a bull called Nandī. Śiva contains within himself the seeds of creation. He is symbolized by the *Śivaliṅgam*. He is totally unconditioned, in a continual state of *nirvikalpa samādhi*, with total absence of duality, of this and that. Śiva is the king of all *yogī*s (Yogeśvara) for he represents the supreme experience. He is also known as Kuleṣaṇa, Lord of the Kaulas, those who have reached the highest stage of Tantra (Kaulācāra).

Śiva also means many other things, in different moods or aspects. Don't be confused by these. Sometimes, for example, he is called Rudra, the destroyer, who seems to be more like Śakti in nature (the dissolving aspect). But the important thing to understand or at least appreciate is that there is really no contradiction between regarding Śiva as the inactive, passive personification of consciousness (as we have already emphasized) and also regarding him as a more active personification in the form of Rudra, the destroyer. This merely further emphasizes that the active and the inactive, the manifest and the unmanifest are really one and the same. All these deities, Śiva-Śakti or whatever, really represent exactly the same thing: The Absolute. Only the symbol, the representation is different. And why not? If you wish you can create your own deity and it will be as vaild as any other. This widespread worship of vast numbers of deities indicates the incredible complexity (yet such simplicity when understood) and tolerance of the all-embracing spiritual climate of India.

Śakti is known by many names and aspects. She is known as *prāṇa* when associated with the organization and growth of matter in all forms of life. She is known as *kuṇḍalinī* the power that lies dormant in everything, including man, and which can be unleased through yogic and tāntric practices, as well as all other spiritual practices. She is known as Kālī, the dissolver (not the destroyer) of the world, who withdraws everything into her womb at the end of the allotted life span. She is known and depicted in many pictures and statues as Pārvatī, the epitome of the loving, faithful wife of Śiva. She is called the primordial power — Ādya, the Universal Mother Īśvarī, the consort of Īśvara, the Lord of the Universe. She is also known as

Avidyārūpiṇī (the form of ignorance) for it is she who produces ignorance and individuality. Conversely, she is also known as Vidyārūpiṇī (the form of knowledge) for she is the means to removing bondage and knowing liberation or enlightenment. As the *Kulārṇava Tantra* says:

By that which one falls, so one will raise oneself.

In other words, she is the mind of each of us, which can either enslave us or free us. She is known as Māyā (the creator of illusion) for it through her power that one fails to see unity and know higher awareness. At the same time, it is through the power of Śakti that the world is experienced. Without Śakti, you would not be able to experience the world, for it is she who creates the mind and body. It is through Śakti that Śiva can experience himself. Śakti is also *Para-Brahman*, the Absolute, when she becomes *Brahman* at the time when Śiva and Śakti unite. Endless different forms of her are worshipped in India — Umā, Gaurī, Durgā and so on. Her forms are infinite, for there is no end to her power and things that she manifests. Her forms are as numerous as the reflections of the moon. She is continually active, creating, sustaining and then reabsorbing or dissolving everything into Śiva, only to be recreated. This is a continual process without end.

Remember, as we have already pointed out, the concept of Śiva and Śakti is not confined to India. We have already said that Tantra is universal and indeed it is. For example, in a book of ancient Greece called the *Phaedrus* by Plato it says:

> "What is on earth (Śakti) is merely the resemblance and shadow of something that is in a higher sphere, a resplendent thing that remains in an unchangeable condition (Śiva)."

This clearly illustrates the principle of Śiva and Śakti. There are many other examples. Consider the ancient Gnostics. These were really a European tāntric sect, which interpreted Christianity with far deeper meaning than understood by most people. They interpreted it in the light of higher experience. But let us get distracted; we want to point out of similarities between Śiva and Śakti and this ancient system of Gnosis (enlightenment). One of the Gnostic mystics, Simon the Magus, is reputed to have said the following:

> The universal eons (cyclic periods of creation as given in Tantra) consist of two branches, without beginning or end, which spring up from one root (the Absolute) . . . the invisible power and the

> unknowable silence. One of these branches is manifested from above and is the universal consciousness ordering all things and designated male (surely this Śiva); the other branch is female and is the producer of all things (Śakti).

The next continues but we will not. The Gnostics even divided human beings into three distinct groups, which are exactly the same as Tantra. The lowest group, in terms of awareness, are those who worship and only know of the existence of the material world. This group is called *paśu* instinctive man in Tantra. The second group includes those who worship an underlying reality without experience, but with blind belief. This is similar though not exactly the same as the second classification of Tantra, namely *vīra*, or heroic man, the third group of humans is those who know and live in higher awareness. In Tantra these are known as *divya* or divine man. So the ancient system of Gnosticism is fundamentally tāntric in nature. There are many other systems in the world that are very similar. These will not be discussed here through lack of space.

Energy, including matter and consciousness are functioning together in the cosmos as well as in each and every human being. This combination gives rise to the world we see around us; it gives rise to time and place. Energy is controlled by consciousness, and consciousness cannot express itself except through energy. In a tāntric book of Śaṅkarācārya called *Saundaryalaharī*, it says:

> "How can Śiva function without Śakti?"

Therefore Tantra says that to merge with consciousness one must use Śakti as the means.

There is a supreme experience where Śiva and Śakti no longer exist as separate entities. Some call it *Brahman*, others call it "not this, not this", to show that it is inexpressible. Others say that it is one without a second. It is the state of *nirvāṇa, samādhi*, perfect oneness and so many other words. This is the meaning of many of the sculptures of personified male and female Śiva and Śakti in India. It depicts the state of being, the enraptured embrace where self-identity and separateness disappears. This is the divine embrace.

At the centre of the two intersecting triangles a *bindu* is found. *Bindu*[32] is

[32] David Frawley, *Tāntric Yoga and the Wisdom Goddesses*, Delhi: Motilal Banarsidass, 1996, vide Glossary of Sanskrit Terms, p. 239.

point or drop of pure awareness in which time and space collapse into a single point. *Bindu*[33] is explained as the point of potential energy and consciousness, nucleus, in Tantra and *haṭha-yoga* it also represents a drop of semen.

The modern Orissa province of India is fortunate that a tāntric scholar Lal Saheb Prafulla Chandra Bhanja Deva was born on this land, on CE twentieth century who was an adept of tāntric-yogic heights. His "Jyoti Darśana" or the sight of divine light as explained, fulfils or confirms the archaeological yogic interpretations given by the author.

The renowned astronomer Varāhamihira[34] in his *Bṛhat-Saṁhitā*, Kūrma Vibhāga 8, puts Kosala, Kaliṅga, Vaṅga, Upa-Vaṅga, Jathar, Aṅga, Sailik, Vidarbha, Vatsa, Āndhra, Cedi, Udharva, Kani, Brusa, Naliker and Charmadip in the Āgneya-Koṇa (i.e. south-east). The grouping of states indicates that Kosala here, refers to Dakṣiṇa Kosala or South Kosala.

In the modern set-up, the present Chhattisgarh and Orissa provinces form the centre of the ancient states mentioned by Varāhamihira. It is in this Great Mahānadī River Valley, Sapta-Mātṛkās, Sixty-four Yoginī cult, cult of Puruṣottama Jagannātha, temple architectures of Kosali and Kaliṅga styles, and erotic sculptural arts originated and developed. Its impact or contribution is found in the Great Indian tradition, which had civilized the ancient world.

Orissa is a place for the study of Paippalāda *śākhā* of *Atharvaveda*. From the Mayūrbhañj district area, palm-leaf manuscripts are abundantly discoverd. The brāhmaṇas of that *śākhā* are still chanting those *mantras*.[35] Prafulla Chandra Bhanja Deva[36] in one of his written speeches *alias* lectures "The Mysticism of Tantra", in England, had said:

> One of the main reasons for my citing a typical indigenous Sanskrit poem of Orissa here is to convey to you at the beginning that Orissa is and has been the seat of tāntric culture, art and philosophy at all times and is not the land of sentimental Vaiṣṇavite effervescence, having its centre in

[33] Swami Muktibodhananda Saraswati (Commentary), *Haṭha-Yoga-Pradīpikā*, Munger: Bihar School of Yoga, 2nd edn., 1993, p. 544.

[34] J.P. Singh Deo, *Cultural Profile of South Kosala*, New Delhi: Gyan Publishing House, 1987, p. 36.

[35] Prafulla K. Mishra (ed.), *New Dimensions in Atharvaveda*, Delhi: Pratibha Prakashan, 2003, *passim*.

[36] *AMCPCBD*, 2005, pp. 134-37 and *ATSATBWOBS*, 2007, pp. 92-94.

Nabadvīpa of Bengal, that is only usually noticed by the superficial observer of my homeland and its people. It is true that the moss lying on the surface of the lake, containing beautiful lotuses, betrays the veneer of green cults popularly known as Vaiṣṇavism, but alas, how few people pause to reflect that even these have their roots in Tantra and the type of Vaiṣṇavism that is prevalent in Orissa is embedded in the highest form of the tāntric way of life and thought, namely the much misunderstood and much abused "Kaulācāra", of a carefully thought-out way of life for the adept, who has achieved a balanced equilibrium of the conflicts facing man in the multifarious departments of existence and behaviour.

The best that my province has to give in art, culture, thought and beauty from antiquity comes from Bhubaneswar, the great Śaivite centre of Orissa and from Jajpur or Yajñapura, the sacrificial town, dedicated to Mahāśakti, the creatrix of the universe, seated on the lion-throne of heaven. Hence all the Brāhmaṇas, versed in the sciences and the Tantras, along with the gems of original manuscripts and manuals on the Vedas, the Tantras and other sorts of esoteric communion, based on these, come and are diffused throughout Orissa from this ancient centre, situated on the river "Vaitaraṇī", and mentioned as a pilgrimage in the *Mahābhārata*.

The art of Purī, compared with the efflorescence of genius showered on the architecture of these two ancient sites, as well as on what remains of the broken Sun-temple of Koṇārka, is crude and prosaic, showing the direction of the predilection of the ethos of our people from very ancient times. But even here, namely at Purī, which is popularly believed by most men to be a centre of Vaiṣṇavism, because of Caitanya's influence there, towards the later part of his life, it is the Tantras which prevail and the famous Kaula doctrine of (in Sanskrit):

antaḥ śākta-a bohiḥ saibaḥ
sabha-yam vaiṣṇava mataḥ

is practised up to this day here, in religious field. Few people know that which those who are versed in the doctrines of Puruṣottama-Kṣetra are familiar with, as self-evident truth — namely that (in Sanskrit):

lokenāthaḥ śivo yatra tīrtha-a
maho-dadho-u vimala bhairavī yantra
jagannāth-stu bhairavaḥ

fig. 12.2: *Tripura Bhairavī-Yantra.*

and that in the *Pīṭha-Pūjā* of the Goddess Durgā in my province, in the enumeration and worship of the "Pīṭha-Śaktis" that is the presiding energies of the principal altar and their respective "Bhairavas" or the Śaivite Lords of these Divine Powers, the formulae (in Sanskrit):

vimala bhairav-vye namaḥ and *jagannāth bhaira-vye namaḥ*

will be invariably found in all the palm-leaf manuscripts dealing with this subject.

How many people know, indeed, that the sacred diagram of Mahāvidyā Tripura is buried in the *vedī* (altar) on which the images of Jagannātha, Subhadrā and Balabhadra are installed and that the daily worship of the temple, concerned mainly with the altar and not with the rough images thereon, is carried out with tāntric formulae and formalities?

It is generally not known either that the (in Sanskrit: Anukalpa's) or substitutes for wine, meat and *mudrā*, i.e. sacrificial cake, recognized and recommended in the Tantras, are offered every morning in the form of "Sherbat" made from the fruit of the "Jatipatri" plant along with salted ginger flakes, embedded in a cake made of Mash (*Phaseolus radiotus*), at the shrine of Jagannātha at Purī.

Not only this, the famous *mahāprasāda* of this temple is only efficacious after the final offering made to the Goddess Durgā, named Vimalā, who is established in the form of Bhairavī within the precincts of the shrine. It is on this principle and practice of the well-known communion, that the temple is regarded as the Bhairavī-Cakra or the circle of the Goddess Bhairavī-Durgā and hence no caste restrictions are observed according to the tāntric dictum (in Sanskrit):

prāpte tu bhairavī cakre
sarve varṇa dvijātīha.

Therefore, it is plain that the aforesaid Kaula manner of behaviour is observed at Jagannātha temple of Purī, which is dedicated to the esoteric worship of Śakti within, but proclaims allegiance to Śiva as Bhairava, in reasoned discourse of learned brāhmaṇas externally, while to the fool outside, the emotional camouflage of Vaiṣṇavism is paraded with flourish.

13

A Grave Folly of Kedarnath Mahapatra

KEDARNATH Mahapatra[1] stated that he discovered a hypaethral temple of Sixty-four Yoginīs at Hirapur and, regarding the date of the monument, he discusses:

> The Circular Cloister at Bherāghāṭ has been assigned to a period ranging from the tenth to twelfth century on the strength of evidence furnished by the inscriptions found there. As regards the date of the Circular temple at Rānīpur-Jharial, Cunningham writes as follows:
>
> > Of its antiquity there can be no doubt as in style of work and execution, it approaches closest to the great inscribed temple, which I have already assigned to the eighth century of our era; I cann't assign it to a later date than the ninth century.[2]
>
> But there is no inscription in this Circular temple at Hirapur or nearby, with the help of which its date can be fixed somewhat definitely. So its date can be fixed with the help of archaeology and the extent literature on tāntric religion.
>
> The predominance of the standing as well as the two-handed figures in the Circular temple at Hirapur is a sure sign of its antiquity and as such it may be taken to be earlier than those at Rānīpur-Jharial and Bherāghāṭ. The sculpture of the images at Bherāghāṭ and Rānīpur-Jharial is much more elaborate than that of the images at Hirapur, there being the figures of attendants and worshippers near the *yoginī* images in those two places, which are completely absent at Hirapur, which tends to prove its greater antiquity.
>
> Thirdly the *yoginī pīṭhas* were established, when the Brāhmanical tāntric religion became very popular in the society and began to vie with the

---

1 *OHRJ*, vol. II, no. 2, July 1953, pp. 23-40.

2 Ibid.; Cunningham's *Archaeological Survey of India*, vol. XIII, p. 132.

Vajrayāna of the Buddhists, which originated in Uḍḍiyāna in the sixth-seventh century. From the *Kālikā Purāṇa* which was written in Assam in the eleventh century,[3] it is known that the first Brāhmanical tāntric *pīṭha* in India, originated and developed in Oḍradeśa, the presiding deity of which was Jagannātha.

जालन्धंर लिखेत पीठं मुत्तर पश्चिमे लिखेत्
ओड्रपीठ दक्षणेतु कामरूपन्तु पूर्बत ॥[4]
ओड्राख्यं प्रथमं पीठ द्बितीयं जालशैलकं
तृतीयं पूर्णपीठन्तु कामस्यं चतुर्थक
ओड्रपीठ परिमेतु तथैबो ड्रेखरींशिवा
कात्यायिनीं जगन्नाथमोड्रशाचं प्रदूजयेत् ॥[5]

The *Kālikā Purāṇa,* which describes in great details the origin, development, religious significance and the rituals of the *Yoginī Pūjā*, speaks in unmistakable terms that in Oḍra or Orissa, the Brāhmanical tāntric religion was first developed. This statement of *Kālikā Purāṇa* is corroborated by the existence of a lot of temples in the coastal region of Orissa, some of which are pure Hindu tāntric *pīṭha*s, while others have been greatly influenced by the tāntric faith. The temple of goddess Virajā at Jajpur, which finds mention in the Sanskrit *Mahābhārata*, is one of the oldest tāntric *pīṭha*s of the Hindus. The images of the Sapta-Mātṛkās on the Vaitaraṇī at Jajpur and those near the Mārkaṇḍeśvara temple at Purī have been assigned tentatively to the eighth century. The Paraśurāmeśvara temple at Bhubaneswar, which is assigned to the seventh century, contains the images of Sapta-Mātṛkās:[6] (1) the Kapālinī, (2) the Mohinī, (3) the Urrarāyaṇī, (4) the Gaurī, (5) the Rāmāyaṇī, and (6) the Dakṣiṇa Caṇḍī temples of Bhubaneswar are regarded as famous tāntric *pīṭha*s and the existing temples of the first four deities have been assigned to the eighth century by all the reputed historians. Only in the temple of Kapālinī, sixteen images, besides the images of Kapālinī, who is the presiding deity of the temple, have been set in the walls inside the *garbhagṛha*. The Kapālinī is a Cāmuṇḍā image and of the other sixteen, seven

[3] *OHRJ*, vol. II, no. 2, July 1953, pp. 23-40; *Kālika Purāṇa*, a compilation of the time of Dharmapada of Kararupa by Sarma, *Indian Historical Quarterly*, vol. XXIII, pp. 322-26.

[4] Ibid.; *Kālikā Purāṇa*, edited and published by Panchanana Tarkaratna in Beṅgālī Script, ch. 63, v. 11.

[5] Ch. 63, vs. 43 and 44.

[6] Ibid.; K.C. Panigrahi, "Date of the Parasurameśvara Temple at Bhubaneswar" *Journal of the Royal Asiatic Society*, vol. XV, no. 2, p. 110.

> are the figures of Mātṛkās, and four are *Yoginī* images. In this respect, the temple of Kapālinī seems to be intimately connected with the Circular temple at Hirapur, where the entire pantheon of Causaṭha *Yoginīs*, nine Kātyāyanīs and some Bhairava images are worshipped, which indicates the gradual development of the tāntric cult. From this point of view, the temple of Hirapur seems to be later than that of Kapālinī. On the grounds stated above, the temple of Causaṭha *Yoginīs* at Hirapur may be assigned to the eighth or early ninth century CE when Brāhmanical tāntric religions became predominant in Orissa, and most of the famous tāntric temples of this region raised their heads. "Oḍrapīṭha", being the first tāntric *pīṭha* in India, according to *Kālikā Purāṇa*, which is taken as an authority on Hindu tantra, it can legitimately be assumed that the Yoginī cult which originated in the coastal region of Orissa somewhere near Purī, gradually spread in the adjoining hilly tracts of Orissa and Madhya Pradesh, having its centres first at Rānīpur-Jharial, which is also another small city of temples, like Bhubaneswar, and then in Bherāghāṭ, near which are seen the monuments of different ages.

The given opinion of Mahapatra came out when the field surveys, explorations, excavations and archaeological and historical studies were in their infancy. Without sound comparative studies, scholars like S.N. Rajguru,[7] H.C. Das,[8] Rajnath Singh,[9] Ekadashi Padhi,[10] and many have followed the opinion of Mahapatra blindly as his was a pioneering study.

While dealing with the Yoginī cult of Orissa, Rajnath Singh,[11] chronologically discusses, first the Causaṭha Yoginī temple at Hirapur, second the Causaṭha Yoginī temple at Khajurāho, third the Causaṭha Yoginī Temple at Rānīpur-Jharial, fourth the Causaṭha Yoginī temple at Bherāghāṭ, and fifth the Causaṭha Yoginī temple at Dudhai.

---

[7] S.N. Rajguru, *Odisara Itihas* (Oriya), p. 453.

[8] H.C. Das, *Cultural Development in Orissa*, Kolkata: Punthi Pustak, 1985, p. 226; H.C. Das, *Śakti Pīṭhas: A Study*, Bhubaneswar: Bharati Prakashan, 1999, pp. 69-70.

[9] Rajnath, Singh, *Religious Tāntricism*, vol. 2, New Delhi: Dominant Publishers and Distributors, 2001, p. 111.

[10] Ekadashi Padhi, "State and Society During Bhaumakara Rule", *Exploring Orissan History*, N.R. Patnaik (ed.), Cuttack: Kitab Mahal, 2005, p. 107.

[11] Rajnath Singh, op. cit., pp. 126-31.

Ekadashi Psdhi[12] quotes Rajguru and states, "Hīrāmahādevī is known to have established at village named Hirapur near Jajpur after her name and constructed the Causṭha Yoginī temple there." Hirapur site is situated in between Bhubaneswar and Purī, far away from Jajpur. Mahapatra[13] himself had said:

> Hirapur stands not far from the south bank of the river Bhārgavī, on which runs the well-known Jagannātha road to Purī, at a distance of nearly three miles straight to the east of famous temple of Bhubaneswar. Śiśupālgaṛh, which has come to prominence during the recent years, stands midway between some other ancient monuments, the chief of which is the temple of Kuṇḍaleśvara Mahādeva in the neighbouring village of Umādei-Brahmapura, nowadays called Taṅkapāni, which marked the eastern limit of the ancient Ekāmra-Kṣetra, according to the verse quoted below:
>
> खण्डाचलं समासाद्य यत्रास्ते कुण्डलेश्वर ।
> आसाद्य बलहांदेवी बहिरङ्गेश्वराबधि ॥
>
> — *Svarṇādri Mahodaya*, Chapter I, p. 4

The Yoginī cult was a major cult of India and in recent years through archaeological surveys, Yoginī temples have been found and traced at the following sites:[14]

(1) Hirapur and Rānīpur-Jharial in the Orissa province.

(2) Bherāghāṭ, Khajurāho, Mitavali, Naresar, Badoh, Hiṅglājgaṛh and Shahḍol in the undivided Madhya Pradesh province.

(3) Lokhari, Varanasi, Rikhiar and Didhai in the Uttar Pradesh province.

(4) The Yoginī cult appears to have been well-known in the Rajasthan and Gujarat provinces. The area of Rajasthan still abounds in papers and cloth cakras of Sixty-four Yoginīs, and must have once erected Yoginī temples as well.

(5) The adjoining area of Gujarat also appears to have several temples. A *yoginī* temple once existed in Kamli village of Siddhapur district of Rajasthan, near a temple dedicated to the Mātṛkā Brāhmī, when the temple crumbled to ruins, a new one was built to replace it, and within this modern structure

---

12 Ekadashi Padhi, op. cit., p. 107.

13 *OHRJ*, vol. II, no. 2, pp. 23-24.

14 Shantilal Nagar, *Indian Gods and Goddesses* (*Yoginī Shrines and Śakti Pīṭhas*), vol. 4, part I, Delhi: B.R. Publishing Corporation, 2006, pp. 54-92.

is a long slab of stone with small engravings of Sixty-four Yoginīs.[15] It is also reported that an old *yoginī* temple existed in Palodhar village of Mehsānā district, but this too has apparently crumbled away. Gujarat once had a famous *yoginī* temple, as per Jaina texts which refer to four towns, renowned for *yoginī* shrines: Broach (in Gujarat), Ajmer (Rajasthan) Ujjain (Madhya Pradesh) and Yogi-nīpura (Delhi). But none of these temples survives at present.

(6) According to a tradition, a festival[16] was organized in honour of the *yoginī*s in Maharashtra. The *Yoginī-vrata* was performed by the womanfolks on the new moon day of Śrāvaṇa (July–August) in order to ensure safety of their children. The story, related to this *vrata*, tells us about the unfortunate Videha who had lost her children and was driven out of the house by her mother-in-law. Wandering in the countryside in search of her children, crying in despair, she arrived at the temple of a Yoginī and she adored her. She appeared before the unfortunate mother and restored her children to her.

(7) Śrīparvata in Andhra Pradesh appears to have been a tāntric centre from the late Gupta period. Bāṇa (CE 606-47) refers in his *Harṣacarita* and *Kādambarī* the important towns of the Śākta faith. It is suggested that the Śaiva sects of Kālamukhas and Kāpālikas rose in the south, where Śaivism had always been predominant. Though there is no evidence of the prevalance of the Yoginī cult in Āndhra Pradesh, a manuscript in Telugu, pertaining to the worship of the Sixty-four Yoginīs, has been discovered which testifies the prevalence of the cult in the region.[17]

(8) On the basis of the inscription in the Kolaramma temple of Karnataka, dating back to CE 1000, it has been presumed that the Yoginī cult was followed there. This temple relates to seven Mātṛkās, in which Cāmuṇḍā is the principal deity and is worshipped by the name of Kolarammā or the Mother of Kolar. A later record mentions about the offering of the wine to the goddess Yoginī. Otherwise, there is hardly any specific evidence for the prevalence of the Yoginī cult in Karnataka.[18]

---

[15] Shantilal Nagar, *Indian Gods and Goddesses* (*Yoginī Shrines and Śakti Pīṭhas*); Vidya Dehejia, *Art International*, March-April, 1982, p. 80.

[16] Vidya Dehejia, *Art International*, March-April, 1982, p. 82.

[17] Ibid., p. 83.

[18] Ibid.

(9) Eleven images of yoginīs are reported to have been recovered from the area around Kāñcīpuram (Tamil Nadu[19]). *Takka-Yoga*, a twelfth-century Tamil text of Dakṣa-yajña story dealing with the Dārasaram temple provides a graphic description of Kālī seated under an *aśvattha* tree (*Ficus religiosa*) and attended by Bhairava and other yoginīs. A temple of Sixty-four Yoginīs was reported from Coimbatore district of Tamil Nadu. But Vidya Dehejia has contested the claim saying, "The original reference mentions a stone pillar and surrounding it in a circle were eight images with their faces turned inwards." This description of eight images perhaps of Mātṛkās was somehow turned and transformed into a temple of Sixty-four Yoginīs. An extensive survey of the village in Udumulpat taluka (in which the Trimūrti temple of the original report is located) does not reveal the existence of a temple of *yoginīs* and the local village authorities rule out the possibility of its existence without their knowledge. South India, may have had a *yoginī* temple, but not at Coimbatore.[20]

The Yoginī cult appears then to have been formulated around seventh century CE and, the earliest representation of the *yoginīs* (a group of sixty four) belonging to this period, is found in the Śakti temple Chatrari in Himachal Pradesh, where they serve as attendants of the Goddess. In due course of time, they were conceived in the groups of eighty-one, as at Bherāghāṭ, sixty-four or even in forty-eight. It is possible that the early mode of worship was through *cakras*, *maṇḍalas* and *yantras*, painted on cloth or drawn on the ground with powdered colours or engraved on the metal sheets. Probably, it was only with the royal patronage of the cult that stone temples were built with niches to have images of *yoginīs*, thus leaving us with tangible evidence of the popularity of the Yoginī cult. The cult became popular the medieval times and after reaching its zenith, it was relegated into oblivian.

Though the temple of Yoginīs could not be traced in the south, but some sculptures, believed to be of the female deities were discovered from there in the beginning of the twentieth century and carried to Europe, which are currently preserved in the museums in Europe and America. Eleven of them have been illustrated by Vidya Dehejia in her work on Yoginīs, published by the National

---

[19] Vidya Dehejia, *Art International*, March-April, 1982, p. 82.

[20] Ibid.

Museum. Indeed, all these eleven sculptures do not appear to represent the Mātṛkās like Brāhmī, Māheśvarī, Kaumārī, Vaiṣṇavī, Aindrī, Cāmuṇḍā and others, though the *Kālikā Purāṇa* and other texts also include Mātṛkās in the list of Yoginīs. Therefore, it would be no surprise if these images form part of the Sixty-four Yoginī temple, which is now extinct. All these images are carved against the slab of granite stone with a rounded top, wherein each *yoginī* sits cross-legged on the ground with her vehicle neatly carved on the narrow bound below. These faces are oval with exaggeratedly arched eyebrows meeting at the centre. The lips are kept open to project the fangs. The Goddesses have gently sloping shoulders, full breasts and narrow hips, characteristics of the early Coḷa sculptures. They are adorned with several necklaces and the sacred threads, which lie in the cavity between their breasts. Placed below on the hips is the skirt covering half of their thighs. The snakes serve as the armlets, while the hair is dishevelled flowing on all the sides. Three sculptures currently preserved in the Muse Gamet, Paris, are the magnificent examples of these Yoginīs.

With these descriptions, Shantilal Nagar,[21] while dealing on "Historical Overtones", mentions, "Besides the Yoginī temples in Madhya Pradesh, similar temples have been found at Hirapur and Rānīpur-Jharial in Orissa. The *yoginī* temple at Hirapur was possibly built by Hīrā Mahādevī, the Queen of Śāntikara, belonging to the Bhauma-Kara dynasty, which ruled Orissa for 200 years. Out of the eighteen rulers of this dynasty, five chief queens ruled the country at different stages. During the reign of this dynasty, the Brāhmanical tāntric religion had been quite popular. The other *yoginī* temple of Orissa is located in Rānīpur-Jharial, which was built by the rulers of Soma dynasty. The place was the main centre of the worship of Śiva and Śakti during the period from seventh to tenth centuries CE and several temples were built during this period.

This statement of Shantilal Nagar, proves that he has been carried away by the early opinion of Mahapatra, as stated, without investigating further. Such erroneous repetition is continuing because academical world of India has neglected the study of the yogic conception of the Indian archaeological remains.

From the chronology and genealogy of the Bhauma-Kara dynasty,[22] it is known that there were female successions or queens of this dynasty as rulers. They were: the

---

[21] Shantilal Nagar, op. cit., p. 98.

[22] Umakanta Subuddhi, *The Bhaumakaras of Orissa*, Kolkata: Punthi Pustak, 1978, pp. 40-42.

eighth successor Tribhuvanamahādevī I *alias* Sindagaurī; the twelfth successor Pr̥thvīmahādevī *alias* Tribhuvanamahādevī II *alias* Sindagaurī II; the fifteenth successor Gaurīmahādevī; the sixteenth successor Daṇḍīmahādevī; the seventeenth successor Vakulamahādevī; and the eighteenth successor Dharamahādevī. Queen Hīrāmahādevī was the wife of the ninth Bhauma-Kara ruler, Śāntikaradeva II *alias* Gayāḍa II *alias* Loṇabhara.

Because the Sixty-four Yoginīs temple is found at Hirapur village, scholars imagine that this village might have been established by Hīrāmahādevī, without any evidence. It is a forced opinion from their imagination.

The 12th ruler of Bhauma-Kara dynasty was Pr̥thvīmahādevī *alias* Tribhuvanamahādevī II *alias* Sindagaurī II. From her Bauḍ copper-plate[23] it is known that she was the daughter of the King Svabhāvatuṅga, the king of Kosala, who belonged to the Soma-vaṁśa and had compared herself with Kātyāyanī. The author had mentioned[24] that Kātyāyanī, Vairocanī, Durgī and Kanyākumārī are first mentioned in *Taittirīya Āraṇyaka*. Goddess Kātyāyanī of later Vedic period gained wide popularity in the Purāṇic period. *Harivaṃśa, Vāyu, Brahmāṇḍa, Viṣṇu, Mārkaṇḍeya, Varāha, Vāmana* and *Matsya* Purāṇas give high epithets to this Śakti and conceive Kātyāyanī as a war Goddess.

> In *Skanda Purāṇa*, she is said to be leading the unmarried life and residing in Vindhya range. The action of killing Mahiṣāsura is accrued to her. She is said to be born of anger of the Gods and named Kātyāyanī. She is ascribed and attributed with many arms and holding the weapons given by Gods. Mounting on a lion given by Gaurī, she went to kill demon Mahiṣāsura. As she is regarded as war Goddess, she is worshipped mostly by the warriors at the time of actual fight. Bhauma-Kara Queen Tribhuvanamahādevī II (reigning period CE 896–905), wife of Bhauma-Kara King Śivakaradeva III, assumed imperial titles of Paramabhaṭṭārikā, Mahārājādhirāja, Parameśvarī and compared herself with Kātyāyanī. She mounted the lion-throne like Goddess Kātyāyanī (Durgā) and her lotus like feet were kissed by all feudatory chiefs with loyalty. This shows that Goddess Durgā in the name Kātyāyanī had become very popular in Orissa, during the period ninth to eleventh centuries CE when religious eclecticism was prevalent in Orissa.

---

[23] *EI*, vol. XXIX (1951-52), pp. 210-20.

[24] J.P. Singh Deo, *Tāntric Art of Orissa*, Delhi: Kalpaz Publications, 2001, pp. 59-60.

During that period Kātyāyanī gained wide currency and crept into Buddhist and Jaina pantheons. Apart from the Hindu Tantras, the Buddhist Tantra like Havajra Tantra, compiled around seventh century CE mentions the names of four tāntric *pīṭhas* including Oḍḍiyāna (it should be Uḍḍiyāna) which is convincingly located in Orissa (including the entire Mahānadī River Valley) and mentions that Jagannātha is worshipped as Bhairava and Kātyāyanī as Bhairavī in Oḍḍiyāna. The name "Jagannātha", used in Hevajra Tantra, a Buddhist tāntric literature, is used for Lord Buddha. Even in *Jñānasiddhi*, Indrabhūti, the king of Sambhala in Uḍḍiyāna, during eighth century CE, has made invocation of Lord Jagannātha, in many places of his work. It is to be observed that King Indrabhūti has addressed Lord Buddha as Lord Jagannātha.

In Oriya *Kālikā Purāṇa*, composed in the eleventh century CE Sixty-four Yoginīs and Nabakoṭi (nine) Kātyāyanīs of fierce appearance are created to kill the demons. The legendary account of the origin of Kātyāyanī, as found in *Kālikā Purāṇa*, indicates the triumph of Śāktism over Śaivism. As it is a Śākta Upa-purāṇa, it gives great emphasis on Śakti and highlights Śakti more than other Gods. This *Kālikā Purāṇa* identifies as Uḍḍiyāna *alias* Oḍradeśa and mentions that God Jagannātha and Goddess Kātyāyanī are worshipped there.

Further, *Kālikā Purāṇa*, says that Kātyāyana Muni first invoked Mahādevī and thus she, popularly, came to be known as Kātyāyanī.

In *Brahma Purāṇa*, Ekānaṁśā is identified with Kātyāyanī. In Puruṣottama Māhātmya of *Skanda Purāṇa*, Subhadrā, the central figure of Jagannātha trinity has been identified with Kātyāyanī.

In *Bata Abakāśa*, of the Oriya saint poet Balarāma Dāsa, written in the sixteenth century CE, mentions that Lord Jagannātha is attended upon by Sixty-four Yoginīs, Kātyāyanī, Sapta-Mātr̥kās, Vimalā, Virajā and refers to seventy-two local goblins. Kātyāyanī images are rare in Orissa. Nine images of Kātyāyanīs are found in the outer surface of the enclosure of Sixty-four Yoginī temple at Hirapur. They are two-armed, and standing on the trunkless head of the demon with skull cup and dagger in their hands, associated with jackals or dogs flanked by their attendants holding *chatra* over their heads.

Kātyāyanī is associated with Sixty-four Yoginī's cult and find mention in the following lists of 64 *Yoginīs*:

(1) *Kālikā Purāṇa*, (2) *Bṛhad-Nandikeśvara Purāṇokto Durgā-Pūjā-Paddhati* (*Viśvokośa* (?), vol. 16, 1312, p. 73), (3) *Causaṭha Yoginī Nāmāvalī* (2nd and 3rd lists), and (4) *Durgā-Pūja* (a palm-leaf manuscript of Orissa State Museum, Dh. no. 345, Folio 22-23).

Only because 12th successor Pṛthvīmahādevī *alias* Tribhuvanamahādevī II *alias* Sindagaurī II of Bhauma-Kara dynasty, compared herself with "Kātyāyanī" and nine images of Kātyāyanīs are found on the outer circular wall of Hirapur, Causaṭha Yoginī temple, it should not be regarded as the construction during the Bhauma-Kara ruling period. All round sculptural arts have also to be subject to comparative studies. No doubt, Yoginīs were worshipped during the Bhauma-Kara ruling period, because a Yoginī image was found at Kualo,[25] the capital of the Śulki dynasty, which was a feudatory *alias maṇḍala* state under the Bhauma-Kara rulers.

According to tāntric text, *Haṭha-Yoga-Pradīpikā*, a Yoginī is one who practises *vajrolī*. Swami Muktibodhananda Saraswati[26] illustrates it:

पुंसो बिंदु समाकुंच्य सम्यगभ्यासपाटवात् ।
यदि नारी रजो रक्षेद्वज्रोल्या सापि योगिनी ॥
— Chapter 3, Verse 99

If a woman practises *vajrolī* and saves her *rajas* and man's *bindu* through contraction, she is a Yoginī.

Just as a man should be adept in the practice, the woman also has to be practised and adept. There are few references in the *haṭha-yoga* texts that the practices are meant for women but it is clearly stated. Just as a man should practise gradual contractions of the urogenital muscles so should the woman. According to Tantra that is *sahajolī*:

> The *Haṭharatnāvalī*, states that: "*Rajas* is permanent, like red lead, in the reproductive organ of a woman. The *rajas* should be saved during menstruation like *bindu* is to be saved. The woman should practise *vajrolī* after that she should draw up the *rajas* is possible. The *nāda* in her body moves like *bindu*. *Bindu* and *rajas* produced in the body should be mixed through the *vajrolī* practice of *yoga*. Then success is at hand. The woman who does not know the science of *yoga*, should

---

[25] Saroj Kumar Patel, *Cultural History of Early Medieval Orissa* (*Śulki Rule*), New Delhi: Sundeep Prakashan, 1991. Plate no. 22 Yoginī, Kualo.

[26] Swami Muktibodhananda Saraswati, *Haṭha-Yoga-Pradīpikā*, Munger: Bihar School of Yoga, 2nd edn., 1993, p. 362.

> not practise *vajrolī*. This *yoga* is successful, to the courageous and pious *yogī*s who have an insight into reality."

> Just as a man prepares for *vajrolī* by practising contractions and then drawing up air/water through a catheter, via the urethra, so a woman can practise in a similar way. Instead of inserting a catheter into the urethra, however, a tube (0.8 cm wide and 10 cm long) should be inserted into the vagina so that a portion of it extends outside. Then sit on a bucket of water and practise *uḍḍiyāna bandha*. If water is not sucked into the vagina through this process, then practise *vāma*, *dakṣiṇa* and *madhyama nauli*. When this has been perfected, try to retain the water inside for as long as possible. Try to hold it while standing upright. Then practise *nauli* by "churning", the abdominal muscles. This cleanses the vagina of old secretions. After these practices are perfected, practise without the use of a tube. Only sit on the bucket and practise *uḍḍiyāna* or *nauli*. Again try to retain the water inside and stand erect. When the water can be retained inside only by the practice of *mūla bandha* and without *uḍḍiyāna*, the perineal muscles associated with *mūla bandha* and *vajrolī/sahajolī* have become strong.

It is also known from *Haṭha-Yoga-Pradīpikā*,[27] that a Yoginī conserving her *rajas* attains *khecarī*.

> रक्षेदाकुंचनादूर्ध्वं या रजः सा हि योगिनी।
> अतीतानागतं वेत्ति खेचरी च भवेद् ध्रुवम्॥
> — Chapter 3, Verse 102

> "She is verily a Yoginī who conserves her *rajas* by contracting and raising it. She knows past, present and future and becomes fixed in *khecarī* (i.e. consciousness moves into the higher realm)".

> All the attainments which a man attains by perfection of *vajrolī*, a woman can also achieve. A woman is normally compelled to experience the mental and physical fluctuations of the menstrual cycle. The loss of energy which accompanies the shedding of menses is obligatory. However, if the ovum is withdrawn by the practice of *vajrolī*, this continuing loss of energy is averted, and the menstrual loss diminishes. Whereas a man is bound to the grosser dimensions of awareness by his instincts and passions, which cause his body to produce and shed supermatozoa within the semen, the woman is bound to physical consciousness by the menstrual cycle.

---

[27] Swami Muktibodhananda Saraswati, *Haṭha-Yoga-Pradīpikā*, 2nd edn., 1993, p. 369.

> A Yoginī, who withdraws the *bindu* (ovum), overcomes this bondage. She experiences the awakening of a higher energy force within her body and her consciousness effortlessly expands into transpersonal awareness. This occurs very readily because a woman can intuit the nature of higher consciousness and understand the hidden power underlying the acceptance and surrender, whereas for a man the barrier of personal ego many times proves insurmountable.
>
> Traditionally, woman has been regarded as the weaker sex but it is clear that she has a greater capacity to suffer, sacrifice and endure. Up to the monarche, the female body is as strong as the male, but with the descent of *bindu* and the commencement of ovulation, vitality begins to be drained in the menses.
>
> A Yoginī, who has perfected *vajrolī* and withdrawn the *bindu*, becomes very powerful. *Siddhi*s manifest more easily to a woman because her intuitive faculties are by nature more highly evolved. She has actually always been aware of them in a rudimentary, dormant form. A woman is more aware of her own subconscious mind than of others, and if she can withdraw the *bindu* by *vajrolī*, the individual consciousness very easily moves into universal mind space (*cidākāśa*), and the attitude of *khecarī-mudrā* spontaneously occurs. As the tongue moves back into the upper palate, becoming fixed there without support, so the mind moves from the centres below *viśuddhi* and enters the total space of consciousness where the barrier of time dissolves, and the past, present and future become known.

With these backgrounds, the development of *yoginī*s and Yoginī cult took place.

It is known from tāntric text *Kāmakalā-Vilāsa*[28] that, in the beginning of *Kṛta* or *Satya* age, Śiva imparted the *tantra-vidyā* (knowledge) to his own Śakti, in Uḍḍiyāna Pīṭha. From critical studies,[29] it has been established that Uḍḍiyāna Pīṭha comprised the Mahānadī River Valley, which is the centre or centrally located in the *Āgneya-Koṇa* (south-east) of Bhāratavarṣa.

According to Rajnath Singh:[30]

> The central feature of the cosmogony of the Tantras is the female principle, the male principle having only a secondary position. This female-dominated world-view is in substantial agreement with that of the Sāṁkhya, according

[28] Sir John Woodroffe, *Tantrarāja Tantra and Kāmakalā-Vilāsa*, Madras: Ganesh & Co., 1971, p. 234.

[29] *THOMV*, 2004, pp. 80-92.

[30] Rajnath Singh, op. cit., vol. 2, New Delhi, 2001, p. 260.

to which the material *prakṛti* conceived as a female principle, is the cause of the universe and the *puruṣa* or the male principle is nothing but a passive spectator. There is reason to believe that the Sāṁkhya philosophy was originally a development of the primitive proto-materialism which formed the substratum of Tāntricism itself.[31] The anomalous position of the male principle of the Sāṁkhya and the Tantra can presumably be traced to the anomalous position of the males in the primitive female-dominated societies, in which the male had something to do in the matter of procreation but in the family he is insignificant and a passive spectator, exactly like the *puruṣa* of the Sāṁkhya.

We have already dealt in Chapter 1 that Sāṁkhya Darśana was originated in the Boden Block area of Nuāpāḍā district. In Chapter 2, we have seen that spiritual *kuṇḍalinī* is the gift of the Kālāhāṇḍī region to the mankind. While dealing on "Kuṇḍalinī-Yoga", Rajnath Singh[32] states:

> There are a number of traditions in the Tantras itself, but broadly the Tantra conceives that there is one reality, absolute, pure, self-existent. When it gets into a mood to manifest, to create, it poises itself into two; the Para-Śiva, the Supreme Reality poises itself into two — Śiva, the presiding, the static reality, and Śakti, the dynamic, the executive power, and this polarization of reality, of consciousness is the beginning of creation. It splits itself into a number of principles which go on to develop this universe. This universe is meant for the display of the glory of God. It is the power of God, Śakti, that executes, builds, presents the cosmic field, the cosmic play for the enjoyment of the Lord, the Divine Lord. There is really no ultimate difference between the Lord and his power, for the power is the Lord as power, just as there is no difference between the sun and his light, fire and its power to burn, similarly the Lord and his power, puissance, Śakti — they are really one. For purposes of play, of creation, they bifurcate as if into two, but always they are one.
>
> This is the setting of this cosmos, which is the tāntric perspective, has been created for the joy of the Lord. Man is an epitome of this universe; in each human being this whole universe is, as it were, recreated. And he is intended to participate in this cosmic enjoyment of life and render it to the Supreme Lord; not to enjoy it for himself, but become one more centre, one more

[31] Rajnath Singh, op. cit.; Debiprasad Chattopadhyaya, *Lokayata*, New Delhi, 1968, p. 360.

[32] Rajnath Singh, op. cit., vol. 2, pp. 229-30.

> station for taking the joy of life and offering it to the Lord. In other words, each one must develop his consciousness, knowledge, so that he becomes one with the consciousness of the Lord, the consciousness of the Śakti, so that they take through him their legitimate enjoyment of life.

As we have already seen in early chapter of this book, the *yoga* of sexual transformation developed in the Central Mahānadī River Valley. The author[33] had found that stone sockets in two parts in semi-circular shapes at the Mohangiri site of Kālāhāṇḍī district. They represent the union of male and female principals and their shape owes its origin to the rock art of Yogīmaṭh Ḍoṅger. Such a set of sockets has been discovered at Kharligaṛh site of Bolaṅgīr district. Another two sets were found within the dilapidated Śakti temple, on the left bank of the Udanti River, Baṛgāon village. One half of such a socket was found at Pātālgaṅgā site in Nuāpāḍā district. One set was discovered from layer III (early historic phase) from Veerapuram in Guntur district of Andhra Pradesh, where it is interpreted as a votive *liṅga*.[34] It is researched and assertively established that *yoga* of sexual transformation was discovered in the Mahānadī Valley[35] and later included in *Bṛhadāraṇyaka Upaniṣad*, of *Śukla Yajurveda*.

With these backgrounds, it can be asserted that the ladies who practised *yoga* of sexual transformation came to be known as Yoginīs. According to R.P. Mishra,[36] the concept of Yoginīs in India began to grow in the lap of Śāktism from the sixth century CE onwards . . . Ādipīṭha of sixty-four *yoginī*s is with the Someśvara-liṅga, as described in the *Yoginī Tantra*, which is probably a work of the eleventh century CE. As Someśvara temple[37] is found at Rānīpur-Jharial site of Bolaṅgīr district, it may be accepted that the first Causaṭha *yoginī* temple was built at Rānīpur-Jharial site and from here this cult spread to different parts of India and abroad.

The *summum bonum* of the spiritual yogic concept of both the *Yoginī Tantra* and the *Yoni Tantra* is the *yoga* of sexual transformation or from sex to super-

---

33 *THOMV*, 2004, pp. 57-142 and 173-84.

34 Ibid.; T.V.G. Shastri, M.K. Bai and J.V.P. Rao, *Veerapuram*, Hyderabad: Bhavani Printers, 1984, *passim*.

35 *THOMV*, 2004, pp. 5 and 75-85.

36 R.P. Mishra, *Fragments of Indian Culture* (*Rānīpur-Jharial*), Kolkata: Punthi Pustak, 1995, pp. 207-08.

37 Dipakranjan Das, *Temple of Orissa: The Study of a Sub-style*, Delhi: Agamkala Prakashan, 1982, pp. 26-29.

consciousness. So, it seems that both these Tantras were originated and developed in the central right Mahānadī River Valley and gradually shifted to Bengal, Cooch Behar, Kāmākhyā, coastal Orissa and other parts.

While dealing on the topic "Primal Yoginī-Pīṭha Rānīpur-Jharial", Ram Prasad Mishra[38] states that the *Yoginī Tantra*, while describing the Tāntric *pīṭhas* or *upa-pīṭhas* in Oḍra or Oḍhra as Sindhubhadraka (modern Bhadrakha), Virajā (modern Jajpur), Ekāmra (modern Bhubaneswar), Bhāskara Mahākṣetra (Arkakṣetra Koṇārka) and others, narrates one Someśvara-Liṅga Ādipīṭha in this realm.[39] It proves that Ādi *alias* Primal Yoginī Pīṭha (site) located at Rānīpur-Jharial site and the opinion of Mahapatra is a folly.

While dealing on art and architecture of Orissa, K.C. Panigrahi,[40] assigned Rānīpur-Jharial monuments to the ninth-tenth century CE and about the Causṭhī Yoginī temple of Hirapur,[41] and mentions:

> We have already referred to this monument and to a similar shrine at Rānīpur-Jharial. One great difference between them is that the Hirapur *yoginīs* appear with their respective mounts, whereas Rānīpur-Jharial images have no such attributes. The Hirapur images are the marvellous pieces of art and are comparable to those of the Brahmeśvara and the Liṅgarāja, and were evidently the creations of that period. It seems that the Somavaṁśī rulers, when they lived in Orissa, created this shrine or helped the creation of it, in the model of the Rānīpur-Jharial which lay in their original seat of power.

Umakanta Sibuddhi,[42] in his PhD thesis submits,"The Bhauma-Karas of Orissa do not include the Sixty-four Yoginī temple at Hirapur, among the art and architecture of the Bhauma-Kara period." The opinion of Mahapatra cannot be sustained owing to the great discoveries, and research findings. The Sixty-four Yoginīs in Tantra represent the 64 Tantras, 64 perfections of Yoga and 64 qualities of nature. The 64 *yoginīs* are first worshipped in *Yantra-Pūjā* (*yantra* worship) and it is a living practice.

---

38 R.P. Mishra, "Parimal Yoginī Piṭha Rānīpur-Jharial and Its Influence on the Culture of Western Orissa", *Souvenir, Bolangir Loka Utsav 2001*, Bolangir, 2001, English Section, pp. 107-17.

39 Ibid.; K.L. Mishra (ed.), *Yoginī Tantra*, Lakṣmi Venketsvar Press, Saṁvat 2013 and Sakabda 1878, Uttara Khaṇḍa Prathama Paṭala, pp. 241-42, verses 15-19.

40 K.C. Panigrahi, *History of Orissa* (*Hindu Period*), Cuttack: Kitab Mahal, 1981, p. 444.

41 Ibid., p. 454.

42 Umakanta Subuddhi, op. cit., pp. 129-44.

14

Two Academical Follies

THE academical world of India is following the British legacy of education, which is bequeathed from the Education Policy of Macaulay.[1] Only two instances of academical follies are discussed in this chapter. The first is the chronology of the history of Bhāratavarṣa and the second is the myth of the holy cow.

Chronology of the History of Bhāratavarṣa

While giving the definition and scope of history, Amarnath (Pen name of P.N. Oak)[2] mentions:

> In western language, the word "history" derives from the Greek word *historia*, meaning "inquiry". Obviously, this is a very misleading root since inquiry is common to every branch of knowledge. In fact, ever since a child is born he is always very inquisitive and is anxious to know many things about the world around him but he cannot be said to be thereby educating himself in history. Therefore, no one can have a clear notion of what "history" is, if he were to be guided solely by the etymological meaning of the western word "history".
>
> As against this, the Sanskrit word for history — *itihāsa* — is far more evocative. Nay, we may even say that the word *itihāsa* embodies a complete definition of what "history" is. That word is composed of these syllables. *iti* means "such and such (a happening or event)", *ha* means "definitely", *aas* means "happened". All that can be said to have definitely happened in the past is history. As such history may be defined as a factual and chronological account of past happenings.

As we discussed in Chapter 4, demeaning of the ancient history, religion and culture

---

1 *THACOTIP*, vol. X, part II, 1991, p. 37.

2 Amarnath, *Some Missing Chapters of World History*, New Delhi: Itihas Shodh Sansthan, 1973, pp. 19-20.

had been done by the imperialistic historians, and the Indian History Congress is still following the chronology of the history of ancient India as established during British rule. D.S. Trivedi[3] revolted against the established and taught chronology of history and wrote a book, *Indian Chronology (8231 BCE to CE 1963)*, which was published by Bharatiya Vidya Bhavan, Bombay in 1963. He states:

> It may look strange to present a chronology of India from the eighth millennium BCE to-date as the date history of no other country goes back to such a remote period. The Oxford and Cambridge histories of India do not take us beyond the fifth or the sixth century BCE. As a matter of fact, the history of no other country can be traced beyond. 1000 BCE on the basis of written records with the doubtful exception of Egypt and Babylon, but even there only the western scholars have come forward with their spades and the local scholars are silent.
>
> Indian scholars and archaeologists generally owe their allegiance not to India or the truth but their so-called preceptors and founders, the British, who did their best to belittle our history and culture. The real history of India is yet to be written based on indigenous sources and supplemented by all other sources wherever available.
>
> Rāṣṭrapati Dr. Rajendra Prasada says: "In a country like ours, where history is outweighed by what is known as the pre-historic period, the task of reclamation of more and more ground from the latter is of the utmost importance. The gaps in our knowledge of even the historical period pose another problem for Indian historians." (Message to the Indian History Congress, XII Session, Gauhati.)
>
> Modern history books and researches are based on two hypotheses, viz. the Aryan invasion of India and the Alexander-Sandracottus synchronism.
>
> All the dates of early Indian history before Harṣa are yet controversial. No date is acceptable to any two independent authorities. The Alexander-Sandracottus or Candragupta Maurya synchronism has been accepted by all modern historians, as a gospel of truth. But this has no acceptance anywhere in Indian literature, tradition or authority. It runs counter to all.
>
> The history of a country must be based on indigenous sources. The author claims no originality. He has only endeavoured to present the dates based

[3] D.S. Trivedi, *Indian Chronology* (8231 BCE to 1963 CE), Bombay: Bharatiya Vidya Bhavan, 1963, Preface and *passim*.

> on and revealed from original sources, unalloyed, unpolished, as he thinks that no scholar has ever attempted a consolidated and comprehensive chronology of India so far. The truth must triumph, as the author has adopted his motto, "to write nothing without basis and to say nothing unwarranted". He may be mistaken at many a steps. But he can only crave the indulgence of learned and impartial scholars to correct him.
>
> The writer cannot claim the same degree of exactness in dating the history for the pre-*Mahābhārata* period as the entire structure is built-up on an average reign per king. The king and events of the Kali age are traced from their original sources, Purāṇas, historical records, literature, inscriptions and coins, etc. During the historical period the author differs from all the recognized authorities. He has pronounced his definite views after discussing all the pros and cons on the subject in first rate research journals. One may judge the veracity of his statements in the following pages only after going through the papers cited in the foot-notes.
>
> His may be a voice in the wilderness and opposed to all. But truth comes out of dispassionate examination and discussion. He would request the scholars to throw light on it.

The struggle of Trivedi to reveal the true history of India finds expression in later works.

While dealing on "History and Ancient India Revisited", Deba Prasad Chaudhary[4] mentions:

> Whatever historical sense grew in ancient India, it is to be found in the Itihāsa-Purāṇa tradition, which is of pretty hoary origin. The Sanskrit word *Itihāsa* literally means so indeed it was (*iti-ha-asa*) which sounds rather familiar to us when we recollect Ranke's famous dictum *wie es eigentlichgewesen* (as it actually was), though the great connotative difference between the two does not escape us. The other word *purāṇa* literally means "old". These two words frequently occur conjointly in Vedic literature like the Brāhmaṇas, Āraṇyakas and Upaniṣads. They were allied classes of work consisting of secular tales, anecdotes, and songs which were composed, compiled and classified along with religious hymns since time immemorial. This secular

[4] D.P. Choudhary, "History and Ancient India Revisited", *The Quarterly Review of Historical Studies*, vol. XLIII, nos. 1 and 2, April to September 2003, Kolkata: Institute of Historical Studies, pp. 10-13.

literature included the Gāthā and Nārasaṁsī (which were hero-lauds and eulogies) mentioned in the *Ṛgveda*. There were thus two parallel trends, religious and secular. According to F.E. Pargiter,[5] after the religious hymns were separated to constitute the Vedas, the secular tales, anecdotes and songs were collected in a Purāṇa. This original Purāṇa, though now lost, was the source of all the later Purāṇas. All these suggest the existence of an oral tradition of great antiquity embodied in a kind of historical literature distinct from, but simultaneously developing with, the religious hymns which were later collected to form the Vedas. While from the early Vedic age we have evidence of the Gāthā and Nārasaṁsī, from at least the later Vedic age we have, in addition, evidence of the Itihāsa-Purāṇa which eventually absorbed all genres of historical compositions — the amorphous mass of history and legend — which had been developing from earliest times.[6]

Thus the great antiquity of the Itihāsa-Purāṇa tradition cannot be doubted. But what is more relevant in the present context is to see if this tradition spanning perhaps a few millennia has got any historical value. For this purpose one has to look into the Purāṇic genealogies which are believed to provide the very foundation for the reconstruction of the political history of ancient India. Pargiter in his two seminal publications — *The Purāṇa Text of the Dynasties of the Kali Age* (1913) and *Ancient Indian Historical Tradition* (1922) — convincingly established the historical worthness of the Purāṇic genealogies of ruling dynasties. In spite of gaps and errors, they exhibit a remarkable degree of consistency even though they are drawn from different contexts. They give us history as preserved and transmitted by a professional class of people, the *sūtas*, whose business it was to preserve the memories of the past. The Jain and Buddhist historical traditions also supplement and support the Purāṇic accounts. Besides, archaeological excavations, coins and inscriptions are increasingly confirming the Purāṇic genealogies. Noted scholars like U.N. Ghosal, A.D. Pusalkar and H.D. Sankalia also admit the historical merit of the Purāṇic data.[7]

The historical worth of the Purāṇas is mainly to be found in the *vaṁśānucarita*

---

[5] D.P. Choudhary, op. cit.; F.E. Pargiter, *Ancient Indian Historical Tradition*, Delhi, 1962, pp. 21-22.

[6] Ibid.; V.S. Pathak, *Ancient Indian Historian of India*, Bombay: 1966, pp. 1-8 and 14; G.P. Singh, *Early Indian Historical Tradition and Archaeology*, New Delhi, 1994, p. 17.

[7] Ibid.; G.P. Singh, op. cit., 1994, pp. 22-23, 209-10, and 212.

sections, which state royal genealogies till the middle of the first millennium CE. They are essentially chronological. Although the Purāṇas supply some reliable evidences relating to the dynasties prior to the Kurukṣetra War,[8] the dynastic and genealogical accounts of the post-war period increasingly became precise and credible, even mentioning the regnal years of kings, as they approach historically established time, especially from the sixth century BCE to the rise of the imperial Guptas. Their mode of time reckoning also significantly changes from the cosmological *mahāyuga* and the start of the *Kaliyuga* to the more practical historical time. The accuracy of this reckoning is borne out by reference to historical eras like the *Kṛta* (58 BCE), Śaka (CE 78), Cedi (CE 249), Gupta (CE 319-20), Harṣa (CE 606) and so on, and by the very precise dates recorded in inscriptions in era, regnal year, and even the season, month and day.[9]

The Purāṇic royal genealogies come to a close after the Guptas. In the post-Gupta period one notices a generic change from the Purāṇic *vaṁśānucaritas* to the *vaṁśāvalīs* and the *caritas*, two new forms of historical literature, which as it were taken up the narrative from where the major Purāṇas leave off. The *vaṁśāvalīs* occupy an intermediate position between the Purāṇic genealogies and the *caritas*. A *vaṁśāvalī* was the chronicle of a particular dynasty ruling in a specific region and, as such, it was also the chronicle of that region. By linking the local traditions with the Purāṇic accounts it sought to legitimize the group in power. The *vaṁśāvalīs* became the typical historical literature in various parts of India in the early second millennium CE, like the *vaṁśāvalīs* of Kangra, Kumaon, Garhwal and Rajasthan. The *caritas* were biographies of individual rulers. Eulogizing the royal patron the *carita* links him with a major Purāṇic lineage or some new lineage which had acquired status. The *carita* literature developed in the hands of many authors like Bānabhaṭṭa (*Harṣacarita*), Vākapati (*Gauḍvaha*) and Sandhyākaranandi (*Rāmacarita*).[10]

This mainstream development of the historical sense was paralleled by the growth of the Buddhist tradition which exhibited a keener sense of history.

---

[8] V.S. Pathak, op. cit.; G.P. Singh, op. cit., pp. 20, and 209; R.M. Smith, *Dates and Dynasties in Earliest India*, Delhi, 1973, p. 1.

[9] Ibid.; G.P. Singh, op. cit., p. 19; R. Thapar, "Society and Historical Consciousness: the Itihāsa-Purāṇa Tradition", in S. Bhattacharya and R. Thapar (eds.), *Situating Indian History*, Delhi, 1986, pp. 275, 372,

R. Thapar, *Interpreting Early India*, New Delhi, 1992, pp. 162-63.

[10] Ibid.; Ibid.; R. Thapar, *Interpreting Early India*, pp. 166-71.

As rebels against the great tradition, the Buddhists must have felt the need of establishing their authenticity by situating themselves in actual events rather than legends. They linked the major event of their sect with the political events and personalities of the time. For various practical purposes they carefully preserved historical records of transactions and decisions of their order. Their tradition supplements and supports the Purāṇic accounts and thus proves the existence of the definite sense of history in ancient India. Warder observes that since they built on pre-Buddhist tradition, there is no reason to suppose that their activity was not paralleled by that of other sects.[11]

Thus the historical sense originating in an embryonic form in a remote past subsequently matured by stages into articulated forms. It began in oral traditions of which possibly the earliest known specimens were the Gāthā and Nārasaṁsī, and then we come across the *vaṁśānucaritas*, *vaṁśāvalīs* and *caritas* which exhibit an increasing manifestation of the historical consciousness. This process was further supplemented by the parallel growth of the Buddhist tradition since pre-Christian times. But in spite of this rather creditable achievement of ancient India, she has often been disparaged for her lack of historical consciousness. To examine this charge we need to investigate certain closely interrelated issues, viz., who brought this charge, when and why it was brought, and if it is tenable in the light of our knowledge of the ancient Greco-Roman tradition, modern philosophy of history and even modern science.

At this juncture much magnitude discoveries are done. The politics of history[12] is now exposed; Bhāratavarṣa, i.e. India is now awakened;[13] and both critical and comparative studies of history and culture regarding ancient India are continuing in great speed. The publication of His Divinity Dharm Chakrvarti Swami Prakashanand Saraswati's book, *The True History and the Religion of India*[14] has exposed the true chronology of the history of Bhāratavarṣa since its origination, which is given in Appendix I.

---

[11] R. Thapar, op. cit.; A.K. Warder, "The Pali Canon and Its Commentaries as a Historical Record", in C.H. Philips (ed.), *Historians of India, Pakistan and Ceylon*, London, 1962, p. 55; Thapar, *Society and Historical Consciousness*, pp. 373-74; G.P. Singh, *Early Indian Historical Tradition and Archaeology*, New Delhi, 1994, pp. 22-23.

[12] N.S. Rajaram, *The Politics of History*, New Delhi: Voice of India, 1995, *passim*.

[13] David Frawley, *Awakend Bharata: A Call for India's Rebirth*, New Delhi: Voice of India, 1998, *passim*.

[14] Swami Prakashanand Saraswati, *The True History and the Religion of India*, Delhi: Motilal Banarsidass, 2001, *passim*.

The Myth of the Holy Cow

Amarnath[15] rightly states that India's history has been written by her enemies. With the advancement of modern science, speedy progress in every walk of human life and consciousness is taking place. There is a saying that "Time creates a man (*alias* an individual)". At such a cross-road of world happenings, the book, *The True History and the Religion of India,*[16] solves great problems of the misunderstanding of Indian history, religion and culture.

Suresh Chandra Banerji[17] has also found out the foundations, on which the global cultural edifice has been built. The world civilization is like a mighty old tree that ramified through centuries and India played the roles of both the lender and the borrower in different facets of culture, architecture, sculpture, music, astronomy, mathematics, medical science, literature etc.

To the edification of Indian history and culture, the work of Bharatiya Vidya Bhavan in publishing eleven volumes of *The History and Culture of the Indian People* is commendable. The group of scholars who wrote these volumes have followed the established political chronology of Indian history as established by the British imperialistic historians and, therefore, not free from the British influence.

While dealing on marriage and the position of women in the Vedic Age, V.M. Apte[18] states:

> A hymn in *Ṛgveda* (X.85), which may be called the wedding hymn, gives us some idea of the oldest marriage ritual. The bridegroom and party proceed to the bride's house (X.17.1.) where the well-adorned bride remains ready (IV.58.9) to join the marriage-feast. The guests are entertained with the flesh of cows killed on the occasion (X.85.13).

Further, while dealing on the food and drink, Apte[19] mentions that meat also formed a part of the dietary. The flesh of the ox, sheep and goat was normally eaten, after being roasted on spits or cooked in earthenware or metal pots.

---

15 Amarnath, *Some Missing Chapters of World History*, New Delhi: Itihas Shodh Sansthan, 1973, pp. 12-18.

16 *TTHATROI*, 2001, *passim*.

17 Suresh Chandra Banerji, *Cultural Reciprocation between India and the World*, Delhi: Sharada Publishing House, (?) *passim*.

18 V.M. Apte, "Social and Economic Conditions", *THACOTIP*, vol. I, *The Vedic Age*, 1965, pp. 392-93.

19 Ibid., V.M. Apte, p. 396.

Further, on food and drink and of the social and economic conditions, Apte[20] says that meat-eating seems to be fairly common, as in the Ṛgvedic age. The *Śatapatha Brāhmaṇa* prescribes the killing of a great ox or goat in honour of a guest. Generally, meat was eaten on the occasion of some ceremony or other, but such ceremonies were performed almost everyday. Its use is forbidden during the observance of a vow. It appears that the killing of cows gradually came into disfavour. The normal meat-diet consisted of the flesh of the sheep, the goat and the ox, the usual sacrificial victims. Man offered to gods what he himself ate.

At first, let us consider a work of D.N. Jha named *Holy Cow in India* (2001), and other book *The Myth of the Holy Cow* (2002). Academically Jha did a beautiful work by quoting all the published materials, which are the source materials. This is academical method of research works, going on in India, i.e. Bhāratavarṣa.

Now the question arises about the authenticity of the source materials studied by Indian scholars of history and culture.

We Indians are not aware about the great politics of British India administrators. Swami Prakashanand Saraswati[21] has exposed all the mis-deeds of fabrications, and has dealt in chapter 3 of *The True History and in the Religion of India* on the eternity of the Sanskrit language, the diplomatic schemes of the British during the eighteenth, nineteenth and twentieth centuries to destroy the culture, language, religion and history of Bhāratavarṣa, and their effects on Hindu writers.

Max Müller, a paid employee of the British government, who translated the *Ṛgveda* in a demeaning style, had some hidden agenda. Going by the letter between him and his wife one has to believe that Pandit Taranath of Calcutta was given money by the British to misinterpet certain words of the Vedic Saṁhitā to reflect the meaning, according to Max Müller's translation of the Vedas. The Sanskrit dictionary *Vācaspatyam*, that Pandit Taranath compiled is still being used by the scholars of Sanskrit. There are certain uncommon words in the Saṁhitā or *mantra* section of the Vedas which are not used in Purāṇas. So, the Sanskrit scholars generally do not notice the artfulness of Taranath in corrupting the meanings of those Vedic words, and they take it for granted that all the word-meanings of the *Vācaspatyam* are correct. That is what the Britishers wanted, that the dictionary by a Hindu *paṇḍit* would be accepted to all the Hindus and, in that way, they could claim that whatever Max Müller wrote about the Vedas was according to the dictionary of the Hindus.

---

[20] V.M. Apte, "Social and Economic Conditions", *THACOTIP*, vol. I, *The Vedic Age*, 1965, p. 461.

[21] *TTHATROI*, 2001, chapter 3, pp. 223-404.

Now, it is worth quoting Swami Prakashanand Saraswati,[22] to know about this background.

1. Max Müller was a British agent, especially employed (in 1847) to write the translations of the Vedas in such a demeaning way so that the Hindu should lose faith in them. His personal letter to his wife dated 9 December 1867 reveals this fact.
2. He was highly paid for this job. According to the statistical information given on page 214 of the *English Education, 1798–1902*, by John William Adamson, printed by Cambridge University Press in 1930, the revised scale of a male teacher was £ 90 per year and for a woman, £ 60 in 1853. The present salary of a teacher in London is £ 14,000 to £ 36,000 per year, which averages a minimum of at least 200 times increase in the last 146 years. Max Müller was paid £ 4 per sheet of his writing which comes to £ 800 of today (1999). This is an incredibly high price for only one sheet of writing. But it's the general law of business that the price of a commodity increases with its demand. The British were in such an imperative need to get someone to do this job and Max Müller was the right person, so they paid whatever Max Müller asked for. His enthusiastic letter to his mother dated 15 April 1847 reveals this fact.
3. Max Müller's letters dated 25 August 1856 – 26 February 1867 and 16 December 1868 reveal the fact that he was desperate to bring Christianity into India so that the religion of the Hindus should be doomed.

His letters also reveal that:

4. He lived in poverty before he was employed by the British.
5. His duplicity in translation was praised by his superiors.
6. In London, where he lived, there were a lot of orientalists working for the British.

Swami Prakashanand Saraswati[23] has exposed many letters and diaries of Max Müller. The author is quoting, only a few of them here.

---

[22] *TTHATROI*, 2001, pp. 261, 263, 265 and 272.

[23] *TTHATROI*, 2001, pp. 268-272.

LETTERS OF MAX MÜLLER
First published in 1902 (London and N.Y.), reprint in 1976 (USA).

(1) To his wife, Oxford, 9 December 1867

. . . I feel convinced, though I shall not live to see it, that this edition of mine and the translation of the Veda will hearafter tell to a great extent on the fate of India, and on the growth of millions of souls in that country. It is the root of their religion, and to show them what that root is, I feel sure, the only way of uprooting all that has sprung from it during the last 3,000 years.

(2) To his mother, 5 Newman's Row Lincoln's Inn Fields, 15 April 1847

I can yet hardly believe that I have at last got what I have struggled for so long. . . . I am to hand over to the company, ready for press, fifty sheets each year, for this I have asked £ 200 a year, £ 4 a sheet. They have been considering the matter since December, and it was only yesterday that it was officially settled.

. . . In fact, I spent a delightful time, and when I reached London yesterday I found all settled and I could say and feel, thank God! Now I must at once send my thanks, and set to work to earn the first £ 100.

(3) (a) To Chealier Bursen, 55 St. John Street, Oxford, 25 August 1856

India is much riper for Christianity than Rome or Greece were at the time of St. Paul. The rotten tree has for some time had artificial supports. . . . For the good of this struggle I should like to lay down my life, or at least to lend my hand to bring about this struggle. Dhulip Singh is much at Court, and is evidently destined to play a political part in India.

I should like to live for ten years quite quietly and learn the language, try to make friends, and then see whether I was fit to take part in a work, by means of which the old mischief of Indian priestcraft could be overthrown and the way opened for the entrance of simple Christian teaching. . . . Whatever finds root in India soon overshadows the whole of Asia.

Much more could be said about this; a wide world opens before one, for which it is well worth while to give one's life. And what is to be done here? here in England? here in Oxford? nothing but to help polish up a few ornaments of a Cathedral which is rotten at the base.

(b) To the Dean of St. Paul's (Dr. Milman), Staunton House, Bournemouth, 26 February 1867

I have myself the strongest belief in the growth of Christianity in India. There is no country so ripe for Christianity as India, and yet the difficulties seem enormous.

(c) To the Duke of Argyll, Oxford, 16 December 1868

India has been conquered once, but India must be conquered again, and that second conquest should be a conquest by education. Much has been done for education of late, but if the funds were tripled and quadrupled, that would hardly be enough. . . . A new national literature may spring up, impregnated with western ideas, yet retaining its native spirit and character. . . . A new national literature will bring with it a new national life, and a new moral vigour as to religion, that will take care of itself. The missionaries have done far more than they themselves seem to be aware of.

The ancient religion of India is doomed, and if Christianity does not step in, whose fault will it be?

With this much exposer of the deeds of Max Müller, let me quote:

How did the impious statements of animal killing and meat eating enter certain scriptures? as told by Swami Prakashananad Saraswati[24] thus:

The earliest Sanskrit commentary on *Manu-Smṛti* which is available is of Medhātithi (मेधातिथि) who was somewhere here between CE 820 and 1050. There are such statements in the existing *Manu-Smṛti* which relate to the animal killing and meat eating as a regular routine of the Vedic *yajña*s and they specifically prescribe to serve meat in the *śrāddha*. (*śrāddha* is a pious religious ceremony related to the appeasement of the souls of the elderly members of the family who are dead. In this ceremony pious brāhmaṇas are invited to dine.) Another important commentary is of Kullūkabhaṭṭa (कुल्लूकभट्ट), a Beṅgālī brāhmaṇa who was between CE 1150 and 1300. There are many more commentaries on the *Manu-Smṛti* but all of them have used the same text.

It shows that such impious statements of animal killing and meat eating, etc. in the *Manu-Smṛti* have been interpolated long before Medhātithi. But

[24] *TTHATROI*, pp. 330-36.

still the question remains that in those days there were no printing presses, so all the copies of *Manu-Smṛti* were in hand written form, copied by different people. So, there was a definite possibility that there must have also been such copies in existence that would have been pure and genuine. Thus, there must have been both kinds of copies. Corruptedly interpolated ones and the genuine ones. Medhātithi belonged to north India somewhere near Kashmir.

The copy he got was the interpolated one. There was greater chance of getting a genuine copy of *Manu-Smṛti* in Kāśī (Varanasi) because Kāśī has remained the centre of scriptural wisdom and scriptural learning for a very long time and a lot of Sanskrit scholars always lived over there. But Medhātithi probably did not care much to do proper efforts to obtain the genuine copy; and his such sloppiness confirms the quality of his being that either he himself was a non-vegetarian (as many Kashmiris are), or he was only a worldly intellectual who did not care much about the holiness of the Hindu religion and showed his scholarly wisdom in writing the comments.

The commentators like Kullūkabhaṭṭa and others used the same interpolated text without giving any thought that how could such impious statements of animal killing and meat eating have entered in the text when *Manu-Smṛti* strongly admonishes that one should never drink and should never even smell any intoxicant like wine (11/146-149) and assert that selling, buying, cooking and eating meat is a sin which is as great as killing an animal itself (5/15). However, the question still remains that: When were those interpolations done?

We have to look into the history before the advent of Gautama Buddha when there were kṣatriya kings who ruled various parts of India. Those non-vegetarian worldly and ambitious kings, presuming to receive heavenly luxuries, had started doing animal sacrifices in the name of *yajña*. It is the nature of *Kaliyuga* that once a wrong and unholy tradition starts in the world, it grows like a bush fire. The same thing happened with this tradition and all the kings and the landlords, big or small, excessively started doing animal sacrifices and the poor brāhmaṇas, in the greed of getting money, supervised and conducted such *yajña*s.

This was the time when the powerful kings, to religiously justify their wrong deeds of killing and eating the animals, made the brāhmaṇa scholars create such verses and chapters that should exactly match the literary style of the scriptures and added them in the Smṛtis, Gṛhya-Sūtras and Dharma-Sūtras, etc. as they were the main religious books related to the ritual performances. Statements of meat eating in *śrāddha* and offering it to God and offering meat to guests as a compulsory act was also added in the Smṛtis, etc. whenever there was a chapter on *śrāddha*. During that period Gautama Buddha came and taught the lesson of compassion to all the beings, and this was the main reason of his descension.

Buddhist community, after the death of Buddha, became totally critical of Vedic religion and did a lot of damage to it by destroying our religious books. Later on, when Jagadguru Śaṅkarācārya descended, he contradicted Buddhism and re-established Sanātana Dharma. During his time there must have been some interpolated copies of Smṛtis, and the Sūtras, but most of the copies especially in Kāśī would have been in their genuine shape.

There was again a big change in the history of India when the Hūṇa and Śaka tribes began to invade and started settling in north India. They were selfish, ambitious and meat eaters. The Śakas began to rule certain parts of India. There is a great possibility that during that period also a lot of similar interpolations concerning the animal killing and meat eating would have been done in the Smṛtis and the Sūtras and subsequently the interpolations of offering meat in *śrāddha* to brāhmaṇas and the Gods would also have been added in the Purāṇas. The Śakas were quite powerful before Vikramāditya and also during the time of Śālivāhana (CE 78).

So we see that such impious interpolations in Smṛtis and Sūtras, etc. were not the work of one single period; they were done during the span of thousands of years and under the instructions of the ruling kings of that time, because the wordings themselves give a smell of perverted sovereignty.

Take an example: In the seventeenth chapter of *Matsya Purāṇa,* there are *śrāddha*-related five interpolated verses, from verses 31 to 35.

While describing the procedure of *śrāddha*, verse 30 says that the vegetarian food prepared with pure butter, milk, sugar and curd, etc. are most pleasing to *pitṛ* gods; and verse 36 says that apart from that cow's milk, honey and the sweet pudding made of milk, rice and sugar with dry nuts (called खीर — *khīra*) satisfies *pitṛ* gods for ever. Verses 31 to 35 describes the acts of cooking and offering all kinds of meat to *pitṛ* gods which is totally out of place and out of context and it evidently appears that it has been deliberately interpolated. These five verses name the flesh of all kinds of beings: fish, gazelle, sheep, special birds, goat, deer, black deer, pig, buffalo, rabbit, turtle, a special deer and rhino.

The mention of turtle and rhino especially indicates towards the royal affiliation. The flesh of turtle and rhino is considered to stimulate sexual efficacy and especially a preparation of the horn of rhino is known to be a potent aphrodisiac, which was desired by the indulgent kings of those days. Another thing is that the rhinos were hunted for royal purposes as their skin was used to make shields for the warriors. The last thing is that when the *pitṛ* gods are perfectly appeased with *khīra* and vegetarian food that could be prepared at a very nominal cost then why should one go around looking to procure an almost impossible thing like the flesh of a rhino, unless he is totally mindless. Thus, these impious interpolations which, on one side, reflect the low wittedness of the people who added such verses in religious books, and on the other side, they also expose the pervertedness of the ruling kings of that time who directed such insertions just to justify their sinful acts of killing an animal and eating its flesh. So, such statements were added in Bhāratīya scriptures in many ways and in many styles. At one place an interpolated verse of the *Manu-Smṛti* says that Brahmā created all the birds and animals for the human beings to eat (5/ 28). See some more examples of such interpolation and the style of their fabrication.

They created such verses and Sūtras which exactly fitted with the style of the writing of that particular scripture, and added them at a convenient location in the book. There are three kinds of fabrications: (a) altering only a few words of a verse to change its meaning, (b) creating a new verse of the desired meaning, and (c) creating a full new section of a chapter to elaborate the killing and meat eating episodes.

Such passages were liberally added in the Smṛtis, Śrauta-Sūtras and Gṛhya-Sūtras because these are the books that describe the details of the rituals, ceremonies and the codes of conduct. We will give you a couple of examples.

There is a book called *Āśvalāyana Gṛhya-Sūtram* by sage Āśvalāyana (EBC, Delhi, 1976). After the ritualistic description of the full moon ceremony, there is a section (section 11 of chapter 1) that tells about an animal sacrifice. The full section is a fabrication. There are detailed descriptions in chapter 4 about the funeral ceremony and śraddha (the Vedic ceremony for the deceased in the family). At the very end of this chapter a section of 45 *sūtras* is a fabricated statement which is called *śūla-gavaḥ* (शूलगवः). It tells about the ox or bull sacrifice for Śiva for the full family prosperity (wealth, cattle, merit and longevity). The blunder of this fabrication is that the divine carrier of God Śiva is a bull, and in this fabrication his own carrier bull is being cut, killed and sacrificed to appease him. Isn't it a doltish fabrication? But it is there in that book. This *śūla-gavaḥ* is repeated in other Gr̥hya-Sūtras also. Take one more example.

The *Manu-Smr̥ti* is one of the most popular names in Hindu religious code books. It has been cleverly fabricated at many places with the alteration of the wordings of a verse, addition of a verse, or adding a whole section of fabricated verses in a chapter. But one thing is certain that, except the killing of an animal and the meat eating fabrications the rest of the writings of the book are in original form because those people had no interest in our philosophical (or *līlā*-related) descriptions.

These are the strict admonitions of the *Manu-Smr̥ti* (11/94, 95 and 5/48, 51). It means, "Brāhmaṇas, kṣatriyas and vaiśyas should never drink wine, liquor or intoxicants of any kind, because intoxicant, wine, liquor and the meat of animals are the food of demons and *rākṣasa*s. So they must not be consumed". Further it says, "Flesh of an animal is obtained only after killing him which is a sin and the killer of animals never enters the celestial abode. All the people who are involved in the killing, consenting the killing, helping the killing, carrying, selling, buying, cooking and eating the meat of an animal or any living being are equally sinful as the killing of that animal or that living being itself."

Now look to a few of its fabricated verses: one verse says that Brahmā has created the animals for the purpose of killing them in the *yajña* (*Manu-Smr̥ti* 5/39); in the Vedic *yajña* it is prescribed by God that meat must be eaten (5/31); and in the *śrāddha* the host must serve the best kind of meat to the brāhmaṇas to eat (3/123).

Considering the nature and the style of the writings of the *Manu-Smr̥ti*, these additions, on their face value appear to be totally out of place as if they have deliberately patched up. We have given just a few examples. There are a lot of such disgusting and insulting fabrications that show the character of the fabricators. Sometimes they go to such an extent that at one place a fabricated verse (5/35) says that the brāhmaṇa who does not eat the meat offered by the host on a ceremonial occasion is punished to be born into the lower species and becomes an animal after his death. In the fifth chapter of *Manu-Smṛti* there are 24 verses of that kind, all in a row, and in the third chapter there are seven verses of that kind which are related to *śrāddha*.

Such fabricated interpolations were liberally done in most of the places where there is a description of *śrāddha* and the wordings (as shown above in the *Matsya Purāṇa*) exactly match everywhere without much change, as if they were done by one group of people and then blindly further interpolated by the others. *Mārkaṇḍeya Purāṇa, Garuḍa Purāṇa, Vāyu Purāṇa, Brahma Purāṇa* and *Yājñavalkya-Smṛti*, etc. they all have same kind of fabrications.

Apart from that, in *Śatapatha Brāhmaṇa, Taittirīya Brāhmaṇa, Aitareya Brāhmaṇa, Āpastamba Dharma-Sūtra, Vasiṣṭha Dharma-Sūtra* and other Dharma-Sūtras and Gṛhya-Sūtras, there are such statements that were inserted not only to justify the meat eating but to prescribe animal killing and meat eating as a compulsory rule on certain occasions and ceremonies. But, at the same time, it is also a well-known fact that all of the scriptures and also the Smṛtis have profoundly stressed on pious living and explained the hellish consequences of the sinful acts of consuming wine, eating meat and killing an animal for any reason. Even then, such evil statements were created and inserted in our religious books.

A question still remains: Whether all the existing hand written copies of our religious books were interpolated at that time, or were there some of them in their fully genuine shape? The answer is simple. Although there is more evil in the world due to *Kaliyuga* but still there are always some good people in the society. So, there were definitely some handwritten copies with some pious Sanskrit scholars; that were unblemished. But those books slowly disappeared during the English rule.

This narration of Swami Prakashanand Saraswati makes the readers aware of the politics, policies and fabrications done during British regime. It seems Jha[25] was not aware of these, therefore academical mind of him had been duped of cheated, hence, he wrote the earlier mentioned two books and fell victim to the trick of British politics and policies. His works are unacceptable and are academically unfit.

---

[25] D.N. Jha, *The Myth of the Holy Cow*, London/New York: Verso, 2002, *passim*.

Appendix I

Chronology of the History of Bhāratavarṣa Since Its Origin

(*Source*: His Divinity Dharm Chakravarti Swami Prakashanand Sarasvati, *The True History and the Religion of India*, Delhi: Motilal Banarsidass, 2001, pp. 500-03.)

Period	*Description*
(Trillion Years ago)	
155.521972	Birth of Brahmā, the first *kalpa* called the Brahma-kalpa.
(155.521971961600 in 1998)	Brahmā meditates and conceives all the Vedas and Purāṇas with the Grace of Kṛṣṇa. His homage to Kṛṣṇa at that time is called the *Brahma-Saṁhitā*.
155.513332	The second *kalpa*. Brahmā creates the *brahmāṇḍa*, produces the first ten *ṛṣi*s, *deva*s and *asura*s (Gods and demons are created.) They are called the celestial Gods and demons. The main abodes of the Gods are: *bhū*, *bhuva*, *svaḥ* (the abode of God Indra), *maḥ*, *jana*, *tapa* and *satya* (the abode of Brahmā). (The general term for the abode of the demons is *pātāla-loka* which is below the celestial abodes of Gods and near *bhū-loka*. All these abodes are in a separate space and dimension. Later on the ozone layer is formed on the earth planet. Brahmā produces Svayambhuva Manu and Śatarūpā, the *ṛṣi*s on the earth planet conceive the Vedas and Purāṇas; and gradually the human civilization develops. (There are 14 *manvantara* in a *kalpa* and in every *kalpa* similar divine historical events happen. Uptil now 18,000 *kalpa*s have already elapsed. One *kalpa* along with Brahmā's night is 8,640 million years.)
(Million years ago)	**(The existing *kalpa*)**
1971.961600 (as in 1998)	Beginning of the existing day (*kalpa*) of Brahmā and first *manvantara* of Svayambhuva Manu and Śatarūpā. Svayambhuva Manu had two sons and three daughters.

	Bhakta Dhruva was from his second son Uttamapāda, sage Kapila was from his daughter Deohūti and Bhakta Prahlāda was in the family succession of his first son Priyavrat.
1663.3902	Beginning of the second *manvantara* of Svarociśa Manu.
1354.8188	Beginning of the third *manvantara* of Uttama Manu.
1046.2474	Beginning of the fourth *manvantara* of Tamas Manu.
737.676	Beginning of the fifth *manvantara* of Raivata Manu.
429.1045	Beginning of the sixth *manvantara* of Cakṣuṣa Manu.
120.5331	Beginning of the seventh *manvantara* of Vaivasvata Manu.
120.5331[*]	Beginning of the existing (seventh) *manvantara* of Vaivasvata Manu who had ten sons and one daughter. Sūrya-vaṁśa starts from his elder son Ikṣavāku and Candra-vaṁṣa starts from his daughter Elā. Bhakta Ambarīṣa was in the third generation of his son Nābhāga.
57.024	Emperor Māndhātā's rule in Bhāratavarṣa.
39.744	Descension of Paraśurāma.
18.144	Descension of Bhagavān Rāma.
(BCE)	**(From 3228 BCE onward)**
3228[**]	Descension of Bhagavān Kṛṣṇa.
3139	The Mahābhārata war (lasted for 18 days). Beginning of Bṛhadratha dynasty of Magadha, and Yudhiṣṭhira dynasty of Hastināpur. (Bṛhadratha dynasty starts with Mārjari so it is also called the dynasty of Mārjari family.)
3102	Ascension of Bhagavān Kṛṣṇa and the beginning of *Kaliyuga*.
2139	End of Bṛhadratha dynasty (21 kings for 1,000 years).
2139–2001	Pradyot dynasty (5 kings for 138 years).
2001–1641	Śiśunāga dynasty (10 kings for 360 years).
1894–1814	Gautama Buddha.
1641–1541	Nandas (Mahāpadma Nanda and his 8 sons for 100 years).
1541–1241	Maurya dynasty (10 kings for about 300 years).
1541–1507	Candragupta Maurya (34 years).
1507–1479	Bindusāra (28 years).
1479–443	Aśokavardhana (36 years).

1241–784	Śuṅga and Kāṇva dynasty (14 kings for 457 years).
784–328	Āndhra dynasty (30 kings for 456 years).
509–477	Jagadguru Śaṅkarācārya.
328–83	Gupta dynasty (7 kings for 245 years). (Candragupta Vijayāditya, 328–321 BCE and Alexander's invasion was in 326 BCE).
321–270	Samudragupta Aśokāditya Priyadarśin, or Aśoka the Great.
102 BCE – CE 15	Vikramāditya, established the Vikrama era in 57 BCE.
(CE)	
25–85	Śālivāhana (ruled for 60 years), established Śālivāhana Śaka era in CE 78.
85–1192	There were several kingdoms of Rājpūt kings all over India. They ruled for 1,107 years.
1192–1757	In 1192, Mohmmad Ghori invaded Delhi (Hastināpura) the second time, defeated and killed Pṛthvīrāja Cauhāna, and became the king. Since then several dynasties of Muslims ruled India for 565 years.
1757–1947	In 1757, English regime was established in Bengal. British ruled India for 190 years.
1947	In 1947, India got Independence.

---

* The Purāṇas mention more than 50 important personalities of Sūrya-vaṁśa who were between Ikṣavāku and Bhagavān Rāma (102 million years).

** According to the *Sūrya-Siddhānta,* the astrologers have calculated that *Kaliyuga* started on the afternoon of 17 February 3102 BCE. In the *Bhāgavatam,* Brahmā tells in round figures that Kṛṣṇa remained on this earth planet for 125 years.

यदुवंशेऽवतीर्णस्य भवेतः पुरुषोत्तम।
शरच्छतं व्यतीयाय पञ्चविंशाधिकं प्रभो॥

– 11.6.25

Accordingly, if you add 125 years to Feburary 3102, it comes to Feburary 3227 BCE but Kṛṣṇa's descension was in the Rohiṇī *nakṣatra* (asterism) of the 8th waning moon midnight of Bhādoṅ (August) which is about seven months earlier. Thus, his descension date is 3228 BCE and he stayed on the earth planet for 125 years and about 7 months.

Appendix II

Pañca Sāgara Tīrtha (The Pilgrimage of Five Oceans)

(Written in Oriya by Prafulla Chandra Bhanja Deo, tr. (verbatim) into English by Juga Bhanu Singh Deo.)

(*Source*: Juga Bhanu Singh Deo, *A Man Called Prafulla Chandra Bhanja Deo*, Bhubaneswar, 2005, pp. 196-216.)

The event took place four years back. "There existed near my ancestral property an exquisite religious site." Hearing this, I started making arrangements to spend five nights there. Since the place is located between a forest and a mountain, I decided to take a retinue of seventy workers and friends. All the forests are full of wild animals, including elephants and tigers. One can reach the destination after a trek of six miles on foot.

The journey started on 21 January 1954. My two sons and one daughter were with me. Before the start of the journey, I prayed to my *guru* and reached the destination by evening after traversing six miles of jungle path. That moment, amidst the gurgling waters of "Deva" mountain-stream coming down through the rocks, making a waterfall on the serene crystal-clear celestial pond of Deva Kuṇḍa, and the sighting of "Divine Light", created a strange phenomenon which overwhelmed the core of our hearts with peace and tranquillity. Yet the voluminous noise of the waterfall beckons the ears to hear more. I sat down for my evening (*sandhyā*) prayers, and whilst doing so and bringing *guru* into focus, I felt my soul-micro — has merged into cosmos-macrocosm; only the noise of the waterfall brought my outer conscience back, and I saw in the dark night up in the sky thousand stars shining like jewels, and in front of me they appeared as if thousands of them were twinkling their eyes at me. That night we did not get sleep because of the presence of roaring tigers and trumpeting elephants, which shook us rather badly. Early morning, up from bed, oblation and bathing in crystal clear Deva-Kuṇḍa, which brought in immediate peace within me. I felt as if *guru* has decided to send me here for *sādhanā* to this *tapasyā* (penance) ground. Most of my colleagues also experienced this sublime feeling.

Next day (22-1-1954) *ādivāsī*s (aboriginals) living in the wilderness brought fresh honey with the honey-combs, collected from the mountains. After finishing my daily routine, I witnessed a strange happening. We were swarmed with countless bees but they did not harm us; only sat down on the honey-combs and started sucking the nectar. Thereafter all flew back towards the mountain. That day some of my workers had climbed up a hill-top and planted a flag. The same night my middle son, Shri Makardwaj Bhanja Deo, and Narendra Giri said they had seen across the pond in the darkness a blue luminous object — but after closely examining the spot nothing was found, in spite of my spending a long time thereafter.

Third Day's Happening (23-01-1954)

Sitting on a stone inside Deva *nadī* stream, after a bath for my evening prayers, suddenly my forehead was filled with infra-red light of the rising sun. Now not knowing what to do, and thinking it must be something to do with the setting sun, I opened my eyes — there was no sign of the sun or any glow in the sky of the impending dusk, as it was fully covered with clouds. Again I closed my eyes — and then again that luminous object started pounding on my forehead. Somehow in the midst of this experience I could manage to complete my evening prayers.

Some time elapsed thinking about the above. A courier came from Baripāḍā, bringing my *ḍāk* (mails), the news of passing away of my eldest daughter (Kamalā) of Bastar. The enactment of life and death, as well as showering of nectar by the bounteous Devī Bhagavatī, prompted me to proceed to the *kuṇḍa* for *darśana* and completion of my evening prayers. On completion, during the dinner-time my chief aide, Shri Padma Lochan Jena, was by my side looking after me. He was heading west, to bring water for washing my hands, when he shouted aloud "By father, what a big glow over Deva-Kuṇḍa." Saying this he got down from a rock and started running towards the *kuṇḍa* (pond). We all ran behind him and stood still — believers and non-believers — some chanting religious rhymes, other doing salutations, and others with closed eyes offering prayers. The reflection of Divine Light (Jyoti Darśana) from Deva-Kuṇḍa waters stretched towards us, all remained transfixed for about half-an-hour.

Everybody were stunned looking at this strange appearance moving towards Deva-Kuṇḍa. Surrounding me and my three children in the centre, my colleagues moved ahead and collected themselves at the edge of the pond. All were astonished to watch two powerful luminous objects, originating from the mountain opposite us, were heading towards the waterfall. Whilst one in transit got diffused in the forest, but the other one came near the waterfall and stood before us. The colour of "Jyoti" — Fire Ball — was golden, superimposed are two squares and within the squares was *AUṀ* — inside two topsy-turvy inverted triangles having six-pointed ends.

Jyoti Darśana at Deva-Kuṇḍa: It looked like this.

At the end Padma Lochan Jena requested me to make an "offering". Someone collected jungle fruits and after cleaning them in the pond came to me. I asked, "With what *mantra* should I make the offering?" All said, "Whichever comes out straight from your heart — today, because of you, we were fortunate for 'Jyoti Darśana'." I raised my hands, holding in my palms "Footy & Tarbhuj" fruit, and focusing on my *iṣṭa devatā* recited:

suleno pahino devī khaḍgeno cāmbike
ghaṇṭa sva-neno-naḥ pahi-ca padyane
sva-neno-ca.

After recital of this *mantra,* I offered the "offerings" into the Kuṇḍa.

After about fifteen minutes, the Fire Ball slowly retracted and got diffused in the forest. *Ādivāsīs* — workers, frightened to the core, wanted to leave Deva-Kuṇḍa that very night. However, after lots of persuasion for an hour, they were pacified to stay back for a couple of days.

Padma Lochan was confronted in the midnight by an old lady-wearing *sindūra* (vermillion) on the forehead, a red *sāṛī* profusely ornamented all over the body, raised her hands as if expressing to convey a wish. At that moment Padma Lochan questioned, "Mother, you are older than myself — why are you raising your hands to salute me?" Lady replied, "I have not raised them to salute you but to bless you; I am satisfied — now I am going to meet your master." Saying this, she vanished. Towards the end of the night I again got the vision of the Divine Light. Inside the six-cornered *yantra* (symbol/diagram), through a key-hole on the opposite side, I could hear clearly the Sanskrit chanting of a lady message in Oriya says thus:

Hear the history. Ages back, at the beginning of "Svayambhū Manvantara" after desecration of Dakṣa-Yajña, the fingers of my left foot (behind the spot where you saw my Divine Light) got cut-off by Shivdutt Sudarśana Cakra. Where they fell: these fingers have turned into stones — still visible at Vajra Śilā Māyā Pīṭha. The kings of Virāṭ dynasty used to worship me as Ambikā. My other name is Vajra-Prasāriṇī. Behind, where these fingers are located, is the union of "Jukta-Liṅgas" (of male and female sex organs) in *maithuna* (copulation) of the "Jugma Śaktis" (of Śiva and Śakti). This is my true self in esoteric sense.

ākaṣam liṅga mitya-ha pṛthvī-tasya pīṭhikā
pralaye sarva devanaṅg-layana-liṅga
mucyo-te.

In front of the fingers situate the holy "Yonī Pīṭha" of Vaga Mālinī wearing a string of one hundred *yoni*s. She is the creatrix Ambikā in her original self. This is Pañca Sāgara. Here, from its five *kuṇḍa*s or oceans, originate the perennial sound of five oceans. Therefore, these *kuṇḍa*s are addressed as "Ratnākaras"/"Sagars". Where you are present — that is Deva-Kuṇḍa.

1. "Deva-Kuṇḍa" (Celestial Pond) or Deva Sāgar (Ocean of God) or Amṛta Sāgar (Ocean of Nectar). This "Ratnākara's Adhiṣṭhātrī Devī" is Tripura Ratneśvarī and "Pīṭheśvarī" is Tri-Daśāmbikā.
2. On the top of this "Deva-Kuṇḍa" (Pond of the Goddess) or Devī Sāgar (Ocean of the Goddess) which constitutes the Mahā-Piṭha of the fingers "Adhiṣṭhātrī Devī" is Siddha Lakṣmī and "Pīṭheśvarī" is Ambikā Devī.
3. On top of this is "Haridra-Kuṇḍa" or Haridra Sāgar located. "Adhiṣṭhātrī Devī" is Śakti Mātaṅgī and "Pīṭheśvarī" is Gaurīśvarī.
4. On top of this is "Toils Kuṇḍa" or Toila Sāgar. "Adhiṣṭhātrī Devī" is Bhuvaneśvarī and "Pīṭheśvarī" in *tri-pāda-mudrā*.
5. At the top is "Bhūdar-Kuṇḍa" or Bhūdar Sāgar located. "Adhiṣṭhātrī Devī" is Bartali and "Pīṭheśvarī" Vārāhī.

Here, after Dakṣa-Yajña my jaw with teeth fell when *sudarśana cakra* cut my body into pieces. There existed my ancient temple at Padāṅguli Mahāpīṭha (Devī-Kuṇḍa) and on top of it this dazzling *yantra* made of gold was enshrined. My *pūjā* and religious offerings were continuously conducted by sage Haridra and his disciples. One of the kings of Virāṭ dynasty had come to this "Mahāpīṭha" for *darśana*, and getting greedy ordered to take away the golden *kalaśa* (pitcher) and the golden *yantra* from the temple. At midnight, when his henchmen started to break the cupola, which held the golden *kalaśa* for fear of the chief priest the temple attendants, they fled from the site. The temple — which was built on the science and principles of Vāstu-Śāstra and the cupola was the balancing factor — with the breakdown of cupola the whole edifice fell to the ground with a roar. On that very night the king along with his retinue stole my image, *kalaśa*, *yantra* and went away to his mountain-fortress. During the journey his head started reeling and he went beserk. He asked his ministers to procure him a girl, and on reaching the fort, this mad man holding my image started dancing naked on the rampart. At that time Cāṇḍālinī Devī crushed his throat, as he was shouting in pain, and threw him down the moat, where hungry crocodiles and other creatures tore him to pieces as their fodder, and the wicked king was sucked into hell. Next day his clothes were seen floating and the subjects declared that the king died of drowning. Since that day the fort got the dubious distinction and ill-fame as "Dubi Gaṛh" (fort). My statue of *aṣṭa-dhātu* (alloy of 8 metals) is still lying at "Dubi Gaṛh". Today is the conjunction of stars and planets which occurred on that fateful day, and for this reason, I summoned you here to let you know the truth. When morning comes, the spot where you saw this dazzling *yantra*, you shall go there and pay obeisance. You must reconstruct the temple which shall be a boon to your subjects and so also to you. I am present before you as *yantra* of Bagalā-Mukhī or Vegasya Devī. Everyday you must pray to imbibe its essence and sleep after reciting Svapna Vārahī *mantra*. If required you wait for my directives.

mamo yoni-rapswan-tahsamudra.
The whole Universe is my *yoni* as Ambikā.

This *yoni* represents "Sṛṣṭi-Sthiti-Laya" or the Creator, Preserver, Destroyer. In the morning I am Ambā or Tripurāmbā, noon I am Rudra Vaginī, six-armed Ambikā. And I am Vaga Mālinī Ambālikā in the evening.

oṁ huṁ-sa suci-ṣaḍ basu-ratna-
ricks-dhota vedi pada tithi duro-no-yet

nṛ-ṣu dyaras-dṛta śabddhyam-sada-
bal goja-o-dṛja ṛtum-ṛhat

I am like a silver string *tāra*. I am Huṁ-sa — like swans, as Śiva-Śakti in Mānsarovara. I am "Adṛja" or "Girijā" — exist as light. I am "Basu/Vasu" live everywhere. I only exist in space. The word "I" is me as "Hotā". The sages invoke me in the *yajña* — sacrificial *kuṇḍa* and address me by various names. I am seed of *kāla* — time, i.e. exist beyond time and as such, take the mantle of all consuming time — *kālī*. I am always present as the wife. I am also present in animate and in man in the form of energy. I am "Guru-Śakti". I am the season or change, or cause to change them in the universe. I am either in the space and all of it in the nebulous world. I am "Abja" Devī

Padma *alias* Lakṣmī. I am "Go-jab" or sourced from speech — i.e. Devī of Speech/Sound/Voice. I am the cause and effect of mankind. I am gigantic and like energy I am the Truth.

Then the "illumined-one" — the Devī vanished. When I opened my eyes, the time was between 7–8 a.m. After cleaning up, I gathered all and narrated my dream to them. All were astonished. After quickly finishing my daily chore we planned to go up the mountain. With great difficulty and arduous effort we reached there. For arriving, there is need to go down to meet the stream — slowly we started trekking down. By then my young workers had reached exclaiming "wonderful — wonderful", and it seemed they were shouting to us to reach soon. Mustering all our energy and strength we reached the spot near the stream. The sylvan surrounding and panorama all around, gladdened our hearts. Compared to the bottom (Deva) Kuṇḍa this upper (Devī) Kuṇḍa is smaller. But the magnificent surrounding of mountains and forests was so beautiful that it has to be seen to be believed; and not possible to describe it otherwise — approaching the Kuṇḍa we felt the ecstasy.

We saw, yesterday's offering of "Naivedya" of fruit/vegetable, which was as per natural law should have flown down the stream, but instead, a portion of it had most surprisingly ascended the 50 ft. waterfall and was found floating at a corner of the pond (Kuṇḍa). Besides, a piece of "Footy" fruit, even after overnight exposure, had remained fresh.

I lovingly started telling everybody — "Dried rice when devotionally offered to God is accepted as *mahāprasāda*. The Truth: we are experiencing here the Reality. Alas! God has appeared in this *Kaliyuga* (present Age), like in *Satyayuga* (Golden Age). Please accept this 'gift' — the 'eye-witness-experience' of the same — with utmost humility and devotion." Saying so, I distributed the fruit in bits and pieces to each and everyone present and taking one myself.

Looking back, I saw a huge black stone: in the middle "Five Fingers of Her Foot" turned into stone. Left of them is the *yantra* of "Jukta Yoni/Jugma Śakti or Śiva-Śakti (physical sexual union depicted in stone — conveying its esoteric, spiritual, tāntric interpretation), covered all around by countless 'mini-*yoni*' *mudrās*". Later, when counted, it came to 135 (number of alphabets of Vega Mālinī is 135). That day I did all the "Pīṭha *pūjā*" myself and during recitation of *Sapta-Śatī-Caṇḍī* — I heard the conch-shell from inside the *kuṇḍa*. The noise was so sonorous and reverberating that other felt and looked upward, as if an aeroplane had just passed overhead. It became evening by the time we descended to the first bottom *kuṇḍa* (Deva-Kuṇḍa).

During the evening prayers, pitch dark around the forest, the prevalence of universal peace engulfed us, and somewhat broken by the "Jhin Jhin" noise of crickets — as if competing with the pulse of *anāhata* (breathing life force/source). When I picked up handful of water in my palms to offer *śraddhāñjali*, I could clearly hear in the upper reaches the combined noise; the beating of 3 or 4 *mṛdaṅga*s (percussion instrument). My ears heard the soothing pronouncement:

oṁ dakṣya yajñe śiva-skanda clohi-bada-tveno pati-tam
devyaḥ pādāṅguli jyotir-dhiyo sma-kam praco-dayāt
oṁ sahasrāra mahā-kṣa mañjira dhan mañjarī
pādāṅguli no-gha-loka śrī-ratmanam praco-dayāt
oṁ sahasrāra mahā-cakra mañjira dhan mañjarī
pādāṅguli no-kha-loka śrī-ratmanam oṁ praco-dayāt
oṁ pañcāyatan-devana mā-śraya-kara-dhāriṇī
pādāṅguli prava-citte sama-dhyona praco-dayāt
oṁ pañcānan mahā dhyāne pañcāgni jyoti-ra kṛtiḥ
punatu pañca-netras-chi pañca pādāṅguli prabha
oṁ prapañhe pañca bhūtana pañca-mā-caro bondite
pañcānan priye-patu pañca-pādāṅguli prabha

During my evening prayers — I always have with me paper, a fountain-pen and torch-light. Having slowly heard the chantings, I wrote them down lighting the torch-light, and felt as if 7-8 persons deep-throated were chanting them in unison.

Next day, I again climbed up the mountain above to offer my *pūjā* to the Devī. That night there was torrential rain and it was difficult to stay-over on barren rocks without a shelter.

We managed to reach Deva-Kuṇḍa with great difficulty and got fully drenched. But we had to spend the night in the house of an *ādivāsī* subject.

Saw in dream one old lady addressing me pointing to her *sāṛī*:

> Couldn't spend the night near me. Three nights got to be spent on pilgrimage, and one is expected to do *pūjā* for three days. Ambikā is Tri-Śakti (Triple Energy). My *sāṛī* is torn — a red *sāṛī* is required to be offered during the *pūjā*. The *sindūra* (vermilion), that was brought the other day, was of inferior quality. Scented *sindūra* must be used. Inside the *yoni-yantra* of Tripura Devī Ambikā there is a sacred girth of "Pan Kāriṇī" wherein to do the *pūjā* on the "Trikūṭa" chanting my *mantra*.

This is my "Trikūṭa" *mantra* — which was pronounced slowly into my ears. Again said

First — like Śiva, last "Kūṭa" — like Śakti and the middle-one "Kūṭa" — Śiva-Śakti. You must do *pūjā* with full concentration of this in mind. This then is the most secret esoteric *mantra* of Ambikā — saying that she vanished, and getting up quickly I wrote down the theme of the dream.

Heard my servant Surendra Khilar was slapped in the night by an old lady saying "go and quickly make arrangement for the construction of my temple". Within a month of this incident I left for Delhi.

One night in Delhi, I saw in a dream a bearded *saṁnyāsī* (sage), who recited the *ekākṣarī* — one syllabled-*mantra* — of "Ādya" — Premodial Devī saying:

> Now the time has come for your *pūrṇābhiṣeka* and *krama-dīkṣā*; without *krama-dīkṣā* one does not have the right to worship Tri-Śakti. A *vīra sādhaka* (Adept) without "Śāktābhiṣeka" turns *piśāca* (roving unfulfilled spirit after death).

After this how, with the grace of *guru* and his directives, I got these *dīkṣās* — need further explanation. Pursuant to the dream all events took place in a systematic way. The *mantra*, which I had imbibed in the dream at the *pīṭha* of Devī Ambikā, was the same unfolded in my *krama-dīkṣā*.

Meanwhile, I got the news that, before any permission was sought for the construction of the temple, the Forest Ranger of Orissa Government had visited the site and unearthed a small statue of two-handed Mahiṣāsura-mardinī. More interesting news was heard that mercury is trickling from the *yoni* of Devī Ambikā. Doing research on it from the Tantras, I found from *Tantra Cūḍāmaṇi-Pīṭha Nirpana Poṭala*, the truth.

virāṭ deśa-dhye tu pādāṅguli nipātitam
bhairavśca mṛta-khya-śca devī tantra
ambikā smata
adho-dante mahā-rudro vārāhī pañca
sāagare

— *Tantra Cūḍāmaṇi*

The remaining explanation is described in *Gaurī Tantra*, pertaining to various *pīṭhas* and their significance. *Bṛhat Yoginī Tantra, Bidyut Latā Tantra, Ek-Danta Saṁhitā Tantra* also enumerate the significance, type of *pūjā* and application of *mantras* to be used.

Last time during "Rajo Saṁkrānti the *yoni-yantra* of Devī Ambikā astonishingly the colour of water remained blood-red for 16 days. So much mercury used to ooze out from Dakṣinamūrti Śiva-liṅga that one-fourth of the *yoni* used to get filled-up. This mercury is Bhairava — because of this semen old becomes young, mortal becomes immortal, copper turns to gold — as mentioned in *Mātṛkā Bheda Tantra.*

P - means Viṣṇu

A - means Kālikā

R - means Rudra

D - means Prajāpati

Therefore, the meaning of P A R D is the essence of the four above. The happening during "Rajo Saṁkrānti" was witnessed with amazement by the multitude, piercing the forests and mountains and received the benevolent red-cloth. Another strange thing happened — even the die-hard, who never believed in superstition, started having a second-thought. The two "Devī Kumārīs" in flesh and blood standing by the bloody — *yoni* were also worshipped. On the last day of the celebration these two Kumārīs, whilst playing amongst themselves, had unearthed one *aṣṭa-dhātu* statue of Devī Ambikā from Deva-Kuṇḍa. All were awe-stuck after seeing the miracle. Within seven days one worshipping priest saw in a dream, the statue of "Hara Gaurī" and "Śiva" from heaven telling him:

> The statue, which has been unearthed was in the old original temple, was copper-plated. During the construction of the temple, make three copper-plates to cover the "Pīṭha-Sthāna". Enshrine the statue of Devī Ambikā for public *darśana*. Place the *aṣṭa-dhātu* statue of Ambikā on its right and the joined — Bhairava/Bhairavī statue of Vaga Mālinī on the left. From today, the Mahāpīṭha shall not remain vacant. Only the devotees — having gone through *pūrṇābhiṣeka* or *krama-dīkṣā* can get *darśana* here. Keep it a top secret of "Mensurating Mahā Yoni".

The Forest Ranger from Udala belonging to the Orissa Government had come for *darśana*. In spite of stopping him, he defied them. The moment he had *darśana* he became senseless. After a lapse of time, when he regained consciousness, he said "Four white elephants who picked up the silver *kalaśa* (pitcher) were performing *abhiṣeka* — where have these elephants gone?" He returned after doing *praṇāma* from a distance. At home he found the design of red *triśūla* (trident) embossed on his pocket handkerchief.

While constructing the temple, the foundation of the old temple was also found. Lots of broken statues, stone-slabs and pillars have been unearthed. Amongst them, a beautiful unbroken statue of "Baṭuka Bhairava" in black stone is worth seeing. Eight–ten copper-coins from the Kuṣāṇa period were found. In a nearby cave there was a broken statue of Kurukullā Devī. Looking at the inscription of the dates, the coins are (headless coins during Kuṣāṇa period) 2000 years old. *Aṣṭa-dhātu* statue of Gaurī has been reclaimed from Haridra-Kuṇḍa. Near Toila-Kuṇḍa "Jagat-Guru" and "Gaurī Śakti Pada" (foot) on slab-stone has been discovered. From Bhūdar-Kuṇḍa Vajra Vāhinī and Samabhar Bhairava in *maithuna* pose is recovered. Above Bhūdar-Kuṇḍa, the ancient statue of Bhūdar Caṇḍī or Svapna Vārāhī and Pīṭha-Sthāna was lying in despicable condition. The restoration was done with utmost difficulty, and thereafter their purification and sanctification. There were many broken pieces of the image and the Pīṭha-Sthāna was also in ruins which required lot of money for restoration. Even now all the restoration work is not complete. The Bhairava-Sthāna of the Devī has also been found.

Bhūdar Caṇḍī's Bhairava is famous in Tantra Śāstra. This Mahā-Rudra Śivaliṅga has on its body 100 numbers tiny Śiva-liṅgas and as such, is addressed as "Śat-Rudra", held in veneration by the tāntrics and the place is abound with snakes and wild animals. His prayer is thus:

śata liṅgam mahā-rudram lohitā-bhyam jaṭā-dharam
śata-cāpa-dharam haste-yiḥ śata vajre-su dharinam
tri sahasra-jvālā netram garta-sinam nṛ-muṇḍa-
malinam śata-kṣ-ardha śarīram tan mahānandam
bhaga mālīnam anant balayam dhya-ye-co candra
rudham digam-baram.

Dynastically, the disciples of Kapila Muni and Kālāmukha sect have been engaged in the worship of Bhairava. On the right of the *liṅgam* is Devī Bagalā's Yoni-Pīṭha and Mātaṅgī on elephant back. For the liberty that has been taken, for the discolsure of these findings, with the blessing of my *sadguru* with devotion — I am presenting the same as an offering at his lotus feet. How *guru*'s miracle can realize the truth of this pilgrimage, by cleansing their "Pañca Mahābhūtas" (five elements) in this "Pañca Sāgara" and attain salvation, is my prayer, hope and aspiration to you all. With this I end my dissertation.

oṁ raktab-dho oṁ rakta-poterabi-
dala kamala bhyan-tare
rajo-manyam raktāṅgin rakta-mauli sph-
ratesaśikalam smer-baktam tri-netram
bīja-pureṣu pāśa-aṅkuśa madana-
dhanuḥ sat-kalpala niha-styei
pañca-sya-mṛtya kumbha-sta divya
pādāṅguli prabham
bidhyan-tin saryar-kai-bāme bhāga-bantam
bhaje hombi-ka-man

— Dhyāna of Ambikā (in *Ambikā Hṛdaya Tantra*)

By the time the construction of the temple was being completed, there was discovery of a statue of Kurukullā Devī from a cave on the west side. It is worth mentioning that this type of statue of Buddhist Tantra, is not found anywhere in entire Asia, except in Orissa. This unequivocally proves Orissa as "Uḍḍīyana Pīṭha". Two statues have been discovered from Kurukullā village in Cuttack district. It is presumed "Kurukkullā" is a misnomer for "Kurukkila". Second, it has also been found in Deva-Kuṇḍa.

On last December 23 – Śrī Radha Nath Rath, Minister of Forest and Welfare, had visited Ambikā Pīṭha. He was awe-stuck by the attraction and natural beauty of Deva-Kuṇḍa. As per the request of the *sevayat*s (survivors), by many of a memorial, he arranged for 20 *mana*s (*mans*) (0.69 *man* = 1 acre) of cultivable land, as a gift by the government, towards the upkeep and expansion of activities of Deva-Kuṇḍa. Besides, through the good offices, there was financial grant of Rs. 60,000 (sixty thousand) from the Development Department of the government, for a road to connect Deva-Kuṇḍa to help piligrims for an easy access.

During the last Basantī Pūjā priests from Kāmākhyā Dhāma (holiest Tantra Pīṭha in India) came to perform tāntric rites for the consecration of the temple, which was successfully accomplished amidst grandeur and a massive gathering.

At this stage, it would be worth mentioning Bhagavatī's "Adho-Danta Pīṭha" is located on the upper reaches of Bhūdar-Kuṇḍa. The ancient statue of Vārāhī Devī was uprooted, and shockingly had fallen into Bhūdar-Kuṇḍa. With the fall the statue had broken into several pieces, and with the revealation in the dream, they were recovered and lifted from there. During this process Devī's left jaw broke, and from the right jaw many broken teeth started coming out one after another. Those who witnessed the "sighting", I am positive, their life-long-wait to see a miracle, has been amply rewarded. That night the *sevāyat* (priest) was ordered in the dream that whoever sees the "molar-tooth" meant decay of his dynasty — "where you found me there lies a silver casket". After an arduous effort the casket was found inside Bhūdar-Kuṇḍa, and as ordained, all "Teeth" were encashed and sealed for good and kept by the side of the statue. The work had also started for the construction of Vārāhī Devī's temple but it was stopped, as per her instruction, and she was enshrined in her original place in the middle of a bush.

As of now, temple complex of Mahā Rudra Bhairava is not constructed. His blessings has enabled me to progress thus far, and waiting for his grant and strength. I am being operated like a machine, functioning as per his wishes. This "*Sādhanā* — Service," is for me, is the greatest *sādhanā* as enunciated by my *guru*.

I have also been inspired to build a "Sadhana Kendra" for "Tantra Darśana" here. But the design, blue-print and culmination of this ambitious project require enormous finance and help: presently, I feel helpless without seeing any positive sign in that direction.

However, I have already started a library, with the collection of books on Tantra and related field of studies; besides a museum — for the broken pieces of statues already collected. Due to lack of helping hands the work is progressing at a snail's pace. For this, I am not sure if my dream shall fructify? With the grace of the Mother, within a short span of time I am trying and have already achieved the impossible. It is my fervent hope, which is getting strengthened everyday, to see its completion so that I can dedicate the same to Her.

prata-ravya sva-yantan sva-yaḥ-nyat
prata-ran-taram
yat karomi jagannātha sva-dastu
taba pūjā-nām
oṁ śiva-arpa-namastu.

Appendix III

Sixty-four Sexual Bandhas in Pāñcaśāyaka

PĀÑCAŚĀYAKA was composed by Kavi Samrāṭ Upendra Bhañja of Orissa in poetic Oriyā language. Full description of sixty-four sexual *bandhas* (poses) are described here for the first time and are not found in the literature of any other languages in India, before his period. It is a speciality and a gift of Orissa to the entire humanity.[1]

Somanath Rath[2] describes Upendra Bhañja as "the 'Kavi Samrāṭ' of Orissa". This epithet literally means "the emperor of poets". In other words, he is the greatest of poets in the Oriya language. His poetical works have been the centre of severe controversies and scholarly disputations among all sections of readers and writers of Orissa during the past three quarters of 20th century. To some, Upendra Bhañja is far from being a poet in the sublime sense of the term *kavi*, he is only a "mighty literary acrobat who has shown his greatest skill in verbal jugglery". To the others, he is so great a poet that he deserves a place higher than those held by Kālidāsa, Homer, Milton, Rabindranath and the like. Thus, the pendulum of Upendra Bhañja's poetic appreciation oscillates between the two extremities of derogatory denunciations and complimentary commendations. It is needless to point out in this connection that sentimentalism and emotionalism preponderate over all such observations.

Biography

Upendra Bhañja was the grandson of Dhanañjaya Bhañja (and the son of Nīlakaṇṭha Bhañja) who ruled over Ghumsur, now part of Gañjam district in south Orissa, for sixty-five years. The Bhañja kings ruled over Ghumsur for several centuries past and Dhanañjaya is known to have ruled during CE 1636–1701. In addition to his being a very powerful king and a benevolent ruler, he was an accomplished scholar and a poet of no mean repute. He was the author of some *kāvyas* (long poems of the medieval type), the most remarkable of which was the *Raghunātha Vilāsa*. It is a poem based on the story of the *Rāmāyaṇa* and written in an ornate style, characteristic of medieval Oriya poetry. Upendra drew inspiration from his

1. J.P. Singh Deo, *THOMV*, 2004, Appendix, p. 255.

2. Somanath Rath, "Upendra Bhañja," *Sidelights on History and Culture of Orissa*, M.N. Das (ed.), Cuttack (Orissa), 1977, pp. 692-93.

grandfather to engage himself in literary activities. His father Nīlakaṇṭha Bhañja, who too was a man of poetic genious, might have also exerted influence on his ductile mind. Orissa was divided into a number of principalities in those days and many kings, ruling over particular areas, were great lovers of art and literature. Some of them were illustrious patrons of music, dance and drama. Almost everyone of them had a "council of poets and paṇḍits". Occasionally, eminent poets and scholars from the neighbouring states or kingdoms were invited to make a display of their talents. Those who could stand the acid test of scholarly examination by the council of poets belonging to the host king were duly honoured with connotative titles. Ghumsur was noted for such literary activities and this also gave Upendra the necessary impetus to unfold his talents. Thus, providentially the poet was favoured with a congenial atmosphere to acquire profound scholarship and to express himself poetically. . . . However, on the basis of the various views put forth by scholars, it may be reasonably held that the poet was born between CE 1675-80.

Upendra in his composition *Pāñcaśāyaka*, describes sixty-four *bandha*s alias sexual poses[3]:

1. *Kāmaprada bandha*: The woman should raise her two legs, place them on the man's shoulder and place her hands on the neck of the man. The man should then have sexual penetration and kiss her on the lips.
2. *Viparīta bandha*: The woman should spread one leg on the thigh of the male and the second foot should be placed over the shoulder. The man should catch hold of the woman's neck by one hand and should place his other hand on her breast.
3. *Nagara bandha*: The man should sit near the thigh of the woman and have sex in sitting position. The man's hands should get hold of the woman's neck.
4. *Ratipāśa bandha*: The woman should place the man locked within her thighs, and then embrace him tightly.
5. *Koyar bandha*: The woman should squeeze one thigh of the man by both of her thighs and her two hands should embrace the male.
6. *Toṣaka bandha*: The man should lift the woman by catching hold of her

3. *THOMV*, 2004, pp. 263-70.

feet. The woman should place her hands around the man's neck. The breasts of the woman are to placed on the chest of the man.

7. *Samapāda bandha*: The woman should raise her legs towards her chest and the man should catch hold of her breasts, squeeze them and give her biting kisses.
8. *Ekapāda bandha*: The woman should place one of her legs straight, raise the other leg and catch hold of the neck of the man. Then the raised leg should be placed on the man's shoulder.
9. *Sampuṭa bandha*: The woman should lie down flat and the man should enjoy her. After this, different poses may be practised.
10. *Ardhasampuṭa bandha*: Enjoy the woman while she lies down flat by touching her breasts with one's own chest.
11. *Stanabhāra bandha*: The woman should sit on the man's lap with her legs spread apart. Then, the male should lie down and fondle the breasts of the woman extremely.
12. *Ratisundara bandha*: The woman should raise her two legs and touch on her breasts. The man should enjoy her by catching hold of her neck.
13. *Padma bandha*: Catch hold the breasts of the woman, embrace her tightly and enjoy.
14. *Ekarasa bandha*: Catch hold the waist of the woman. Then lift one of her leg and put it on the man's waist. The other legs of the woman should be straight. Then, place one hand round her neck and do movement.
15. *Cakra bandha*: Catching hold of the woman by the left hand the man should make her sit on his feet. The woman's legs should be spread apart.
16. *Second cakra bandha*: Catching hold of the two legs of the woman by the armpits the man should put his hands around her neck and touch the breasts.
17. *Bikrama bandha*: One foot of the woman should touch the man's forehead and her other leg should hold the man's waist. While kissing her the man's chest should touch the woman's breasts and thus enjoy the sexual intercourse.
18. *Vaiṣṭaka bandha*: The woman should raise her one leg and keep touching the man's chest while the other leg of her should encircle his waist. This action should be done in a sitting position.

19. *Haṁsa kīlaka nīlāsana bandha*: Man lies down and the woman sitting on his thighs becomes active.
20. *Haṁsa kīlaka bandha*: Man lies down and the woman sitting on his thighs catches hold of the man's arm-pits and does movement.
21. *Nīlāsana bandha*: Man should lie down and the woman should sit over his *liṅga* (penis) and bend over the man's chest so that the woman's breasts can be caught hold by the man and in the same time the woman's breasts should touch the man's chest.
22. *Siṁha-rīti bandha*: The two legs of the woman should be placed on the man's shoulders. The man should catch hold of the woman's breasts and have sexual intercourse.
23. *Gaja-rati bandha*: Making the woman sit on his thighs, the man catch hold of her. The woman's body shouldn't be allowed to touch the ground.
24. *Aśva bandha*: Making the woman bent her front the man should touch her thigh with his *liṅga* from the back and enjoy by having movement.
25. *Brūśa bandha*: The woman should bend her front side and rest by her hands. The man should kiss her from the side and have sexual intercourse from her back.
26. *Mṛgamata bandha*: Make the woman bend towards her front and while resting her hands on her knee. Then, the man should have sexual intercourse from her back.
27. *Mārjāra bandha*: The woman should lie down on her back. The man should lie on her straight. The man's hands should be spread on her hands.
28. *Rati bikrama bandha*: The man should raise the feet of the woman on the bed and make her spread her hands. He then does sexual intercourse.
29. *Grāmya bandha*: The woman should lie down flat and the man should lie or sit on her so that the thighs of both should touch each other. In the meantime the woman should catch hold of the man's right hand by her left hand and should feel a fist-closed palm.
30. *Karmūka kṛti bandha* (bow pose): The man should sit between the thighs of the woman and bend on her, while clasping hands.
31. *Chanda bandha*: Raising the legs of the woman on his head and sitting close to her buttocks, the man should clasp the thighs tightly and perform the sex act.

32. *Padmāsana bandha*: The man should sit in *padmāsana* (lotus pose) and the woman should sit on his lap. Both of them should clasp their hands to form a lotus.
33. *Cakrabhava bandha*: The woman should sit on the feet of the man. The man should clasp breasts as he moves his hands through her thighs. In this pose, kissing and embracing each other should also continue.
34. *Eśa* (plough) *bandha*: The woman should lie down flat and the man should rest himself on his knees and place his chest on the woman's breasts.
35. *Aśr̥ta bandha*: The woman should lie down flat and keep her one leg straight and the other leg should be placed on the thigh of the man.
36. *Sūraja-kr̥ti bandha*: Raising the legs of the woman and catching hold of her thighs with upper arms, the man should place his hands on her breasts.
37. *Malla bandha*: The man should lie down flat and raise his two legs. The woman should catch hold of the man's thighs and bend her head down like a deer. This can be done the other way also.
38. *Varuṇa bandha*: The man should raise both the legs of the woman and hold them, while the woman should hold the man's neck by her hands, the man should kiss on both breasts and perform the sex act.
39. *Gūḍharāsa bandha*: The woman should spread her legs between the legs of the man. The man should touch the cheek of the woman by one hand and catch her breast by another hand.
40. *Viparīta bandha*: The man should lie down and place one leg on the shoulder of the woman and the other leg should be straight. The woman should perform the act and the man should hold her chin.
41. *Ekapāda bandha*: The woman should lie down with one leg stretched and her other leg should be placed on the shoulder of the man.
42. *Ūrdhvapada bandha*: Let the woman lie down flat and raise her two legs up. The man should hold the woman's legs by both of his hands and do sexual intercourse, energetically and tightly.
43. *Cakra bandha*: Let the woman lie down and spread her both legs and hands. The man should lie upon her and allow his chest to touch her breasts.
44. *Bhadrāsana bandha*: The man should sit in a posture of meditation and allow the woman to sit on his lap, then embrace her and kiss her proficiently.

45. *Jaṅghāsana bandha*: The man should sit over the two feet of the woman and catch hold of her body by both hands. The man's buttocks should touch the ground and enjoy the sex act.
46. *Sūsama bandha*: Sūsama bandha is practised very less. Place both the woman's legs on one shoulder of the man and the man should grasp the two breasts of the woman.
47. *Kūrma* (tortoise) *bandha*: The man should catch hold of the woman's neck after placing her both thighs upon his.
48. *Kaṅkaṇa bandha* (bracelet pose): The woman and the man should embrace each other and have sexual act in standing pose.
49. *Kākarati bandha*: The man should sit down and stretch his legs. Then, the woman should sit on the lap of the man by stretching her legs, towards the back of the man.
50. *Jugala bandha*: The man and woman should stand and put one of their legs round each other's waist.
51. *Dṛḍha bandha*: The man should put his thighs on those of the woman and catch hold of her chin.
52. *Rasajita bandha*: The woman shoud lie down flat. The man then sits on one of her thigh and place another thigh on his own thigh.

    पक्षीबन्धः समुत्पन्नः दडनाम समाचरेत् ।
    युगलः कंकणः प्रोक्तो सारभस्य यथाक्रमः ।।

53. *Uparati bandha*: The man and the woman should lie down side by side, facing each other and perform the sex act.
54. *Saṅkaca bandha*: Make the woman lie down flat on her belly, facing the ground. The man should then lift one thigh of the woman and perform the act from her back.
55. *Trikoṇa bandha*: The man standing on the feet of the woman should stretch her hands apart by catching them.
56. *Mekhalā bandha*: The woman should place her thighs on her breasts by lifting them and hold them by her hands. The man should catch her at the waist and perform the sex act.
57. *Bikaca bandha*: The woman should sit down with crossed legs and then lie down by lifting the crossed legs. The man should penetrate his hands

through the crossed legs of the woman and catch hold of her neck and perform the sex act.

58. *Ghana bandha*: The woman should cover her body with the bedsheet and stretch herself on the bed, being hidden. The man should search the proper place for the sexual intercourse.
59. *Kumuda bandha*: It is a difficult pose. The woman should hold both her feet and lie down, so that she could lift them and keep on the man's shoulders. The man should enjoy sexual intercourse by placing his hands on her breasts.
60. *Bakra bandha*: Make the woman lie down flat, facing the ground. Hold her from back side. The man should bend from the waist towards her and kiss her. At the same time sexual intercourse should go on.
61. *Adhomukha bandha*: The woman should rest on her knees and elbows. The man should penetrate from her back by kneeling and perform the sexual intercourse.
62. *Ūrdhvomukha bandha*: The man should sit down, putting his feet near the vulva of the woman, then lift her face by holding the chin and perform the sexual intercourse.
63. *Padadruta bandha*: Both the man and the woman should stand and catch hold of each other's thighs by one hand and embrace by the other. At the same time sexual intercourse should continue.
64. *Sammukha bandha*: The woman should sit on the lap of the man by stretching her legs. The man should then embrace her by the neck and kiss on her cheeks while having sexual intercourse.

The sixty-four sexual poses are still continued in Orissa (Odisha) province of India and find expressions of *Causaṭhī Rati Bandha*, palm-leaf manuscript, composed by Gopāl Bhañja, a scion of the Bhañja dynasty of ex-Mayūrbhañja state, in *paṭṭa-citra* paintings and palm-leaf etchings, traced in Gañjam district. The illustrated sixty-four sexual poses are free-lance etchings on palm-leaf, as traced in Gañjam district.

Glossary

ādi	Primeval
bīja	Seed, seed state.
bindu	Point, point of potential energy, consciousness and nucleus. In Tantra and *haṭha-yoga* it also represents a drop of semen.
guṇa	Quality of Nature, threefold capacity of manifest Śakti; Prakòti; Nature; namely, *tamas, rajas* and *sattva*.
kriyā-śakti	Activity, dynamic yogic practice of Śāktism.
liṅga	Naturally formed oval-shaped stone; represents the subtle form of individual existence. Śiva-liṅga is especially venerated as the symbol of *ātmā* and individual soul.
māyā	The mistress of illusion or the Lady of phenomena.
nāda	Subtle sound vibration, the vibration created by the union of Śiva and Śakti.
pīṭha	Site.
puruṣa	Male.
prakṛti	Nature.
para	Supreme.
Śakti	Energy.
Saguṇa Śiva	Lord Śiva with divine attributes.
Tantra	A religious system of the Śāktas.
sṛṣṭi	Creation.

Bibliography

Bulletins

Indian Museum Bulletin, vol. XI, no. 1, January, 1976.

Gazetteers

Sahu, N.K. (state ed.), *Gazetteer of India, Orissa, Bolangir*, Nilamani Senapati (chief ed.), Cuttack, 1968.

Kuanr, D.C. (state ed.), *Gazetteer of India, Orissa, Puri*, Nilamani Senapati (chief ed.), Cuttack, 1977.

Madhya Pradesh District Gazetteer, Bilaspur, Bhopal, 1978.

Kuanr, D.C. (state ed.), *Gazetteer of India, Orissa, Kalahandi*, Nilamani Senapati (chief ed.), Cuttack, 1980.

Behuria N.C. (chief ed.), *Gazetteer of India, Orissa State*, vol. II, Cuttack, 1991.

Inscriptions

EI, vol. XXIII.

Rajguru, S.N., *Inscriptions of Orissa*, vol. I, pt. II, Bhubaneswar, (?)

South Indian Inscriptions, vol. IX, pt. I.

Journals

Journal of the Asiatic Society, vol. II, no. 1, Calcutta, 1960.

Journal of the Indian History, Madras, vol. XVI.

The Journal of the Kalinga Historical Research Society, vol. I, no. 4, March, 1947.

OHRJ, vol. I, no. 1; vol. II, no. 2, vol. XIV, nos. 3-4; vol. XXIV, XXV and XXVI; vol. XXII, no. 2; vol. XXX, nos. 2-4; vol. XLVII, no. 3.

The Journal of Orissan History, vol. IX, June 1989.

Monthly

Orissa Review (Monument Special), Public Relation Dept., Govt. of Orissa, Bhubaneswar, January, 1976.

Orissa Review, vol. XXVI, no. 12.

The Youth World, issue no. 27, January 2005, Bolangir, Arabinda Das (ed.).

Caravan, English monthly, June, 1977, no. 60.

Monographs

Rāmaswami, N.S., *Monograph on Temple of Mukhaliṅgam*, Hyderabad: Govt. of Andhra Pradesh, 1976.

Newspapers

The Indian Express, English, Bhubaneswar, 26 February 2004.

Sambad, Oriya, dated 12 October 2005 and 26 February 2007.

Oriya

Das, Siba Prasad, *History of Sambalpur*, Sambalpur: Viswabharti Press, 2nd edn., 1969.

Jagannāth Chaitamruta, Cuttack: Union Printing Works, 1913.

Rajguru, S.N., *Śrī Purushottam-o-Śrī Mandira*, Bhubaneswar: Orissa Sahitya Academy, 1996.

Mohanty, A.B. (ed.), *Mādalā Pāñjī* (Prachi edn.), Cuttack: Prachi-Samiti, 1940, rpt., Bhubaneswar: Utkal University, 1969.

Rajguru, S.N., *Odisa-ra-Itihasa* (Oriya), (?)

Mishra, Nilamani and Laxman Panda, *Sālabega*, Cuttack: Rashtrabhasha Samavaya Prakashan, 1985.

Sutar, Subhransu Bhushan, *Kanika*, published by Malla Ghara, Raj Kanika, Kendrapara, 2000.

Singh, Jagabandhu, *Prachina Utkala* (?), Puri, 1929.

Mullick, S.C., *Odisa Itihas* (Manuscript), (?).

Mohanty, Surendra, *Odia Sahitya-ra-Madhyaparva*, (?)

Banerjee, Haradhar, *Daibi Śākti* (Oriya spiritual monthly magazine), Sirlonabagram, Raghunathpur, Cuttack, September, 1995.

Quarterly

Indian Historical Quarterly, vol. XXXI.

The Quarterly Review of Historical Studies, vol. XLIII, nos. 1-2, April to September 2003, Kolkata: Institute of Historical Studies.

Souvenir

Souvenir, Bolangir Loka Utsav, Bolangir, Orissa, 2001.

Patalganga (Souvenir), Patalganga Utsav, Boden, Orissa, 2006.

Souvenir, Bolangir Loka Utsav, Bolangir, Orissa, 2006.

Souvenir, Swarna Kshetra, Sunabeda, Śrī Śrī Jagannāth Seva Samittee, Sunabeda, 2006.

Secondary Sources

Agrawal, D.P. and D.K. Chakrabarti, *Essays in Indian Proto-History*, Delhi: B.R. Publishing Corporation, 1979.

———, *Art Traditions of Orissa*, Bhubaneswar: Orissa Sahitya Akademy, 1983.

Amarnatha, *Some Missing Chapters of World History*, New Delhi: Itihas Shodh Sansthan, 1973.

Avalon, Arthur (ed.), *Sarada Tilak Tantram*, Delhi: Motilal Banarsidass, rpt. 2001.

Bäumer, B., R.P. Das and S. Das (eds.), *Śilpa Prakāśa*, Delhi: Motilal Banarsidass, 2nd rev. edn., 2005.

Bandyopadhyay, Pranab, *The Aryans and Holy Vedas*, Kolkata: Firma K.L.M. Private Ltd., 1993.

Bandyopadhyay, Pranab, *The Goddess of Tantra*, Kolkata: Punthi Pustak, 1987.

Banerjee, J.N., *Purāṇic and Tāntric Religion*, (?)

Banerji, Sures Chandra, *Cultural Reciprocation Between India and the World*, Sharda Publishing House, (?).

Basham, A.L. (ed.), *A Cultural History of India*, Delhi: Oxford University Press, 1975 and 2nd impression, 1984.

Behera, S.C., *Rise and Fall of the Sailodbhavas*, Kolkata: Punthi Pustak, 1982.

Bhagwan Shree Rajneesh, *From Sex to Super-Consciousness*, New Delhi: Orient Paperback, 2nd edn., 1976.

Bharati, Swami Agehananda, *Great Tradition and Little Traditions*, Varanasi: Chowkhamba Sanskrit Series Office, 1978.

Bhargava, P.L., *India in the Vedic Age*, New Delhi: D.K. Printworld, 1956, 1971; 3rd rev. and enlarged edn., 2001.

Bhattacharya, N.N., *History of the Tāntric Religion*, New Delhi: Manohar, 1987.

Bibby, Geoffrey, *Looking for Dilmum*, New York: New American Library, 1974.

Bombay-Karnataka Collection, no. 93, of 1940-41.

Bose, Nirmal Kumar, *Canons of Orissan Architecture*, New Delhi: Cosmo Publications, 2nd rpt., 1982.

Burton, R. and F.F. Arbuthnot (trs.), *Vātsyāyana's Kāmasūtra* (*A Classic of Love*), Orient Paperbacks, rpt., 1982.

Carleton, P., *Buried Empires*, (?), London, 1939.

Chakravarty, Minoti, *Religious Life in the Kalachuri Empire*, Kolkata: Punthi Pustak, 1999.

Chawdhri, Jyotis Shiromani L.S., *Practicals of Yantras*, New Delhi: Sagar Publications, 1984.

Chinmayananda, Swami, *Vedānta: The Science of Life*, pt. I, Central Chinmaya Mission Trust, rpt. 1983 and pt. III, 1982.

Danino, Michel, *The Invasion that Never Was*, Mysore: The Mother's Institute of Research, Mira Aditi, 1996.

Das, Chittaranjan, *A Glimpse into Oriya Literature*, Bhubaneswar: Orissa Sahitya Akademi, 1982.

Das, H.C., *Śākta Pīṭhas: A Study*, Bhubaneswar: Bharti Prakashan, 1999.

———, *Tāntricism: A Study of Yogini Cult*, New Delhi: Sterling Publishers, 1981.

Das, M.N. (ed.), *Sidelights on History and Culture of Orissa*, Vidyapuri, Cuttack, 1977.

Dash, M.P. (ed.), *A Descriptive Catalogue of Sanskrit Manuscripts of Orissa*, vol. V (Tantra Manuscripts), Bhubaneswar: Orissa State Museum, 1965.

Davies, H.A., *An Outline History of the World*, London: Oxford University Press, 1959.

Dwivedi, Shivakant, *Temple Sculptures of India*, Delhi: Agam Kala Prakashan, 1991.

Elder, J.W., Jr. Dimoak, C. Edward and A.T. Embree (eds.), *India's Worlds and U.S. Scholars*, 1947–1997, New Delhi: Manohar, 1998.

Elst, Koenrad, *Update to the Aryan Debate*, New Delhi: Voice of India, (?).

Eschmann, A., H. Kulke and G. Tripathi (eds.), T*he Cult of Jagannāth and the Regional Tradition of Orissa*, New Delhi: Manohar, 1978.

Fouerstein, G., S. Kal and David, Frawley, *In Search of the Cradle of Civilization*, Delhi: Motilal Banarsidass, 1999.

Frawley, David, *The Myth of the Aryan Invasion of India*, New Delhi: Voice of India, 1994 and 1995.

———, *Wisdom of the Ancient Seers* (*Mantras of the Ṛgveda*), Delhi: Motilal Banarsidass, 1995.

———, *Gods, Sages and the Kings* (*Vedic Secrets of Ancient Civilization*), Delhi: Motilal Banarsidass, 2nd rpt., 1995.

———, *Tāntric Yoga and the Wisdom Goddesses*, Delhi: Motilal Banarsidass, 1996.

———, *Awakened Bharata: A Call for India's Rebirth*, New Delhi: Voice of India, 1998.

———, *The Ṛgveda and the History of India* (*Ṛgveda Bharata Itihas*), New Delhi: Aditya Prakashan, 2001.

———, *Yoga and the Sacred Fire* (*Self-Realization and Planetary Transformation*), Delhi: Motilal Banarsidass, 2006.

Handebuchder Orientalistik II, Abt. IV, Band 2, Abschn, *Hindu Tantrism*, Leiden/Koln: E.J. Brill, 1979.

Harding, Elizabeth, U., *Kāli (The Black Goddess of Dakshinesvar)*, Delhi: Motilal Banarsidass, 1998.

Jha, D.N., *The Myth of the Holy Cow*, London/New York: Verso, 2002.

Joshi, Arjun, *New Light on the Cultural Heritage of Orissa*, Cuttack: Baneeshree, 1980.

Kareem, C.K., *What Happened in Indian History*, Cochin: Paico Publishing House, 1971.

Kulkarni, S.D. (gen. ed.), *BSOIHAC*, vol. I, 1988, vol. XVI, 1995.

Kumar, Pushpendra, *Śakti Cult in Ancient India*, Varanasi: Bharatiya Publishing House, 1974.

Lal, B.B., *The Homeland of the Aryans*, New Delhi: Aryan Books International, 2005.

Mahatab, H.K., *History of Orissa*, vol. I, Cuttack: Prajatantra Prachar Samiti, 1959.

Majumdar, R.C. (gen. ed.), *THACOTIP* vol. I: The Vedic Age, 1965; vol. V, 1966; vol. X, pt. II, 1991.

Margoliouth, D.S., *Mohammed and the Rise of Islam*, New Delhi: Voice of India, 2005.

Maurya, Vidya (ed.), *Encountering the Indian*, New Delhi: Aryan Books International, 1999.

Mishra, K.C., *The Cult of Jagannātha*, Kolkata: Firma K.L.M., 1971.

——— (ed.), *Studies in the Cult of Jagannātha*, Bhubaneswar: Institute of Orissan Culture, 1991.

Mishra, K.L. (ed.), *Yogini Tantra*, Lakshmi Venkatesvar Press, Samvat 2013 and Śakābda 1878, Uttara Khaṇḍa, Prathama Paṭala.

Mishra, N.R., *Kāmākhyā: A Socio-Cultural Study*, New Delhi: D.K. Printworld (P) Ltd., 2004.

Mishra, P.K., *Archaeology of Mayurbhanj*, New Delhi: D.K. Printworld (P) Ltd., 1997.

Mishra, Prafulla Kumar, *New Dimensions in the Atharvaveda*, Delhi: Pratibha Prakashan, 2003.

Mishra, R.P., *Sahajayana: A Study of Tāntric Buddism*, Kolkata: Punthi Pustak, 1991.

Mishra, R.P. (ed.), *Culture and Collections*, Kolkata: Punthi Pustak, 1996.

Mishra, Ram Prasad, *Fragments of Indian Culture (Ranipur-Jharial)*, Kolkata: Punthi Pustak, 1995.

Mohanty, Phani, *The Concept of Purusa and Purusottama in the Commentary of Sankara on the Prasthanatrayi*, New Delhi: Garg Publications, 1986.

Muller, M., *India: What Can It Teach Us?*, London: Longmans, Green & Co., 1883.

Nagar, Shantilal, *Indian Gods and Goddesses*, vol. 4, Yogini Shrines and Śakti Pīṭhas, pt. I, Delhi: B.R. Publishing Corporation, 2006.

Nigam, L.S. (ed.), *Riddle of Indian Iconography* (*Zetetic on Rare Icon from Tala*), Delhi: Sharada Publishing House, 2000.

Nayak, P.M. (ed.), *Confluence*, vol. I, Registrar, Sambalpur University, Burla, 1992.

Nikhilananda, Swami, *The Upaniṣads* (Abridged edn.), New York and Eva-ston: Harper and Row Publishers, 1964.

Notovitch, Nicolas, *The Unknown Life of Jesus Christ*, Kolkata: Nababharat Publishers, 1981.

Oak, P.N., *The Rationale of Astrology*, New Delhi: Published by author, (?)

———, *Some Blunders of Indian Historical Research*, Delhi: Surya Prakashan, rpt., 1969.

Pani, S. (ed.), *Illustrated Palmleaf Manuscripts of Orissa* (*A Selection from the Orissa State Museum*), A Golden Jubilee Publication, Bhubaneswar, 1984.

Panigrahi, K.C., *History of Orissa* (*Hindu Period*), Cuttak: Kitab Mahal, 1981.

Panikkar, R., *The Vedic Experience: Mantramanjari*, London: Dorton, Longman and Todd, 1979.

Pargiter, F.E., *Ancient Indian Historical Tradition*, Delhi, (?), 1962.

Patel, C.B., *Dynastic History of Nalas*, Kolkata: Punthi Pustak, 1990.

Patel, Satyavrata R., *East and West: A Cultural Dialogue*, Bombay: Bharatiya Vidya Bhavan, 1992.

Patnaik, N.R. (ed.), *Religious History of Orissa*, Delhi: Indian Publishers and Distributors, 2004.

Patnaik, N.R. (ed.), *Glimpses of Orissan Culture*, Cuttack: Kitab Mahal, 2004.

Patnaik, Nihar Ranjan (ed.), *Exploring Orissan History*, Cuttack: Kitab Mahal, 2005.

Pradhan, Sadasiba, *Rock Art in Orissa*, New Delhi: Aryan Books International, 2001.

Praharaj, Gopal Chandra (comp.), *Purnnachandra Odia Bhasha Kosha* (*Oriya Lexicon*), vol. II, 1932; vol. III, 1933 and vol. V, 1936, Cuttack.

Prakash, Satya, *Founders of Science in Ancient India*, New Delhi: The Research Institute of Ancient Scientific Studies, 1965.

Pundit, R.N. Dattasastri (ed.), *Śrī Durgā Saptaśatī* (*Devī Māhātmya*), XXth edn., Gorakhpur: Gita Press, (?).

Radhakrishna, B.P. and S.S. Merh (eds.), *Memoir 42: Vedic Sarasvati*, Bangalore: Geological Society of India, 1999.

Rajaram, Navaratna S., *The Politics of History*, New Delhi: Voice of India, 1995.

Rajaram, N.S. and D. Frawley, *Vedic Aryans and the Origin of Civilization*, New Delhi: Voice of India, 2nd edn., 1997.

Rao, S.K. Ramchandra, *Yantras*, Delhi: Sri Satguru Publications, 1988.

Rath, A.K., *Studies on Some Aspects of the History and Culture of Orissa*, Kolkata: Punthi Pustak, 1987.

Renu, L.N., *Indian Ancestor of Vedic Aryans*, Bombay: Bharatiya Vidya Bhavan, 2nd impression, 1996.

Śākta Pramoda, Bombay: Venkatesvara Press, 1951.

Sah, Ayodhya Prasad, *Life in Medieval Orissa, Circa* CE 600–1200, Varanasi: Chaukhambha Orientalia, 1976.

Sahu, N.K., *Buddhist in Orissa*, Cuttak: Utkal University, 1958.

Saraswati, Paramahansa Satyananda, *A Systematic Course in the Ancient Tāntric Techniques of Yoga and Kriya*, Munger: Bihar School of Yoga, 2nd edn., 1989.

Saraswati, Paramahansa Satyananda, *Kundalini Tantra*, Munger: Bihar School of Yoga, 1992.

Saraswati, Swami Muktibodhananda (comm.), *Haṭha-Yoga-Pradīpikā*, Munger: Bihar School of Yoga, 2nd edn., 1993.

Saraswati, Swami Prakashanand, *The True History and the Religion of India*, Delhi: Motilal Banarsidass, 2001.

Sastri, E.R., *The Buddhist Art of Nagarjuna Konda*, Delhi: Motilal Banarsidass, 1994.

Sastri, T.V.G., M.K. Bai and J.V.P. Rao, *Veerapuram*, Hyderabad: Bhavani Printers, 1984.

Satapathy, N., *Religious Life in Orissa (A Study of the Inter-relation of Cults)*, Kolkata: R.N. Bhattacharya, 2000.

Schmieke, Marcus, *Vastu: the Origin of Feng Shui*, New Delhi: New Age Books, 2003.

Schoterman, J.A., *The Yoni Tantra*, New Delhi: Manohar, 1980.

Sengupta, G.G., *Indology and Its Eminent Western Savants*, Kolkata: Punthi Pustak, 1996.

Sengupta, S.R., *Mother Cult*, Kolkata: Firma K.L.M. Pvt. Ltd., 1977.

Sethna, K.D., *The Problems of Aryan Origins*, New Delhi: Voice of India, 1989.

Singh Deo, J.P., *Cultural Profile of South Kosala*, New Delhi: Gyan Publishing House, 1987.

Singh Deo, J.P., *Origin of Jagannāth Deity*, Delhi: Gyan Publishing House, 1991, and 2nd enlarged edn., 2003.

Singh Deo, J.P., *Tāntric Art of Orissa*, Delhi: Kalpaz Publications, 2001.

Singh Deo, J.P., *Some Tāntric Esotericism of Orissa*, Kolkata: R.N. Bhattacharya, 2003.

Singh Deo, J.P., *Tāntric Hedonism of Mahānadī Valley* (*Uḍḍiyāna Pīṭha*), New Delhi: D.K. Printworld, 2004.

Singh Deo, J.P. (ed.), *A Tāntric Scholar and the British Wrath on Bastar State*, Kolkata: Punthi Pustak, 2007.

Singh Deo, Juga Bhanu, A *Man Called Prafulla Chandra Bhanja Deo*, Bhubaneswar: Published by the author, 2005.

Singh, Bhagwan, *The Vedic Harappans*, New Delhi: Aditya Prakashan, 1995.

Singh, Rajnath, *Religious Tāntricism*, vol. II, New Delhi: Dominant Publishers and Distributors, 2001.

Sunderland, Jabez, T. Rev., *India in Bondage: Her Right to Freedom*, Calcutta: R. Chatterjee, 1928.

Svoboda, Robert E., *Aghora* (*At the Left Hand of God*), New Delhi: Rupa and Co., 1993.

Talageri, Shri Kant G., *Aryan Invasion Theory and Indian Nationalism*, New Delhi: Voice of India, 2003.

———, *Aryan Invasion Theory: A Reappraisal*, New Delhi: Voice of India, (?)

Tiwari, A.N. (chief ed.), *Reference Orissa* (century edn.), Bhubaneswar: Enterprising Publishers, 1999, 2nd edn, 2000, 3rd edn., 2005.

Trivedi, D.S., *Indian Chronology* (*8231* BCE *to* CE *1963*), Bombay: Bharatiya Vidya Bhavan, 1963.

Varāhamihira, *Bòhat-Saṁhitā*, H. Kern (ed.), BI, Calcutta; 1865. English tr. H. Kern, *Journal of the Asiatic Society of Great Britain and Ireland*, London, pp. 1870–75, pts 1-5, London, 1870-73, ed. with English tr. and notes by V. Subrahmanya Sastri and M. Ramakrishna Bhat, 2 vols., Bangalore, 1947.

Varma, V.K., *Indo-Aryan Colonization of Greece and Middle East*, 2 vols., Delhi: Pratibha Prakashan, 2000.

Varma, V.K., *Missing Link of World Civilization* (*Indo-Aryan Colonization*), Delhi: Pratibha Prakashan, 2005.

Vatsyayan, Kapila (gen. ed.), *Kalātattvakośa*, vol. IV, *Manifestation of Nature — Sṛṣṭi Vistara*, Delhi: Motilal Banarsidass, 1999.

Wall, O.A., *Sex and Sex Worship in the World*, New Delhi: Inter-India Publications, 1979.

Yogananda, Sri Sri Paramahansa, *God Talks with Arjuna in the Bhagavat-Gita*, Kolkata: Yogoda Satsanga Society of India, 1999, and 2nd impression, 2002.

Weekly

Gorborsky, A.S. "Ancient India May Have Had N-Arms", *Statesman*, Moscow, 8 September 1986, *passim*. (Vide *The Illustrated Weekly of India*, 3-9 January 1988, Bombay.)

Index